WITH ME EVERYTHING IS POSSIBLE

WITH ME EVERYTHING IS POSSIBLE

Discovering the Greater Self Within

OLADIPO OLAFUNMILOYE

WITH ME EVERYTHING IS POSSIBLE.

Copyright © 2013 by Oladipo Olafunmiloye. All rights reserved. No part of this publication may be reproduced, stored in a retrievable system, or transmitted in any form or by any means - electronic, mechanical, photocopy, recording, or any other - except for brief quotations in printed reviews, without the prior permission of the author. For information please contact:

Oladipo Olafunmiloye

Cover and interior designed by Tokunbo Adegoke
Associate Editor Feial Britton

For more information about special discounts for bulk purchases, resellers agreements or to book
Oladipo Olafunmiloye as a speaker please see contact and booking info
at
www.Lafamediaproductions.com

ISBN 978-0-615-85012-2

Printed in the United States of America

Acknowledgements

With special thanks to my Lord and Savior, my family, and friends who God have used, who has contributed to both my success and life journey, everyone who have encouraged and supported me throughout the years, as these experiences lead me to believe that With Me Everything Is Possible.

I dedicate this to my family. I also dedicate this book to my Mom. Thank you for your prayers, unconditional love and support. There are seldom good enough words to describe all the things you have done for me and the role they had in shaping the person I've become.

This book is also dedicated to anyone that has ever had a dream, anyone who's lost their dreams or whose dream has ever been placed on a shelf due to their unique deflating circumstances.

Dear Readers

Although we can all agree - that is, if we are of a faith-based temperament - that our Creator is the molder of our destiny, and it is through Him that all things are possible and this thought should be encouraged in our daily endeavors, it should also be acknowledged as well that great, indisputably, though His charities are acknowledged to be, it is nevertheless equally obvious that we must necessarily be the active agents of our own wellbeing and well-doing, and that, however many talents and skills and however much intelligence our Creator has bestowed upon us, it is up to us, in the end, to nurture these abilities into a shining destiny. It is up to us in the very nature of things to be our own best helpers - hence, the title: With Me Everything Is Possible.

This title is not an attempt to state the obvious; that, without the Creator as our guiding light, our way will be perpetually obscured. It is to suggest, however, that if He gives us Napoleon's bravery, Newton's ingenuity, Mandela's perseverance, King's tolerance, Plato's brain, Teresa's heart, Shakespeare's imagination and Obama's eloquence, and we sit idly with these qualities, it will be impossible for us to reach the summit of our ambitions.

There are no earthly or heavenly powers that can make us successful without our being an active agent in such success. If we claim any measure of accomplishment without any effort on our part, at best, we will only be a representative of fraud and self-deception.

CONTENTS

Chapters
1. PROLOGUE..9
2. NO MISTAKES, JUST LESSONS.............................13
3. FINDING PEACE..28
4. AROUSING THE HAPPINESS WITHIN 45
5. BECOMING A BETTER FRIEND 62
6. WE ARE OUR THOUGHTS....................................79
7. OUR SPECIAL CALLING.......................................92
8. THE IMPORTANCE OF FAITH.............................106
9. UNBENDING HOPE..119
10. FORGIVENESS...132
11. BANISHING OUR FEARS.....................................143
12. OVERCOMING ADVERSITIES..............................155
13. REGRETS..172
14. TIME IS IMMEASURABLE....................................183
15. HUMAN COMPASSION..193
16. DEFINING SUCCESS..206
17. CHARACTER..219

Prologue

The best institutions in our nation cannot give us active help. Perhaps the most they can do is provide the opportunity for us to consciously develop ourselves and improve our individual condition. Yet, in all times, we have been prone to believe that institutions, rather than our own conduct, are the source of our happiness and wellbeing. Consequently, the value of legislation as an agent in human progression has been greatly overestimated. It is no wonder that every four years we have this burning zeal to go out and cast our votes. This social duty, however carefully performed, can exercise but little active influence upon any man's life and character. It is equally true that national progress is the sum of individual progress, and national failure is the sum of individual failures. Certainly, we may endeavor to extirpate our most depressing failures by means of laws, but they will only spring up again with fresh abundance in some other form, unless the conditions of personal life and character are radically improved. If this view is correct, then it follows that the highest levels of patriotism and philanthropy consist, not so much in altering laws and modifying institutions, as in helping and stimulating men to elevate and improve themselves by their own free and independent individual actions.

    The truth that the function of Government is restrictive rather than active, being resolvable principally in the protection of life, liberty and property, is self-evident. It is clear to see that laws, however severe, cannot make the idlers productive, the spendthrifts far-seeing, or the drunkards sober; it is only self-discipline that can implement such reforms. As a result, if we want to improve our personal life and our community, we need to focus on better habits, rather than greater rights.

THE GREATEST SLAVE IS NOT HE WHO IS UNDER THE WHIP OF A TYRANT, EVIL AS THE TYRANT MIGHT BE, BUT HE WHO IS UNDER THE WEIGHT OF HIS OWN IGNORANCE. Individuals who are thus enslaved cannot see the light of freedom by any mere changes of masters or of institutions. It is a fatal delusion to think that our peace and prosperity solely depend on and consist in governments and institutions. Until this delusion ceases to prevail, we will continue to sink instead of sail, fall instead of rise and exist instead of live. The pillars of liberty, peace, happiness and prosperity rest upon individual character, not institutions. This is the ONLY sure guarantee of social security and national progress.

Therefore, I set out to write a motivational book. I felt a moral obligation to lend a few words of hope to those trapped amidst the dark vista of loneliness, to those whose nights seem like an everlasting monument of darkness, to those who, owing to the difficulties of life, fled to the pit of hopelessness and burned the draw-ladder. Clearly, we are living in difficult times. Uncertainty lingers everywhere. Many of us are facing great challenges and have given up on mortal life. Many of us are watching helplessly as our greatest dreams fade to extinction like the mocking echoes of long-departed youth. Joblessness is frightening. It seems as if we have greater luck in finding diamonds than employment. Thus, we suffer from low spirit and lack of worth and will. This book, I hope, will encourage you, and help you to redeem hope, purpose, peace, happiness and prosperity. I pray that the thoughts and quotations in which I myself have found comfort may be of use to you as well. Perhaps they can breathe you back to life.

Another purpose of this book is to prompt you to take a careful note of the activities of your daily living - your methods of work, habits of thought, and modes of recreation. Are you making the absolute best of life? No matter what our current situation, life can still be fruitful and inspiring. We all have a great and definite cause to serve. To serve this inescapable cause, we have to be passionate, self-sacrificing and gallant, always moving forward with an incurable outbreak of optimism and hope.

A third intention of this book is to help you to bring your brightest characters into expression and to help you to combat the deadliest of adversities on your route through life. It contains a fleet of rich and glowing words which I hope will build your esteem, confidence, affection and morality, so that you can live peacefully and purposefully in thought, utterance and action.

In these trying times, mental efficiency is an absolute prerequisite to any notable personal achievement or any great individual success. Our inner energies are the forces with which we must wage our battles in this world. Are you prepared to direct and deploy these forces with masterful control and strategic skill? Are you prepared to become a better person? Are you prepared to use all your reserves of inner energy in the crises of your destiny?

The greatest of all eras is at hand! Consequently, our mental fitness must be ready to appreciate it and to participate in it. Unmistakably, there is no way we can avoid the discipline of life. Neither is there any means by which we can "load" our fate like gambling dice. Each of us must meet our own troubles and difficulties, each soul must pass through its deep waters, every heart must encounter its own sorrow and anguish. Even so, no one needs to be overwhelmed in the great conflicts of life.

THE GREATEST RESOURCE OF THE WORLD IS THE HUMAN SOUL. One of the leading goals of this work is to strengthen this human foundation. A nation is only a mass of individuals and the true prosperity of a country depends upon the true prosperity of its people. Indeed, our intelligence is a wonderful thing, but if our soul is fragile, we will lack faith, courage, happiness, peace, originality, ambition - those vital elements that make us the defining race. This force can be awakened in every soul and mobilize a force, not only for our personal good, but also for the good of us all.

To make it clear, this book does not offer any vain promises of an easy life - for, if this were possible, it would be the greatest of all disasters. Instead, this book endeavors to show how to become so strong that life looks almost easy by comparison. I hope, as well, that it will help many of us to come into harmony with our life and purpose and thus avoid needless suffering. If we are to be the best that we can be, we must harness the greater self within us and bring into expression our inner forces, thus entering a life of overcoming and almost boundless power. The men of the former centuries have harnessed these forces. We can too, and once we do, we can better serve the whole of humanity.

I trust that this book will prove useful and helpful toward the purpose for which it is intended.

No Mistakes, Just Lessons

"There are parts of a ship which when taken by themselves would sink. But when these parts are built together they float. So it is with the events of my life. Some have been tragic, some have been cheerful, but when they are built together, they form a craft that floats and is going someplace."

-Ralph W. Sockman

The sound of the echoing doorbell suddenly awakened me from my dream on a blazing midsummer afternoon in 2005. The solemn, ponderous sound vibrated through the mansion as through a vault. I drowsily turned my sleep-stained eyes to the clock on my bedroom wall to see what time of day it was. Indeed, the afternoon had just dawned. Who could it be at such an hour? I was not expecting anyone and was more alarmed by the ringing of the bell than the actual noise. Again, it rang twice and forced me to be urgent in my response.

I scurried out of bed, dragged on some clothes and descended the stairs. I was on the verge of asking who was there – possibly even exclaiming 'Leave me alone!' Honestly, I felt irritated and grumpy. Some people do not like to be forced from their sleep abruptly. Such disruption sometimes leaves them with a slight headache. I was one of those persons.

I was ashamed of my weakness even as I quietly peeped through my peephole. There was an unknown man standing outside dressed in an elaborate business suit bearing an attaché case by his side. His face was like a crimson apple with a peachy sheen. He had two watchful green eyes, fringed with thick, heavy blond lashes, which cast a shadow into their depths. Altogether, he looked like a man of relevance, and being that I was a businessman, I deduced the purpose of the meeting to be of some substance and subsequently drew back the chain latch.

I distinguished an older white man standing erect, in the yellowing bellow of the noon. He bore the semblance of an opportunist - those sophisticated tycoons who naturally believe that the world would cease to exist without them. Those arrogant men who think they are exempt from ordinariness or anything that reflects it, who think their sole purpose on earth is to lead humankind to a deeper fate. And that was exactly how he scrutinized me as he asked to speak with the owner of the mansion.

I responded modestly, conveying to him that I was the owner of the property. Once again, his curious eyes, with dimming brows, studied my features with the eccentricity often seen in a detective at a crime scene.

He repeated his request as if he thought, somehow, that I had not heard him correctly. This time a humble smile emerged on my face as I repeated my answer. Frankly, it excited me when this happened. I have been in this situation a thousand times before and had long become an expert in such dramatic response from visitors and passersby alike.

This time, I guess he finally heard me, released an unassuming shrug, took a step backward and measured me thoroughly. He began by glancing at the mansion mildly, trying not to be too impertinent, and then stared me dead in the face almost rudely, with a kind of cynical admiration and a childish affronted vigor. The silent uncanny awkwardness lasted for a moment before the scene-shifting took place.

I was still a little tired and had no time for his theatrics. Come to think of it, his reactions were not theatrical at all. Thanks to shows such as MTV Cribs and these media, our society has become mentally conditioned to think and believe that only movie stars or athletes can afford a mansion such as the one he was standing before. I should not have taken his rational conclusions as an offense. Nevertheless, I asked him what he wanted and he asked me to oblige him with a few seconds of my time. I surmised his engagement was pertaining to some sort of business so I further opened the door and he, prompted by his impulse, released another unassuming shrug and ambled inside.

We stood in the living room and he shook my hand as he introduced himself as Mr. Evans, and gave the purpose of his visit. The negative notions he had earlier assumed were swiftly swept away. He began to marvel and sank into a child-like excitement that lasted for an eternity. His arrogance was hurried away like a feeble voice that is quickly drowned in space. He grew submissive and humble as a peasant often does when met by a man of wealth. He had come to realize that I was indeed the owner of the settlement. Shortly thereafter, he began showering me with all kinds of flatteries about my dwelling. Confessing openly that it was the biggest house he had ever seen, he further added that he used to drive down the dead-end street and park his car right outside my gate admiring the geometrical wonder.

He proceeded to ask me all sorts of questions. Of course, the first one he asked was what I did for a living. I informed him that I was a realtor, and that I had been doing real estate investments, acquisitions and constructions for over ten years. Discovering that we were reading from pages of the same book, he spoke fluently, as a man of experience often does. We got on very well together. The guest from time to time shared his vast experiences with me, describing explicitly some incident in his own personal life. In the perpetual eagerness of my propensity to learn more about real estate, such a professor was a veritable treasure. Our conversation was as edifying as it was open. We held nothing back. He gave me a comprehensive history of his thirty-year real estate career and I told him practically my entire life story. For some odd reason, I grew quite comfortable with this real estate mogul who, by the way, had come to seduce me into selling my house.

I gave the man a thorough tour of the building with an air of reserve. Looking back, I was only being accommodating. Was it so? Or I was being polite? Obliging, I suppose. Conceited perhaps? It could be a mixture of all of the above but certainly not because I wanted to sell my monumental residence.

After a detailed tour of the entire newly-completed but virtually empty mansion, I accompanied Mr. Evans back to the door to conclude our conversation. Right before he exited the monument, he turned around and stretched his hand toward me for a handshake. We shook hands firmly as if we had just closed a multimillion-dollar deal. Yet even after the handshake was finished, he still held my hand as if he was sharing a moment. Indeed he was. He looked me straight in the eyes and told me that for some reason, he felt compelled to tell me to write a book about my journey. A book to help inspire others.

"It will be the source of hope for many in desolation," he stated with an affirmative nod. "Your adversities have made you earnest," he continued sternly, like a man of business laying down the terms of an agreement, "full of alacrity and stirring. No one, I believe, should live without magnificence - without being useful to their country, their family and himself. And the greatest of all, no man should die without leaving a trace of their existence behind to roll this world onward, closer to its goal. Your story, I imagine, will achieve both."

I thanked him for his kind words of support. However, as far as writing a book was concerned, that was not for me. I was already doing well finding, renovating and reselling properties all over Maryland and Washington D.C. I had no time for anything else. Real estate was my pride and joy and I was doing it effortlessly. Success was monotonous. I grew so monumental in the business that money had lost its attraction. I was sincerely helping many people. That was one of my core beliefs. However, I was doing so almost exclusively through real estate. As far as encouraging others was concerned, I was inspiring throngs of people by putting them into beautiful houses. I was also organizing various charity events, gathering canned food and raising money for the less privileged citizens. What inspiration could be greater than those? I promised Mr. Evans that I would keep his advice in mind as we released hands and he bid me goodbye and stepped outside briskly. The afternoon wind carried him away. He strode confidently to his car surveying the premises once again as a matter of form, rather than with any real intention. I watched him until he got in his fancy car and drove away.

Time passed and I continued doing what I did best - finding old buildings, purchasing them, reconstructing them and selling them for a fortune. My life was brilliant and eventful. The world seemed to be turning at my command. I had it all - an enormous mansion with rooms that resembled those of eighteenth-century France. The elaborate antechambers hung with cultural tapestry, illumined by tall bronze candelabra, distinguished bedrooms with upholstery hangings complementing their convenient walk-in closets that led to the bathrooms with whirlpools bathtubs and other such delights. There were spacious living rooms with expensive cabinets containing priceless curiosities. Many expensive high-end vehicles – Rolls Royce, Range Rover, Bentley, Mercedes Benz and BMW to name just a few - were parked in my driveways. Not to mention the latest electronic gadgets I owned. I was hosting the most elaborate parties at my house and only stars were invited; prominent football players, NBA stars and media personnel. I held that I was born with a non-negotiating will. I took vacations to wherever I wanted, whenever I wanted. Whatever I dreamt of I converted into mortal life. Life was heavenly. No, life was immensely heavenly!

  I did not think much of the conversation Mr. Evans and I had had until the latter part of the decade when the real estate market took a turn for the worse. It was months before the terrible disappointment I had initially made with enormous investments on some properties. Then all at once I found myself losing most of these properties to foreclosures. I had to act. I had to do something to save my livelihood. It was as if my life itself was being foreclosed. I was willing to both accept misrepresentations on buyers' applications and also to misrepresent some facts myself. Before you know it, I was charged with mortgage fraud and money laundering, the inevitable fate of all who try to break the law.

  Within months I lost everything! I lost my investment properties, my cars, I lost it all. It took me 17 years to achieve all these things and only a few months to lose them. My life was a cold and lonely place. I grew into a state of physical and mental unhappiness and dejection. My soul was overcast by the dark shadows of doubts and uncertainties. The struggle was dreadful.

A new chapter of depression was dawning for me. My endurance was exhausted by overmuch suffering and loneliness. As much as my wife loved me sincerely and was always there for me, she could scarcely fathom what was going on. She was too overwhelmed by the continual stress of our disrupted domestic life. She was lonely and so was I. By degree, loneliness stung us with a kind of superstitious terror. Even in the company of each other we were still lonely. Thus, this made me feel terribly remorseful and overwrought. I suffered as a man who is condemned to death might. Every night I asked myself the same series of despairing questions, as a torrent of despair doused my heart. I never knew life could hurt so much. I was as afraid of my own thoughts as men are of murderers. I dreaded my vacant, dark, horrible life as equally as a child dreads a haunted house. I suffered from this long poignant grief, which one cannot see, know, or guess, but which breaks forth at night in the loneliness of the darkness. I prayed so long and hard that my prayers outran discretion.

As the allegations strengthened, my life grew even darker and colder. I led a colorless existence, full of pain and without variety. The media painted me in a disdainful light. This led many of my so-called friends to withdraw their support. Even some of my close relatives distanced themselves. It was difficult to rid myself of the bitter hopelessness that lingered within my soul. Happiness was a rare phenomenon. It was during this low era of my life that I was able to learn a lot of things. I learned the importance of true friends, the importance of family, the necessity of God and, last but certainly not the least, I learned a lot of things about myself.

NO ONE CAN TRULY DETERMINE WHO THEIR TRUE FRIENDS ARE UNTIL THE DAYS OF THEIR HARDSHIP. UNTIL ADVERSITY STAMPS ITS MARK UPON US "USERS" MAY BE PASSED OFF AS "CLOSE FRIENDS". I find no quality so easy to counterfeit as loyalty. The fire of my adversities had purged the mass of my acquaintance. All my "close" friends deserted me. This, no doubt, was a painful experience.

Though several of my relatives isolated themselves from me, a few stuck by my side and helped me weather the storm as best they could. Those are the ones who taught me the importance of family and what it means to have unconditional support, what it means to not rush to any harmful conclusion which may be difficult to retract. I remember telling my wife to just focus on the kids and let me fight the battle alone and she glared at me, bitterly offended, and like a preacher cutting loose on a Sunday morning said, "The family which does not sink under misfortune rises above it more lofty than before, and is strengthened thereby." Genuine friends and family are preserved only in the school of adversity, while a state of continuous ease and comfort may easily prove a quicksand to them.

I also grew spiritually. *"God is in control"* was my favorite watchword. And no doubt the showers of his grace fell into my lowly heart and humble soul, helping me to keep on holding on. The more I spoke of God, the less I spoke of my troubles. His name alone was to be what the warming sun and the refreshing rain of spring are to the seeds which have lain dormant in the frosts of winter.

One of the biggest lessons of all was learning about myself - who was I? Who I was is who I am and who I have always been. I was a human, born of flesh and blood, fated to make mistakes. A man of independence. A self-effacing man of vision with a keen sense of purpose and duty, born with the capacity to utter a new word - a new thought - a new idea. A self-willed man morally inclined, who had made a terrible blunder and was paying for it dearly. Oftentimes I looked around and saw nothing but the cold and inescapable walls of hopelessness and defeat. I was bewildered by the maze of adversity and found the obstacles of life very disobliging. When I looked around and saw no friends and only an exhausted wife, I gathered an instinctive understanding of life and all its illusions. Like a lion in his lordly lair, I surveyed the scenes of days gone by when I would have laid down my life for persons who came across as my friends. Now where were they? All vanished like mists that melt before the morning rays. They were never my friends; merely acquaintances who lingered around for the opportunities I could offer. This oppressive realization left a lasting stamp on my mind.

However, it was not about them. It was never about them. It was never about friends or family who had deserted me. It was about me and the mistakes I had made that had cost me my career and all that I had worked so tirelessly to achieve. Therefore, my spiritual temper led me in the end to accept every suffering with acceptance and to regard it as a means to mold me into something monumental. I grew into myself. It was an intimate affair. I wanted to redeem myself and regain the trust and confidence of all those whom I had let down. I wanted, on the whole, to be very instrumental to all humankind. I had this unquenchable passion inside me to lift the lives of others to a deeper destiny. I had a natural instinct to be charitable and compassionate toward others. I had helped many people as a realtor and I did not intend on stopping.

The allegations led to the loss of my license as a realtor. I could no longer practice the art. I was deeply saddened. I was left to start over my life from scratch, like a man who had lost everything to fire. I lost all of my investment properties, my luxury cars, and most of my friends and family. I tell you, I spent some cold and forlorn nights in my life that I would hate to repeat. The biting current of dejection, failures and disappointments that loitered in my home, like a hungry grave that gapes for a living prey, always found me sitting by the table in lonesome deliberation. There seemed no trace of hope beyond the clouds for the grinding force of adversity had eroded it. To live in such hopelessness was to die daily.

I remember vividly one particular night when I had in front of me a bowl of cold mashed potatoes that looked like prison pap. I was dejected like a widowed bride and had to force myself to eat. I did so mechanically, with my eyes glued to the plate, and so stupefied with despondency that I could not swallow without a great effort, as my throat felt paralyzed. By degrees, a great deal of self-pity seized me. My glory days of champagne and elaborate partying ran back to tease me. I was terribly ashamed of the man I had become. There was no NBA player dining with me, no prominent football players, or media personnel. It was only my wife and two children, all dejected and sad. My name was removed from the list of real estate tycoons in the city. I was no longer a victim of jealousy and envy but one of shame and dishonor. At such self-defeating moments of self-pity, hope and faith are dormant, and one swiftly sees the whole of life outside the scope of living.

One evening, I sat by myself on a bench which seemed as if its sole purpose was to host broken souls, musing across the purpling autumnal skies. The silvery sun, in his declining seat, bordered the horizon brilliantly, and in proportion, it softly waned into the blood-red cotton clouds, like an angel leaving her heavenly bed in her long white robe of vapor. A collection of native birds squabbled around the immense expanse of space, freewheeling in the wind. It was a divine scene, one that prompted me to dream at will. Behind my deepest consciousness, reason and wonder blushed face to face and for the first time in years I felt hopeful. The thought of restoring joy to the hearts of my family was so soothing that it abolished the possibility of any other kind of feeling. **HOW SWEET IS HOPE WHEN THE SKIES ARE BLUE AND FAIR!** It is hope that distinguishes men from beasts. It is a miserable state of mind to have nothing to desire, and everything to fear; and yet that is commonly the case of one who has no hope.

That evening I gave birth to an astounding idea. The vast mistakes I had made that cost me everything were the portal of this idea. I was able to see clearly, as if I was going through an epiphany, the direction I wanted to take my life from there onward. As I have mentioned earlier, I had a passion for philanthropic work. I had organized many charities and made many donations to different organizations, raising awareness and helping others. This idea was right in line with this passion. Indeed, it is at our lowest point in life that we should trust our soul to lift us up and out of the rot. When we make mistakes we often acquire a wealth of experience. This experience often bears thoughts and these thoughts often lead to action. Oscar Wilde said, *"Experience is of no ethical value. It is merely a name men give to their mistakes."* The failed experiences are no less important than the ones that bear fruit because all success is a string of edited failures. Mistakes are the highway to self-empowerment and self-education. Men mistook the world for being flat before we discovered it was round.

I was making mistakes long before these mistakes that ruined my real estate career. My first contractual job as a realtor was an indiscriminate failure. I was contracted to renovate a dilapidated home for a woman. I took the job and subcontracted it to another contractor. The contractor was someone I had worked for in the past but this was a much bigger project.

I kept an eye on the progress [or lack thereof] of the task but it seemed as if every time I went to get an update the contractor was nowhere to be found. All I saw were his mediocre workers mostly sitting around idly. In the end the contract had expired with him never fulfilling his obligations. He merely pocketed the money. Windows that should have been replaced were merely repaired, doors that were rotten and useless were only further embarrassed by the cheap paint that was slapped carelessly onto them, and carpets that should have been replaced were further bleached out in an attempt to remove the years of misuse they had endured. The entire experience was a monumental disaster! A vast treason against construction. The employer was greatly disappointed and threatened to file a lawsuit against me. I faced her anger and disappointment and assured her that I would get it done correctly. By this time I had taken on another job and was forced to hire another contractor. This time I had done my homework and made sure he was a professional. Yet as soon as the project resumed the employer started adding more and more demands. She was inclined to add more specifications and upgrades that were not part of the initial agreement. I had little room to disagree given the fact that she had suffered grave inconveniences. I ended up giving her a brand new house at my own expense. A big mistake is certainly an expensive college.

Mistake? I did not think so. It was a learning lesson for me that set the tone for my long and fruitful career as a realtor. The greatest men sometimes overshoot themselves, but then their very mistakes are so many lessons of instruction. It is immaterial to live our lives lying under a shroud of mistakes. "Little minds are tamed and subdued by misfortune; but great minds rise above it," said Washington Irving.

Great minds succeed through failure and mistakes. The best experience of men is made up of their remembered failures in dealing with the affairs of life. Such failures, in sensible men, lead to better self-management and greater tact and judgments, as a means of avoiding them in future undertakings. Our greatest lessons are not learned in the classrooms or through success, but through misadventures and mistakes. Ask the diplomat and he will tell you that he has learned his art through being baffled, defeated, thwarted, and circumvented, far more than from having succeeded.

Precept, study, advice and example could never have taught me as well as failures, disappointments and mistakes have done. They have disciplined me experimentally, and taught me what to do as well as what NOT to do - which is often still more important in any undertaking.

Throughout my life I had made up my mind to encounter failures and mistakes again and again before I succeed. For I know that if I fail, it will only serve to stimulate my knowledge and stimulate my courage to renewed efforts. The severe mistakes that cost me my real estate license have only forced me into another direction of success. It taught me, among other things, to be patient, courageous, far-seeing and persevering. If, whenever we are going through troubling times, we remain patient, optimistic, courageous and persistent, Time will certainly bring about strange revenges. The persecutors and the persecuted often change places; it is the latter who are great - the former who are infamous. Even the names of the persecutors would probably have been forgotten long ago had it not been for their connection with the men whom they have persecuted. It is the struggles of the freedom fighter Nelson Mandela that the world remembers when in dire need of inspiration. *"You may encounter many defeats, but you must not be defeated. In fact, it may be necessary to encounter the defeats, so you can know who you are, what you can rise from, how you can still come out of it,"* said Maya Angelou.

It is amazing what perseverance and hope can do when we are daunted by failures and mistakes. I am terribly ashamed to say that I was advised to write a motivational book years ago, but writing a book was never in my plans. I was too busy with my real estate career. Besides, I thought the changes I could make in this world relating to humanitarianism could only come through real estate; whether helping struggling families to find a decent home or by using my renown as a prominent realtor to organize charity work for the less fortunate. But when I woke up one day without a career, without fame, without wealth, and without connections, my fate took a deep twist. At first I was very ashamed. Aren't failures and mistakes shameful things? Isn't that what we are told when we have failed? We are taught in school, in our families, or at work to feel guilty about failures and mistakes. We are taught to do whatever we can to avoid them. This sense of shame combined with the inevitability of setbacks when attempting difficult things explains why many of us give up on our goals; we are not prepared for the mistakes and failures we will face on our way to getting what we want. It is inevitable that the more challenging the task, the more frequent and difficult setbacks will be, and the more likely it is for us to fail.

  The greater our ambitions, the more dependent we will be on our ability to overcome and learn from our mistakes. This notion of a man being a failure because he has failed a task is one of the most ignorant ones I have ever come across. No one is a failure. The task we set out to achieve, which we may have failed, does not represent us. If we fail an exam we are not a failure. The exam doesn't represent us. If we fail a marriage, we are not a failure. The marriage doesn't represent us. If we make a mistake, we are not a mistake. We should never equate making mistakes with being a mistake! This is not true. This may explain the behavior of some of our high school or college friends, or some of our coworkers. *"To make your mark on the world is difficult. If it weren't so, everyone would have done so. It takes patience, commitment and comes with a lot of failures along the way. The real test is not whether we avoid these failures; it is whether it hardens or shames us into action; whether we choose to persevere."* -Barrack Obama. I could not agree more. To make no mistakes is not in our power. What is in our power, though, is to learn from these errors and mistakes for future success. We learn from these blunders after we have admitted that our route was not the best choice. We learn from our mistakes when we are not swift to cast blame but to courageously stand up and honestly say, "I have made a decision that affected me adversely and I take full responsibility," then the potential for learning will progress toward us. Accepting responsibility makes growth and development very possible. When the allegations left me empty and without a livelihood I blamed everyone. I blamed my friends and business partners. I blamed my wife, who enjoys nice things. I blamed God. It was only after I stood up as a man and took responsibility for my mistakes that the groundbreaking idea was able to germinate within my soul. Admission of a mistake, even if only privately to ourselves, makes learning possible by moving the focus away from blame assignment and toward understanding. Prudent people admit their mistakes straightforwardly. They know progress accelerates when they do.

Mistakes can be very complex and complicated because not all mistakes can be avoided the next time. That is the reason Elbert Hubbard asserts that the greatest mistake one can make is to continually fear he will make one. Mistakes are inevitable. As long as there are dreams to be met there will always be mistakes and errors. As long as there are tough decisions to be made there will be unfavorable results. This, however, should not be a deterrent against tough decision-making or dream-chasing. This is only one of the many things that make our lives interesting. Even Einstein made mistakes and learned from them. The thing to do when we have blundered is to regain confidence in ourselves, pick up the pieces and continue along life's journey. I know this is difficult, especially when the mistake is visible to a lot of people and has impacted their lives. We should continue to believe in ourselves. Study the error and use it as a guideline of what not to do. A lot of us shake off our mistakes with a smile. This is very healthy. When we can laugh at our own mistakes we know we have accepted them and no longer judge ourselves on the basis of one single event. Reaching this kind of perspective is very important in avoiding future mistakes. Humor loosens up our psychology and prevents us from obsessing about the past. It is easy to make new mistakes by spending too much energy protecting ourselves against the previous ones. We should not spend all our caution on the mistakes that have passed so that we have none left to prevent the ones that are ahead.

THE MOST IMPORTANT LESSON IN ALL OF MISTAKE-MAKING IS TO TRUST THAT THERE IS ALWAYS SOMETHING TO LEARN THAT WE CAN TAKE TO ENRICH OURSELVES WHEN MAKING ANOTHER DECISION IN THE IMPENDING FUTURE. After I had lost it all, sitting and thinking there on that park bench moments before I gave birth to the life-bestowing idea, my rationale made light of my mistakes and for the first time I reasoned soberly with myself. I encouraged myself over and over, gently and without pity. And suddenly, I was no longer absorbed in myself. I realized the obstacles of life were not confined to me. I have no monopoly on mistakes, disappointments, failures and setbacks. I realized that the only way I was going to rid myself of self-pity and fear was by not feeling sorry for myself, but rather by confronting my adversity face to face and wrestling with it. It was during that moment of reflection I was able to consciously evaluate what was really important going forward; what steps I needed to take to get back on track and do what I was send here to do, and how I could use those mistakes to my advantage and move on. There is no map designed to guide us away from mistakes and errors. After all, to fall and rise again is the journey of any great life. At that very moment, sitting there on that bench, musing at the brilliant sunset ribboning the sky, I lost all sense of bitterness. I told myself that my mistakes should make me better, not bitter. There is always something abstract in our mistakes that we can use to get something concrete. There is a famous saying that every disappointment is for a good. And had it not been for my mistakes, this groundbreaking idea would never have materialized. I sat there cutting through the thick crust of my mistakes and misfortunes, wondering how I could use them to my advantage. That was when the idea struck me. Why not have a reality television show? I had a natural passion for helping people. All my life I had helped low-income families. There are millions of us who may never enjoy the godly pride of calling the place we live *"our home"* in the fullest sense of the statement. The general idea was to find old, dilapidated houses, repair them, and give them to low-income families who could not afford a house. After all, owning a home is the America dream. Fittingly, I decided to call the show "This Is Your American Dream". I was bent on touching lives and making people happy. Needless to say, when a major network expressed an interest in buying the idea, it was the happiest day of my life! All the mistakes, all the disappointments, all the failures at last made sense, and in the end, they were **NOT MISTAKES, JUST LESSONS**. Throughout my rollercoaster life I have learned a lot and I had no choice but to yield to Mr. Evans' advice and write a book about it all. The subsequent chapters are my very own experiences which I was inclined to share.

Finding Peace

"Our life depends on the kind of thoughts we nurture. If our thoughts are peaceful, calm, meek, and kind, then that is what our life is like. If our attention is turned to the circumstances in which we live, we are drawn into a whirlpool of thoughts and can have neither peace nor tranquility."

-Elder Thaddeus

It is overwhelming how many of us in society today find ourselves increasingly unhappy and unsatisfied with ourselves. We do not like who we are, lodging all sorts of complaints about ourselves, registering how displeased we are with everything. Some of us would go as far as condemning ourselves for lacking the ability to possess or attain certain qualities and abilities such as those of our friends or peers. The traditions of human culture treat us as branches of a machine. They allocate us positions and place enormous weight upon us to fulfill defined roles. They distribute unhelpful opinions that further aid the waning of our faint humanity. A lot of us have feelings suppressed for so long that a mountain of reclusiveness is rooted inside us. There is a voiceless cry resting in the depths of our pining souls, waiting for expression. Only real peace can give that feeling voice and form.

HOW THEN WILL WE FIND PEACE AND CONTENTMENT? How will we find pleasure in ourselves? Surely, we cannot find peace by perpetual complaining; surely, not by looking the other way with untamed admiration, raining praises on everybody's abilities but our own, then wondering why our lives are full of sadness and self-worthlessness. Yet we wonder why we are always stuck in a rut. Yet we wonder why no one seems to think we are of any real purpose or value in this world. Yet we wonder why there is no peace in our lives.

The reason animals have greater peace than humans is that they are born who they are; they accept it, and that is that. They do not spend their lives trying to be everything but themselves, or spend their lives worrying over their inadequacies, or the opinions of other animals, or fussing over the fact that they are not able to do what other species of animals can do. I do not think for a minute that the elephants are disappointed at not being able to live in the ocean as the whales do.

We will not find peace by doing what we see others are doing, unless of course, our soul approves of it. Neither will we find peace by waiting for others to approve of what we are doing. We will not find peace until we are confident in ourselves and until we have permanently rid ourselves of all our insecurities. We will not find peace until we are not dependent on anyone else to define and validate us. If such a compliment comes from outside, it should be well received; however, we should not solely rely on such compliments to approve our worth as a person. We should be secure in what we are making of life, and not what others think we should be making of it. Then and only then will we achieve peace.

WHAT I AM IS ALL THAT CONCERNS ME, NOT WHAT OTHERS THINK. This rule, equally arduous in actual and in intellectual life, may serve for the whole distinction between peace and despondency. It is all the harder because we will always find those who think they know us better than we know ourselves. It is easy to chase after the world's opinion of us and difficult to live on the basis of our own. To find peace, we must be able to maintain independence from others' opinions. We should be able to be ourselves and reinforce our character. Most of us have blinded our own eyes with someone's blindfolds and attached ourselves to several communities, none of which is our own, fettering ourselves with the prison-uniform of the party to which we adhere. We come to wear one cut of face and figure, and acquire by degrees, the gentlest dim expression, counterfeiting, with the foolish face of praise, the forced smile that we put on in company where we do not feel at ease in conversation that does not spark our interest.

LIFE IS A JOURNEY THAT WE SOMETIMES HAVE TO WALK ALONE. Why should we assume the negative opinions of our friends, spouse, or parents, simple because they are close to us? All men are close to us and we are close to all men. However, that is not enough reason to adopt their lowly opinions of us.

At times, the whole world seems to be in a conspiracy to pester us with forceful trifles. Friends, parents, children, sickness, fear, wants, charity, all knock at once at our bedroom door, and say, "I know you are in there! Come on out!" If we want to maintain peace, we should keep our state and stay away from adverse opinions and disbelievers. We should not sell our peace and our soul to save their sensibility.

The trouble is that most of us care more about appearing at peace rather than being at peace. A woman will walk a thousand miles in high heels to appear taller or sexier than she really is while under extreme stress, rather than wearing something far more comfortable but seemingly less elegant. She is more concerned with the views of the public rather than her own comfort. A man will turn his back on his beloved wife and leave her to loneliness, just for public approval; all this time his heart is burning with self-contempt.

This undue regard for appearances is very deep-seated, for it comes from long habit and inheritance. We should recognize it and acknowledge it in ourselves, to take the true path toward peace. So long as we are working for appearances, we are not working for realities. We should refrain from being a slave to compliments and admiration for mere appearances. We should cease relying on others to make us feel secure, to feel worthy, to feel relevant, to feel important, and to feel beautiful, no matter how close they are to us. We should find that confidence within us and use it as a bolster to lift our heads above unfavorable opinions. We should always remind ourselves how beautiful we are. We should wear this concept profoundly, and proudly, like a badge of honor. Let it be the armor that protects our soul and spirit. We are the work of a divine hand. Our beauty should follow no rules, laws or mortal virtue. Our beauty should live above human opinions and approvals. It is not relative to persons or things around us. Therefore, we should never be afraid of it. *"Men seek retreats," said Marcus Aurelius, "houses in the country, seashores, and mountains; and thou too art wont to desire such things very much. But this is altogether a mark of the most common sort of men; for it is in thy power whenever thou shalt choose, to retire into thyself. For nowhere either with more quiet or more freedom from trouble does a man retire, than into his own soul, particularly when he has within him such thoughts that by looking into them he is immediately in perfect tranquility."*

Therefore, the world's opinions of us should not be a factor that determines our peace. Peace is confidence- confidence in our own skin; the confidence to know that we are not perfect, and will never be - neither are we trying to be - but we strive every day to be the best person we can be. Our feet might be dirty and our clothes might be shabby, but our heart is clean. We might have a few extra unwanted pounds but that does not make us unattractive or unlovable. The world might not appreciate us but we are willing to appreciate ourselves. We should learn to cherish the things we admire about ourselves and live to change the things that are in disagreement with us. We might not be the supermodel our companion would like but that is not our problem. As long as we are contented with our current status, while trying to improve ourselves, that is all that matters. Adhere unbendingly to these practices and relieve your nervous system of a great weight, and decrease the income of the nerve specialists, the doctors and counselors to the extent of depriving these gentlemen of many luxuries they now enjoy.

It matters very little how affluent we are, or how much attention we have received; it is the amount of peace we can radiate in our life that counts. Ultimately, our moral duty is to secure the peace in ourselves and transfuse it toward others, not looking toward others to ignite the peace laid dormant within us.

PEACE IS THE SERENITY OF THE SPIRIT. The wellness of the body is relative to that of the spirit. No matter how physically healthy we might be, if our spirit is in discontent, it is difficult for us to recognize the great health of the body. A man whose spirit is full of unrest, no matter how tired he is, finds it difficult to sleep.

It can be difficult to fulfill the conditions of healthiness in the spirit, much more difficult than to keep the body well and strong. People, if they are uncomfortable in their bodies, are very glad to find the cause and to do their part to fulfill the conditions of health until their bodies are comfortable again. This is certainly not the case with the spirit.

Most of us do not even recognize that we have many forms of selfishness. We tend to think that all the faults are with circumstances or with other people. We look everywhere and to anyone or anything rather than look inside ourselves for the cause of our spiritual illness. Looking inside ourselves and acknowledging and repenting is the only way to get spiritually well. To be sure, many of us call ourselves "wretched sinners" every time we go to church, and some of us occasionally call ourselves wretched sinners out of church. What good does that do? How would we feel if we visited our doctor and he told us that we were in a miserable state of sickness and then told us to go home without ever treating our illness?

What could be more dull than us saying day after day that we are miserable sinners, and then taking no means whatever to find out where and how and in what way we are sinning? Common sense and respect for the law of cause and effect would prompt us to find the specific cause of our sin and bring the right remedy to bear upon it. That is the only attitude that will lead us into the atmosphere of wholesomeness.

YE SHALL KNOW THE TRUTH AND THE TRUTH WILL MAKE YOU FREE. Do you suppose that it is the truth about others that will set us free, or the truth about ourselves? The health of the spirit is the only element in the acquisition of peace. The trouble is, it seems to me, that our standards for the health of the spirit are too low. We are altogether too much inclined to take the standards of the world about us, and are entirely too dissatisfied with what other people think of us, rather than who we truly are and can be. We should learn to be independent of the world's opinion of us. What people think of us should be no business of ours. To please everyone is to please none. We spend our entire lives being a slave to others' expectations and opinions, only to have our best efforts turned into mockery and ridicule from these same people we try desperately to impress. Here is a story below that I am sure a lot of us will think is a parody of our lives.

An old man decided to visit a friend miles across his village. His ten-year-old grandson insisted that he accompany him, which the old man did not contest.
They saddled their donkey delightedly and then hopped on blissfully. Moments later, they were riding in the midday wind.
Soon enough, they rode past some people and the old man happened to overhear the opinions of the passing throng. They thought he was inconsiderate: "How could he and the little boy be so heartless, riding the poor old donkey in the broiling sun?" They accused him of lacking compassion and mercy for the animal. Now that I thought of it, they might have been members of the Animal Rights Organization.
The old man felt disappointed and decided to get off the animal, leaving his grandson as he walked tirelessly behind the trotting beast.
Moments later, as they mounted a hill, they encountered another group of passersby. Sure enough, they too had something to say. "That old man is a fool! They uttered chorally. "Why is he dragging behind the donkey breathlessly, when the boy, young and healthy, is sitting comfortably? He is dumber than a box of rocks! The boy should be the one walking."
The old man, indeed, could not have been more saddened. He immediately eased his grandson off the animal and took his place, while the little boy followed behind.
He was just starting to enjoy the heavenliness of the countryside when a flabbergasted couple emerged in front of the beast and shadowed his view.
"Selfish old man!" the woman exclaimed disgustedly, stepping in front of the donkey valiantly. "How could you be so cruel to let the little boy walk while you leisurely ride?"

"Not only are you selfish and cruel," the man added bitterly, "you are arrogant and lazy as well!"

The old man felt emotional and hung his head in shame.

Tired of all the conflicting opinions, he decided he would do what was best - at least, what he thought would meet the public's approval. Hence, he jumped off the donkey and joined his grandson behind the animal. Now they both were walking and the animal hurried along briskly. "This," he thought, "will shield me from criticism."

When he thought he was safe from scrutiny, a group of observers mocked and teased him pitifully. Not only did they mock and tease him, but he became a laughingstock.

"You are a lunatic!" roared the first impishly.

"And a waste!" yelled the second.

"You must be a drunkard!" joined the third; after that, they all burst out laughing uncontrollably.

The old man decided to give up trying to please everyone and followed his own mind.

Whatever his mind was is of little relevance to us. What is relevant is to know that peace is not relative to our surrounding, or the public's opinions, but to our own standard. To find it, one's spiritual health must begin with such a concept. It must grow from work in each separate individual. Every man, owing to his uniqueness, is without rival in the world, until, of course, he chooses to give up his uniqueness, by trying to duplicate the activities and characteristics of his companions. So too, he tries to replicate the happiness and fulfillments of others, and tries desperately to make them his own. Day after day, he digs for that treasure his friends have, treasure which, when found, proves to be no treasure at all. Because it glitters, he thinks it has value and makes believe he is happy because he possesses it, until one day a jeweler comes along who knows genuine gold. He is rudely awakened when the expert tells him that what he has is not only no treasure at all, but that the iron has poison in it, and the sooner it is entirely out of the way, the better! Just think of all that! He will not believe the honest jeweler, because, having traded his poisonous iron back and forth among his peers, he will have come firmly to believe in its intrinsic value.

Perhaps some would laugh and say, "Oh, yes, we discovered some time ago that the iron was of no real worth, but the people about us seemed to think it was, and so long as we could keep ourselves comfortable by continuing to trade with them, we thought it better not to disturb anyone." Then again, they might add, "You see, we are not only comfortable ourselves, but the belief in the iron is keeping everyone else about us comfortable. Would it not have been unkind to enlighten them?"

Let us go farther and imagine a group of people, even a whole town or city, dealing in counterfeit money. Counterfeit gold and silver - counterfeit bills - and the trade of the city continue for some time undisturbed, with the counterfeit money always used. Then, suppose a man comes from an honest country and shows these citizens the difference between the genuine notes and the counterfeit ones. Would not most of the citizens say, "We have kept very comfortable with this money which you say is counterfeit - our city has gone on all right, and we are all having a very good time. We see no reason for changing?" Then, the man with honest money could say, "That appears alright for now, but wait until you have to come in contact more with the world at large. You will find then that your money will not pass, and you yourselves will be terribly awakened. Remember, I have warned you."

THERE IS BOGUS PEACE AND THERE IS REAL PEACE. REAL PEACE BRINGS HEALTH OF SOUL AND BODY WITH IT, WITH AN INTERIOR SENSE OF VIGOR AKIN TO, AND FINER THAN, FRESH MOUNTAIN AIR. When put to the test, real peace grows stronger, deeper, and full of vitality. Indeed, all tests strengthen it, deepen it, and are the means of bringing it more vigor. Fake peace and real peace are so closely in resemblance nowadays that it is surprising, even to one who knows, how often and how exactly it seems to be real. It is like a thick sugar coating over a bitter pill.

If each individual soul would do his homework, if each soul would work with an alert desire to know the root of his own peace and obey it, the peace he would inherit would be wonderful. Each soul should practice the habit of looking entirely to himself for the cause of his suffering, and restrain himself from compromising in the slightest way. Each of us owes ourselves the habit of looking entirely within ourselves and comparing ourselves to others in the very least for our peace. Geshe Kelsang Gyatso said, *"Without inner peace, outer peace is impossible. We all wish for world peace, but world peace will never be achieved unless we first establish peace within our own minds. We can send so-called 'peacekeeping forces' into areas of conflict, but peace cannot be imposed from the outside with guns. Only by creating peace within our own mind and helping others to do the same can we hope to achieve peace in this world."*

The greatest obstacle in the way of our peace is this low standard among us with regard to blaming circumstances or looking toward others for approval, instead of knowing ourselves intimately. Peace is an individual thing. The best textbook that could lead us to peace is right within us. It is a universal habit of blaming circumstances or others for the discontentment of our lives. We should know that displeasure lies entirely within us, not our surrounding elements. It takes courage to look to one's self entirely for pain that we are sure that others inflicted upon us. Once we do this, and are thoroughly clean-cut about it in every thought, word, and action, peace seems almost miraculous.

When I say, *"look to ourselves"* I do not mean that we are to blame ourselves. Oftentimes, we have inherited tendencies of which we are not in the least aware, but if we refuse to cut ourselves off from these hindrances to our peace, then of course, we are at fault. We should work tirelessly to conquer these inherited habits.

It is our own attitude toward life that makes us suffer, not the circumstances and people in life. The tendency is, when we read a book that has in it practical truth, to say, how good this would be for so-and-so, but this book, dear reader, I hope you may apply it where it is most useful - YOU.

It is my purpose and my hope in this book to point out, as far as I am able, the road to real peace. I do not pretend to have found uninterrupted peace myself. If I thought I had, that would prove that I have nothing to teach anyone. On the contrary, I do believe I have found the road to it, and that I am working my way, with many others, toward the peace that lasts.

One thing I know - the finding of it, and the privilege of feeling its strength, does not depend upon others; it does not depend upon environment, it does not depend upon circumstances, or even upon inheritance. In finding it, we should work as if we are alone in the world.

Finding peace does not depend upon family, religion, friends, jobs, affluence or health. Finding peace, as I said before, is not relative to circumstances or surroundings or others' opinions. It dwells within our own honesty of self.

When we indulge in fake peace, we can find no peace. For even though fake peace can be passed off as a real one, we know that the peace we have has no value. It is like a man with a million dollars' worth of counterfeit; he knows that he cannot claim to be a millionaire, for the money has no real worth.

WE CAN ONLY ACQUIRE REAL PEACE BY REMOVING THE OBSTRUCTIONS TO IT. We are apt to carry about an almost unconscious attitude of grumbling at the various interferences to our comfort, when the truth is that no one is responsible for removing our obstructions but ourselves.

There are many obstructions that block the passage of peace. Self-pity, anxiety, self-indulgence, worldliness, jealousy and desire are just a few of these elements that scourge our spirits. Oftentimes, we do not want to acknowledge these obstructions because they are an inconvenient truth. The only way of earning peace, real peace, is to conquer our self-pity, anxiety, self-importance, self-indulgence, worldliness, jealousy and desire.

Indeed, we have the tendency to indulge in self-pity when things are not going our way. This is not the right approach to peace. Self-pity is harmful. It is our inability to get out of our own way of peace or success. Some of us are so self-pitying that every obstacle we face, even though the same obstacles are appearing to others all around us, we view as a personal attack. We cry to the heavens asking, *"God, why us?"* We have no glimpse of the possibility of freedom because we live within the stifling garbs of self-pity. Therefore, this bondage prevents us from seeing past the mist and we can only further suffer from it.

Once upon a time, a beautiful bird was soaring high in the sky. He was free and happy, basking in the warmth of the summer wind, unprepared for the sudden tragedy that would befall him. Yes, indeed, in the middle of his flight, he found himself in a deep, dry well. Fortunately, he was unhurt.

Despite this good fortune, the bird did not try to help himself out of his trouble. He just sat there helplessly, expecting the public to rescue him out of the well.

When people did not come to his rescue, he began wailing and lamenting about his bad luck. He kept saying to himself, "Poor me! What did I do to deserve this? Why me, Lord?"

Next, he started blaming others for his circumstance. He muttered, "It is not my fault that I lay here and suffer at the bottom of this well. It is the fault of the wind. It is the fault of those who dug the well. It is the fault of those who did not cover it. It is the fault of the passersby for not rescuing me from this well. No! No! It's not my fault."

His pity was fixed and final as death. He kept shouting, "Help! Help! Heeellppp! Pleeease! Get me out of here!"

People outside the well kept telling the bird: "You've got wings; you can fly! The well is broad, fly! Help yourself out of it." A man even went as far as to jump into the well to confirm that the bird was indeed alright. His wings were perfect; he had not even suffered a mere scratch.

Yet the bird continued to blame everyone and everything for his mild misfortune. He blamed his mother for not blessing him with stronger wings, he blamed the season, and he even blamed the climate. He bent his mind on blaming, rather than simply making an attempt on his own behalf. He kept on crying, "I can't help myself! If I fly, I will hurt my wings. I will surely dash against the walls of the well. It will cause me pain. No! No! You have to rescue me from here. It is not my fault that I am trapped down here."

SELF-PITY IS ONE OF THE WORST KINDS OF SELF-MUTILATIONS. It keeps one in an emotional penitentiary. Self-pity is one of the elements that interfere with making the right use of adversity. To pity one's self is destructive to all favorable liberation. If the reader finds himself in the pang of this weakness and finds comfort in these words, let him hasten to shun self-pity as he would shun poison. If this emotion overwhelms us, it will only take slight difficulties of any kind to overthrow us.

Why do we get so emotionally entangled in the unfavorable events that are past and over? Can we just let the dead bury the dead? Let bygones be bygones. Why are we strangling our peace in the iron mesh of our past? Some of us keep ourselves in unrest and stagnancy for months, perhaps even years, by holding on to the relics of some gloomy historical memory. Whether the gloomy memory is little or great, we should drop it entirely. If we fall, we should pick ourselves up and go right on. Whatever the stone may be that we have tripped over, we should know that it was there before and others have tripped over it many times, and it will be there and others will be tripping over it many times as well. This act of fate, or the Devil, depending on our belief, is nothing personal. We are not exempt from the adversities of life. Our peace and freedom begin when we are aware of our imprisonment to self-pity. This bondage brings very real suffering, and we may become depressed, but we will have to endure it, unless we decide to use the adversity as a guiding light by which to find peace.

SELF-PITY MAKES US VERY SENSITIVE. Our soul reflects every disappointment like a mirror. If, when a man is complaining of all the troubles that seem to be plaguing him, we tell him, in honest kindness, that not all his sufferings are isolated, in most cases he would disagree. He will assure us that we do not understand. He will tell us how his life is the worst, further authenticating our conclusion, rather than looking the truth in the face and doing the work required in himself to meet his peace.

SELF-PITY IS SPIRITUAL LAZINESS. It is difficult for us to find peace and tranquility if we sit and pity ourselves because we are facing disagreeable winds, instead of searching about until we find the true laws of peace whose application would make the light of our life shine brightly. How ridiculous it is if with every little barrier that we face we throw our hands up and curse the Devil for being a fork-tongued monster. This practice of shame makes us low-spirited, and the more trouble comes our way, the more it increases, until the depression becomes so unbearable that we are pushed to fold into ourselves like a pleated wing and thus, peace, so far as real inner peace goes, becomes more and more unachievable.

Since Shakespeare reckoned that the entire world was a stage and we all agreed, think of self-pity as stage fright. To be a true performer on the stage of life, we must overcome it by getting out of our own way, and by letting the obstinate character we have work through us. The conditions by which we gain peace are entirely within us. When we understand this, we are sure to find our way out of depression and into the arms of peace.

I assure you that finding peace is totally up to us. We should not depend on others to find it. As long as we are willing to work on removing all the obstructions to it, we will find it. The experience is beautiful and beneficial. Many of us spend a lifetime trying to find it. All the while, it is right within us, covered by the obstructions we placed over it. Until we get rid of these impediments, our peace will remain dormant.

When I think of peace, nothing else comes to mind but the satisfaction of my spirit. I am not concerned with how others perceive me. That is a useless worry. I do not waste time or energy on others' opinions of who I am. Why murder my peace by harboring a strong and earnest regard for the opinions of others? That will only keep our peace relative to these opinions and keep us, in the end, in the strain of constant fear. *No one can hurt us without our permission. No one can lock the door to our peace unless we give them the key.* Ralph Waldo Emerson, one of the greatest American writers and philosophers said, *"Nothing external to you has any power over you."*

These little nervous worries are countless. The fear of not being skinny enough, the fear of not being sexy enough, and the fear of not being beautiful enough are terrible things. All these fears will attack us viciously, if we allow ourselves to be influenced by them. When we gain control over these obstructions, then and only then will we be able to find peace.

We should not let ourselves be tyrannized even by that finest faculty of idealizing things; otherwise, both truth and peace will one day part company from us with the insulting remark: "Thou arch-liar, we must now be strangers!" Mother Teresa told us that: *"The peace we own should be so internally fortified that it cannot be swept away by swift-footed Time."* Consequently, we should learn to appreciate ourselves and find comfort even in our dullest features. The quality of life depends not upon external growth or material progress, but upon the inner development. We can see from this that if we want true, lasting happiness, we need to develop and maintain a special experience of peace by removing every obstruction to it. Be careful of our self-indulgence, envy and desires. These worldly material trappings can be very dangerous. The only way to discover peace is to rid ourselves of these vain external trappings. Find comfort in what we have. Peace comes from remembering what we possess and forgetting what we are lacking.

"Oh! I want a new house! Oh! I want a new car! If only I had enough money to go to Disney World. We need to paint the house. This dress is old, I wore it before." We hear it all the time, from our own selves. A lot of us never cease to worry and complain about the things we do not have, instead of finding completion in the things we do have.

There was a husband who stood in front his wife on their wedding night staring her in the face blankly, without ever saying or doing anything. Indeed, he looked ludicrous. She too stood there looking at him blankly as if it was some kind of strange sport called stare-at-me-blankly. She was looking beautiful, the kind of wife that would make many a husband envious.

The strange sport went on for a while with neither party saying a word.

After having had enough of the eerie moment she asked, "How is it that on our wedding night you are just standing there like a deer in front of the headlights?" His reply was, "Baby, you are looking so beautiful tonight. I have never seen you more beautiful. If this world were mine, I would give it all to you. If I had a thousand hearts, they all would love you. If I had a thousand hands, they all would be hugging you right now. If I had a thousand lips, they all would be kissing you. If I had a thousand..."

She irritably stopped him in his long Obama-like speech and said, "Damn fool! Stop pining over what you do not have and use what you have! You have two hands, why are they not hugging me? You have two lips, why are they not kissing me? You have passionate love, why aren't you giving it to me? And," she paused, her eyes opening wide, "I hope the one heart you have is indeed mine!"

WE ACQUIRE NOTHING UNLESS WE ACQUIRE PEACE. We can acquire real peace by turning our attention inwardly and ridding ourselves of the obstructions marring it. We are the vine from which everything springs - peace, love, happiness and hope. The wealthiest men in the world should be able to find the same peace they so much enjoy in their material trappings, in the middle of the Sahara Desert, stripped of all their luxuries. If it is not so, their entire claim to peace is a façade. If we cannot live at peace with ourselves, we most certainly will not be able to live at peace with others. The key to that peace is the technique of self-appreciation. Let us maintain a positive outlook toward ourselves. Let us not think of ourselves as being a failure in life. Think of it; if we think that we are a failure, by whose standard are we judging ourselves? Whose is the definition of "failure"? Is it ours? Surely not! We are undeniably defining ourselves by using someone else's dictionary. To be peaceful, we cannot do this. We cannot define ourselves by using someone else's dictionary. We have to use our own. What do we hold happiness to be? Wealth? Success? Love? These words do not have a universal definition.

I implore everyone; please remove those obstructions to your peace, for peace is imperative. Peace is not everything; it is the only thing! Remove selfish desires. Remove self-indulgence. Remove anxiety. Remove self-pity. When the obstacles of life are upon you, instead of asking, *"Why me?"* challenge it and say, *"Try me."* Faith makes all things possible, hope makes all things work, love makes all things endurable and peace makes all things beautiful. Mahatma Gandhi, an activist for peace, said, *"There is no way to peace; peace is the way."*

PEACE IS THE ABSENCE OF INNER AGGRESSION, INNER VIOLENCE AND INNER HOSTILITY. Peace is untouchable because it is not external. A king may sit arrogantly on his throne of wealth and still be empty. A prisoner may be confined to maximum solitude and still be peaceful. Peace is not dependent on time, place, person or thing. Just as long as we strip ourselves of the external trappings that are obstructing our peace, we will discover peace. The obstructions that cover the peace within us are the source of our unhappiness. If we seek peace from material objects or from others, we will never attain it. The Nobel Peace Prize is ours.

To sum it up: we can never find peace by duplicating the peace of others. The only real peace is that deep peace that comes from within independently; independent of family, friends, spouse, affluence, job - it comes from nothing and no one, except from within us. Therefore, let us try to be consistent in every act that conforms to uprightness. What greater reward can we have than the *"peace that passeth all understanding"?* This peace will never be experienced unless we learn the art of shunning the obstructions to it, unless we learn not to yield to the expectations or opinions of others, but to be content with ourselves.

We can never shun these obstructions except by finding what they are, facing them squarely, acknowledging them in detail and refusing steadily to act, speak or think from any one of them. John F. Kennedy, the 35th President of the United States and a strong advocate for peace, said: *"Peace is a daily, a weekly, a monthly process, gradually changing opinions, slowly eroding old barriers, quietly building new structures. And however undramatic the pursuit of peace, the pursuit must go on."* Of course, the process is slow, and we advance by overcoming difficulties. Sometimes the troubles of life push us down and we are tempted to lay there discouraged. But every time we fall, the right thing to do is to get up and continue. By and by we do not fall so far, and later on, we probably only trip a little.

When life has fleeced us of rank, fame, connections, friends, wealth and property of every kind, we perhaps discover in the end, after the first shock, that we are richer than before. For now we know for the first time what is so peculiarly ours that no robber can touch, and perhaps, after all the disappointment and devastation, we discover that we are a mighty real estate mogul, for we are the sole owner of our soul - the greatest property of all.

Arousing the Happiness Within

"True happiness comes from the joy of deeds well done, the zest of creating things new".

-Antoine de Saint-Exupery

One morning, years ago, when my hair was black, my steps were light, and I never fell asleep forgetting to take my shoes off, the rich burned scent of mint tickled my nose just seconds before the old alarm blared a distorted shriek through its tiny top speakers.

Wiping away the grit of last night's sleep, the starch white sunlight blinded me for a moment as I swung my arm like the limb of a willow along the top of the alarm searching for the off button. While stretching my hands and feet to the four posts of my bed, my eyes opened after several watery blinks.

Now that I could see the resplendent sun and the magnificent blue clouds soaring in the sky edged aflame, I realized that the happiest day of my life was at hand - my first day of elementary school.

I immediately crawled out of the comforter, edging awkwardly like a butterfly from a cocoon, swinging my legs over the side of my bed, getting up in preparation for my big day. The butterflies in my stomach, fuelled by the unquenchable excitement I was feeling, sent ripples spiraling from my ankles to the nape of my neck.

After I went to the bathroom and brushed my teeth, and did the usual things one often does the first thing in the morning, I headed to the breakfast table.

"Nervous yet?" My mother asked jovially, with warmth as friendly as her love.

"No, Mommy," I answered shyly.

"This is your big day, Son," my father followed with his thick raspy accent, his words wild with excitement.

The moment was one of those moments that are sweet, rare, delightful, and unforgettable. Indeed, it was. We could hardly contain ourselves. We smiled from ear to ear so that it was difficult to eat the egg sandwich.

Moments later I was sitting in the back of my parents' car marveling at the enormous skyscrapers, the hordes of pedestrians decking the city streets, the uniformed policemen directing the sluggish traffic, the blaring fire truck speeding by, the long curling train that bent like a cat playing with its tail and the airplane ascending overhead. Of course, I may have seen all these activities before, but not in such a light and definitely not on the most exciting day of my life! I was thinking of all the new friends I was going to meet, the new environment, my teachers, the girls, everything! My heart was as bright as the day and overcrowded too, with joy, with a delight similar to that of first love. The joy often experienced on a wedding day. I felt a sense of uncontrollable happiness.

We finally arrived at the school and my parents, being the overprotective guardians they are, decided to accompany me to my class. It was a delightful walk. Everyone we met seemed to be smiling; an air of happiness appeared to pervade everything in the warm light of the autumn morning. It is safe to say that a breeze of love was blowing through the school, and the sight of parents and children alike, whom we met walking to and from the school in a sense of brotherly kindness, swiftly brought to my imagination the vision of angels in the halls of heaven. In every face lurked an open tenderness, and as my parents and I walked on in languid grace, my heart was filled with happiness that was immeasurable.

A warm and affectionate woman met us the moment we arrived in my classroom, and after the brief good-humored railleries, she guided me to my seat.

Five minutes later, it was time for class to begin and the teacher asked us to stand for morning devotion. She had a charming smile on her face, as she tapped her ruler on the table and broke out with the song "If You're Happy and You Know It, Clap Your Hands!"

Spontaneously, we all clapped our hands in harmony. "If you're happy and you know it, clap your hands! If you're happy and you know it, and you really want to show it, if you're happy and you know it, clap your hands!"

This went on for at least five minutes; we innocently sang and danced, getting lost in the much-anticipated fellowship, before our teacher restored order. After that, we prayed and moved into the introductory phase.

That day, for sure, was the happiest day of my life! I was young, innocent, aspiring, motivated, with an all-surveying sense.

Now that I am much older, my hair is tinged with grey, my steps are heavy, and I often fall asleep forgetting to take my shoes off, I see happiness in a different light. I see it as more than just the mere anticipation of something new, interesting or exciting. I see it as the end of man's main eternal aim. Happiness is the thing for which we dare to live or dare to die. It is a daily quest for everyone alike! Deep in every human heart is a burning desire for happiness. The soul desires happiness just as much as a flower desires air and water. The soul desires happiness like the night desires the moon and stars, or drought desires rain, or the summer desires the sun, or a blind man desires to see.

The desire for happiness is good, for it leads us through innumerable experiences so that the soul can realize, by practical experience, the emptiness of self-seeking, and thus learn wisdom. After we have run the whole gamut of experiences, our souls learn at last what true happiness is and how to arouse it.

The way in which we pursue this ultimate human destination is often pitiful! Firstly, happiness cannot be pursued, for the reason that it is not a dream or an ambition; neither is it a goal. The pursuit of happiness would be like that of an aggravated greyhound in the summer evening, spinning around and around breathlessly, trying to catch the end of its own tail. How comical such a scene always appears! When happiness is being sought in such a way, it becomes a satirical allegory, like Judd Isaacs' The Story of An Ostrich, in which something new is constantly sought, but seldom found. Happiness can only be aroused, for it is already within us, laid dormant until we do the things that stimulate it.

LIFE IS A PRECIOUS GIFT, AND WE SHOULD CHERISH IT WITH A GREAT DEAL OF CARE. It is not enough merely to live, but to live well. Many of us live without a design. We simply wander through this world aimlessly, like leaves in a gust. We spend all our days searching for a meaning, for a purpose, for a reason. But if we take our time and be patient with ourselves, if we try our best, if we look resolutely at the bright side of things, if we avail ourselves of the many blessings that surround us, we cannot help but feel that life is indeed a glorious inheritance.

TO BE BRIGHT AND HIGH-SPIRITED OFTEN REQUIRES AN EFFORT. There is a certain art in keeping ourselves happy and in this respect, as in others, we need to watch over and manage ourselves, almost as if we were somebody else. For there are many pleasures in life, but we must not let them rule us, or they will soon hand us over to sorrow.

Our lives should have a selfless purpose. Few of us, however, realize the wonderful privilege of living, or the blessings we have inherited, the glories and beauties of the infinite universe, which are all ours if we choose to have it so, to the extent to which we can make ourselves whatever we wish to be.

IT IS IMPERATIVE FOR US TO UNDERSTAND THAT LIFE IS A PARADOX: THE TRUE OBJECT OF LIFE IS NOT NECESSARILY THE ATTAINMENT OF HAPPINESS, YET IF WE ATTAIN THE TRUE OBJECT OF LIFE, WE ATTAIN HAPPINESS. Those who are ignorant of life's true purpose and who seek happiness high and low, year after year, fail to find it. On the other hand, those who recognize the true object of life, and follow it, attain happiness without seeking it.

Each of us, as we travel the way of life, has the choice, according to our deeds, of finding that happiness that stirs our soul. However, we must know what it takes to arouse the happiness that is already within us. It will be difficult for many of us to arouse this happiness, for too often we think only of the happiness of the body, and sacrifice that of the soul. Joy is naturally within us, it is owning up to the selfishness within us, in all ages, which has sown vanity to reap sorrow.

My dear reader, materialism cannot stimulate happiness. Materialism is certainly the baggage of happiness. Wealthy men are slaves to their own vaunts. They spend their precious time oppressing the lustful, jealous and covetous paupers with their self-satisfying vaunts. We should all learn from the history of the many mistakes made in arousing happiness the wrong way. Anthony sought for happiness in love, Brutus in glory, Caesar in dominion: the first found disgrace, the second disgust, the last ingratitude, and in the end, they all found destruction. Material possessions often bring danger, trouble and temptation. They require care to keep, and can only arouse true happiness when graciously dispersed. Where it can be a down payment to happiness, it should only bring out the charitable person whom we have always wanted to be. He who rests his happiness upon material possessions will forever be a stranger to happiness. For happiness cannot be aroused in wealth and all that it can command. It allures at first and promises happiness, but fails us miserably, and finally reveals itself as vanity at best. *"There is but one way to tranquility of mind and happiness,"* said the Great Philosopher, Epictetus. *"Let this therefore, be always ready at hand with thee, both when thou wakest early in the morning and all day long, and when thou goest late to sleep, to account no external thing thine own, but commit all these to God."*

I remember a conversation I had previously with a close friend, who is accustomed to relentlessly pursuing the superficial happiness of vanity. Blinded by the black mists of traditional misrepresentations and false indoctrinations, he holds that money is the only way to his happiness. I told him that such a pursuit is old, a misleading tradition. I told him that he could find happiness wholly from within, every time he does something to uplift the human race. He went on to state that this was only metaphysical, but the only sacred way to happiness is riches and more riches. I responded simply by telling him that the only way to happiness is doing right; the only way to sadness is doing what is opposite to it. I asked him if it is our earthly endeavor to heap up vanity, oftentimes doing so without the splendor of official dignity. He insisted that he who is in need cannot be happy; thus, he must chase riches. Naturally, I contradicted him by bringing to his attention the many who squander their happiness in the desperate hunt for affluence, thinking wealth, fame and rank alike can secure the happiness they so desire, only to be rudely awakened to the harsh truth that they were immensely deceived. Many, after such a disappointing discovery, turn to drugs, some to drinking, gambling, even suicide, everything but virtuous service; the only source of true happiness. Needless to say, we went back and forth for a while before he was finally able to see, with his own heart, the merit of what I was saying.

If we separate ourselves so much from the interests of those around us with whom we do not sympathize in their sufferings, we shut the door to our own happiness. If we avoid sympathy and wrap ourselves in a cold chain armor of selfishness, we exclude ourselves from many of the greatest and purest joys of life. How often do we labor for that which does not satisfy us? Most of us give ourselves an immense amount of useless trouble; we encumber ourselves on the journey of life with a dead weight of unnecessary baggage. Helen Keller wrote, *"Many persons have a wrong idea of what constitutes real happiness. It is not obtained through self-gratification but through fidelity to a worthy purpose."*

A LIFE OF SO-CALLED PLEASURE AND SELF-INDULGENCE IS NOT A LIFE OF REAL HAPPINESS. IF WE GIVE IN TO OUR MATERIAL DESIRES, WE FALL UNDER AN INTOLERABLE TYRANNY. Narcotics, alcohol, gambling, infidelity, at first, perhaps, may seem delightful, but there is bitterness at the end of them. We drink to satisfy the desire created by previous indulgence; so it is in other things. Repetition soon becomes a craving, not a pleasure. Resistance grows more and more painful. To resist is difficult, to give way is painful; until at length the wretched victim to ourselves can only purchase, or thinks we can only purchase, temporary relief from intolerable craving and depression, at the expense of far greater suffering in the future.

THE PLEASURES OF THE BODY CANNOT AROUSE HAPPINESS. Lust is full of uneasiness and emptiness. Sex, at times, is no different, and even at the times when it is all-pleasing, pleasure is not happiness. All these bodily pleasures rarely make good on the delight they promise. Neither do they lead as by-ways to happiness; nor do they make us completely happy. It is beyond doubt, then, that these paths do not arouse happiness.

TRUE HAPPINESS HAS LITTLE, IF ANYTHING, TO DO WITH RANK OR POWER. History has taught us such a lesson very well. Napoleon, the greatest military general of modern times, who had resolved on universal dominion, was summoned to answer for the violation of humankind. The Great Emperor was reduced to being an exile at Elba, and then a prisoner on the rock of St. Helena, and finally there on a barren island, in an unfrequented sea, in the crater of an extinguished volcano, there was the deathbed of the mighty conqueror. All his remarkable years of sublime events had come to that! His last hour had come; he, the man of destiny, he who had rocked the world was powerless, and so he died. On the wings of the tempest that raged with unusual fury. Behold! The fiery soul of that wonderful warrior, another witness to the existence of that eternal decree, which they who do not rule in righteousness shall perish from the earth. *"All rising to great place,"* said Bacon, *"is by a winding stair;"* and *"princes are like heavenly bodies, which have much veneration, but no rest."* Until we can find that honest zeal in our daily service as it relates to the betterment of humankind, we will always be a kingdom divided against itself, which, as our Lord said, cannot stand. Happiness, then, must be of a spiritual character. Until this harmony exists, there can be no real happiness.

HAPPY PEOPLE LIVE LIGHT AND CHILDLIKE, AS IF THEY ARE DAILY REHEARSING THEIR CHILDHOOD INNOCENCE. They are forever young and free in spirit. There is no universal measurement for happiness. What makes me ultimately happy may not be the same thing that makes you happy. What is universal about happy people however, is the heart of gratification and appreciation they feel when employed in the service of their fellow human being. Aristotle contended that: *"Happiness is the meaning and purpose of life, the whole aim and end of human existence."*

Can one attain a true state of happiness? Surely! However, it is also with the recognition that it is almost impossible to achieve if the source hinges on something external. What is it that makes you happy? I hope that you will not say money or some material object. Certainly, happiness does not depend on our material acquisitions. It is not something our spouse, family or friends can give us. It is not something the world can give us. It is something we have to find within ourselves.

We can stimulate this joy within us when we have put our hearts into our work and done our best. Anything contrary will not give us any happiness or peace. Society is often in conflict, in conspiracy against us. It is a vast cooperation in which we, the workers, are forced to agree, so that we can better secure our bread. Its ordinary duties such as commerce, manufactures, agriculture - the pursuits to which the vast majority are and must be devoted - are most often incompatible with the dignity or nobility of life. Oftentimes we have to surrender our liberty, peace, happiness, even our virtues, to maintain employment. The only way we can be truly happy is when we have done our earthly duty in a true spirit of service, to enhance our society, rather than just activities that whip at financial acquisitions.

We are seldom satisfied with our lives. We are forever seeking something that is better. Until we learn wisdom, we look for it in pleasure, in gratification of various kinds; namely, wealth, luxury and possession. The less evolved we are, the more convinced we are that happiness can be gained in these ways. Many of us seem to think that we have fallen on an age in the world when life is difficult and anxious. Many of us seem to think that there is less leisure than in earlier years, and the struggle for existence is keener than ever. All of us who hold such views should remember how much we have gained in science, in technology and in art. Subsequently, if we have less leisure, one reason is that life is so full of interest. Happiness is the daughter of employment, and overall I believe there never was a time when modest merit and virtuous industry were surer of reward.

HAPPINESS COMES FROM OUR OWN SOUL. We cannot expect to be happy if we do not lead pure and useful lives.

Let us try our best every day to arouse, by fellowships, friendships, and in pure human love, the happiness within us. These more evolved types get much more pleasure through the senses than do those who are more elemental. To be good company for ourselves we should store our minds well; fill them with pure and peaceful thoughts; with pleasant memories of the past and reasonable hopes for the future. We should, as far as may be, protect ourselves from self-reproach, from lust, and from vain pleasures. We will make our lives pure and peaceful, by resisting their obstructions, by placing restraint upon our appetites, and perhaps even more by strengthening and developing our tendencies to good. We should be careful, then, on what we allow our minds to dwell, for the soul lives and dies by its thoughts.

Although work well done brings a quiet sense of satisfaction and success in one's career and may be a source of gratification for a short time, this still may not satisfy the deep longing of the soul. This longing rests wholly upon our service. Not if we seek happiness in service, but if we serve others naturally, for the sake of serving. Then and only then will we find the only happiness that will endure and satisfy. Within all of us lies the ability to extend courtesies without expecting anything in return, outside of the rewarding feeling that accompanies a benign act.

All humans have a measure of kindness within them. All humans get a sense of worth from doing a kind deed to his fellow human. They feel a sense of duty, purpose and pride from it. I doubt that there is one person who has ever voluntarily done a kind deed and felt any kind of sadness from doing the deed. This is a clear indication that true and honest happiness is from service. It is from doing a good deed to a fellow citizen. Just imagine if every day when we got up, all we did was to give to people who are in need; if we had some vast warehouse of supplies that we just gave away to whoever was struggling. Oh! How we would live in an eternal happiness. *"Happiness is the only good. The time to be happy is now. The place to be happy is here. The way to be happy is to make others so."*- Robert Green Ingersoll. All I can say about such a quote is, "Brilliantly put!"

The problem is that most people are not in a position to give as they would like, or help as often as their hearts desire, so they just give up on the whole idea of service. Make no mistake about it, when I say 'Give,' I am not necessarily talking about material things. A simple piece of advice or words of encouragement can do the trick at times. Helping an elderly woman cross the street is service; visiting a neighbor for a social chat is service; visiting a nursing home and spending time with the elderly or the lame is service; volunteering at a school or church is service; a missionary trip to developing nations is service; helping out at a youth program is service. Charity is not confined.

True, we can find comfort, pleasure and security in success, self-realization and love. Surely, we can find comfort and pleasure when somebody loves us and we love them back. However, none of this self-gratification is happiness. This sentiment of which I speak lingers in human virtues and universal values that are given to a man from birth and are inalienable. It is always within in, ready to be aroused, not from heaping material possessions, but from being a dealer in virtuous services.

There is a tendency in society to confuse personal pleasures with happiness. We all see people flaunting various material possessions and sometimes we do envy them, this is human nature. However, we should not think for a second that they are happier than us because of it. I am not saying that we cannot be wealthy and happy; absolutely that is not the case. Happiness does not come from material possessions; it comes from the manipulation of the resource. It is also impossible without satisfaction and a sense of worth and usefulness. To shut oneself up from humankind, in most cases, is to lead a dull life. Our duty is to make ourselves useful, and thus, life may be most interesting. Therefore, a man who has no intimacy with society is a mere beast. From this perspective, only in social harmony resulting from service can we find true happiness.

I do not intend to dismay any of my readers. Neither do I intend to send a message of hopelessness. If you are "well off" there is nothing inhumane or immoral about that, but you must know that happiness cannot be aroused by heaping more wealth for ourselves, and forgetting our fellowmen. A true star is not a star because everyone around him thinks him so. He is a star because he makes everyone around him a star as well. That should be the same concept that we apply to our talent, skill or resources; whatever we can do for the greater good of our society should be evoked and applied. If we take all the wealth of the planet, give it to one man, and send him off on a remote island to live by himself, we would be surprised to see how swiftly he returns to the general population. To further state my claim, America is one of the wealthiest countries in the world, and yet, it never even ranks in the top five for "Countries With the Happiest People". The surprise is, it is a developing Latin nation, Costa Rico, which has been the steadiest in terms of happiness for some time now. If it were not too depressing, I would elaborate on the many wealthy celebrities who abruptly cut their own lives short because they cannot arouse the happiness laid dormant within them.

Chasing after material possessions, or chasing after lust and bodily pleasures, can never arouse our happiness. One only has to observe the lives of those who are always selfishly seeking and grabbing, hard in their dealings, to see how impossible it is for self-seekers to be happy.

No doubt, wealth entails more labor than poverty, and certainly more anxiety. Still it should, I think, be confessed that the possession of an income, whatever it may be, which increases somewhat as the years roll on, does add to the comfort of life. Nevertheless, the possession of wealth is not the possession of happiness. Moreover, it is as difficult to keep or enjoy money, as it is to make it. Keeping it is a dull and anxious labor. The fear of losing it hangs like a dark cloud over our life. Furthermore, the value of money depends mostly on knowing what to do with it. The poor man, as Emerson said, is the man who wishes to be rich, and the more a man has, the more he often longs to be richer. It does not matter whether they acquire riches or remain poor, they are equally unhappy.

Midas is a renowned case in point. He prayed that everything he touched would turn to gold. When his prayer came through, his wine turned to gold, his bread turned to gold, even his clothes turned to gold. How unhappy he became.

MANY OF US CHOSE TO GIVE UP THAT GOD-GIVEN QUALITY OF PHILANTHROPY. In contrast to this, we have only to go out of our way to do a kind and perfectly disinterested action and experience the glow of sheer happiness that it brings, to realize that we are dealing with a law of life that is as sure and unalterable as the law of gravity.

We all have a purpose in life, and this must have for its object the betterment of the lives of others, either few or many. The law of service should be obeyed; otherwise, there can be no happiness. Again, this may fill some readers with dismay, for they may be employed in an occupation that apparently does no good to anyone other than themselves.

We have only to do our daily work, not as a task which must be "got through," in order to bring us a living, or because it is expected of us that we should work, but as an offering of love to life and the world, to come into harmony with the great law of service. Our ideas of values with regard to occupations are altogether erroneous, from the internal wisdom point of view. The gathering of garbage from our city streets, if faithfully done in a true spirit of service, is of as much value and real importance as flying an airplane, saving a life in the surgical theater or defending our country's liberty. We can never truthfully say that one act of service is of greater value, or is more important than another. All that the higher law looks at is the motive. Therefore, if our motive is right, honest and godly, we can have the humblest and, apparently, most useless occupation, and yet be happy because we satisfy the law of service.

THE ONLY WAY TO HAPPINESS IS THROUGH SERVICE. The man who cannot find happiness in being of service to his fellow-man will not find happiness at all. It is, I believe, our moral duty as humans to use our talents, skills and intelligence in a philanthropic manner to enhance all those around us. He who does not practice the law of service will not be able to reach others and it will be difficult for others to reach him. This is the universal law of service. We cannot expect to attract others unless we are of service to them. The businessperson who has something to sell should have something to give, and he should talk about it from the point of view of the people to whom he wants to sell his goods. In the same way, the journalist, the preacher, and the politician must look at things from the point of view of those they intend to reach. They must feel the needs of others, then reach out and meet those needs. They can never have a large following unless they give something. The same law runs into human relationships. How we dislike the man who talks only about himself, the man who inquires about no one else's problems, the man who never puts his feet in others' shoes, but dully and uncaringly goes on and on, egotistically hammering away on the only subject that interests him - namely, himself.

HAPPINESS CAN ONLY BE AROUSED THROUGH SERVICES THAT ARE KIND IN NATURE. A heart without it is a pure and absolute tyranny in which no happiness can abide. The deeds of kindness put life and spirit into our fellow humans and happiness into our own hearts. It serves justice, peace and love, which are instrumental in arousing the happiness within us. Happiness is inevitable when the habits of kindness, directed by the right reasons, are demonstrable in our duty to each other. Only in these kinds of virtue can we find perpetual exuberance. The inclination to it is imprinted deeply in the nature of kind service; so much so that if it is issued not toward men, it will take unto other living creatures, as it is seen in people who found completion in giving alms to dogs, cats, birds, and other living creatures.

Happy is the man who makes it his point of duty to be gracious and courteous to strangers; it shows he is a citizen of the world, and that his heart is no island, cut off from other lands, but a continent, that joins to them. Happy is the man who is kind-hearted toward the suffering of others; it shows that his heart is righteous. When we forgive our transgressors and remit their offenses, it shows that our minds are above malice. If we are thankful for even the least charity, it shows that we are grateful.

GENTLE KINDNESS HELPS TO SHIELD A BROTHER AGAINST THE WAVES AND WEATHERS OF TIME. It will not allow us to pass our brother by who lowers himself in the humble posture of petition. Blessed is the house that houses a stranger in need.

Half of this world knows nothing about the other half. The Discovery Channel often shows us people eating their dinner off human bones. Others set up their housekeeping, with two or three mud pots, a stone to grind meal, and a mat that is the bed. The house - namely, a tomb - is ready without rent or taxes. No rain can pass through the roof, and there is no door, for there is no want of one, as there is nothing to lose. If the house does not please them, they walk out and enter another, as there are several hundreds at their command. Some live in dumpsters, worrying the least about their daily meals. Some feast upon rats, mice and all kinds of rodents. Some live among corpses and rags. Some live in sandy deserts, caves or igloos. Some of them, when they speak, sound like the shrieking of bats or the whistling of cardinals. Some have no proper names and are called by their height, thickness, or other accidental quality. Still, I do not suppose for a minute that these various kinds of human are strangers to happiness. Indeed, they are not. If, indeed, we cannot arouse happiness, the fault is generally in ourselves. Socrates lived under the Thirty Tyrants. Epictetus was a poor slave, and yet how much we owe them!

This is what Epictetus said in prison while addressing his captors: *"How is it possible that a man who has nothing, who is naked, houseless, without a hearth, squalid, without a slave, without a city, can pass a life that flows easily? See, God has sent a man to show you that it is possible. Look at me, who am without a city, without a house, without possessions, without a slave; I sleep on the ground; I have no wife, no children, but only the earth and heavens, and one poor cloak. And what do I want? Am I not without sorrow? Am I not without fear? Am I not free? When did any of you see me failing in the object of my desire? Or ever falling into that which I would avoid? Did I ever blame God or man? Did I ever accuse any man? Did any of you ever see me with a sorrowful countenance? And how do I meet with those whom you are afraid of and admire? Do not I treat them like slaves? Who, when he sees me, does not think that he sees his king and master?"*

HAPPINESS, I CONTEND, IS NOT IN MATERIAL POSSESSIONS. All one has to do is participate in a worthy service, and behold the joy it puts on his fellow man's face. What greater joy is there than helping a friend in need, a family in need, or a stranger in need? The result is always refreshing as the summer wind. I am apt to shut the door of my heart against any service that is contrary to this joy. I am not here to tell you that I am happy all the time, or that I am virtuous all the time. Man is an ever-erring beast, and surely, that includes me. However, I have eyes to see, therefore I use them; I have ears to ear, therefore I hear; I have a mind of my own; subsequently, I use it to influence my words and deeds independently of social, political, or economic powers. I try as often as I can to be guided by the light of uprightness in service to my fellowmen, not because I am in search of happiness, but because in my heart I feel that that is the reason I was born - to service humanity. I do not know of a way to measure happiness. On the other hand, just like pain, it cannot be measured but by the one who feels it. I do not think for a second that a wealthy man who walks around arrogantly, flaunting his riches with a broad insidious smile, is any happier than an anchorite or a peasant in some developing nation. For I reckon true happiness does not come from possessions; it can only be aroused through service to a fellow-man.

To put it all together in a nutshell: I am not ashamed of my obstinacy to badges and names, to large societies and dead institutions, to erring traditions and ideologies, or to any opposition to my definition of happiness and the only way it can be aroused. The truth of the matter is, wealth is not necessarily an advantage, but that whether it is so or not depends on the use we make of it. The same, however, might be said of most other opportunities and privileges; knowledge and strength, beauty and skill, may all be abused. If we neglect or misuse them we are worse off than if we had never had them.

Wealth is only a disadvantage in the hands of those who do not know how to use it. Mark Twain once said that a man who can read and does not, has no advantage over the man who is illiterate. It is so, too, with a man of wealth who cannot manipulate it for the greater good of his friends, family and community. Wealth should only have one power, and that is the power of virtuous service.

It would be easy to exaggerate the advantages of money. It is well worth having, and worth working for, but it does not require too great a sacrifice, not indeed to offer our souls for it. If wealth were to be valued because it gives happiness, clearly it would be a mistake to sacrifice happiness in the struggle for it.

One should not spend his life in a vain pursuit of happiness, for the soul does not find it from seeking. We can only fuel this emotion within us when we have put our hearts into our work and done our best, when we have demonstrated a loving kindness to our fellow humans. We can only find happiness when we freely offer our service to others and see the smiles upon their faces, knowing that it is owing to the service that we have provided them.

OUR PURPOSE ON EARTH IS TO REACH FOR THE BETTERMENT OF THE LIVES OF OTHERS, THROUGH OUR WORTHY SERVICES, NOT ONE WE CHOOSE TO DO BECAUSE WE ARE GRABBING AT HAPPINESS, BUT BECAUSE IT IS THE RIGHT THING TO DO. Title and rank are of no importance, just as long as we do our duty faithfully in a true spirit of service. We will certainly find happiness if we have done our best to make others happy, to promote peace on earth and goodwill amongst men. Nothing can do more to release us from the cares of this world, which consume so much of our time, and embitter so much of our life. When men on earth have done their best, angels in heaven cannot compete. Therefore, there is no unhappiness in doing a good deed.

We should always bear in mind that deeds of kindness put life and spirit into our fellow humans and happiness into our own hearts.

"If a man is unhappy, this must be his own fault; for God made all men to be happy." - Words of wisdom from Epictetus.

This knowledge is very important for practical, everyday life; for the one who possesses this quiet joy can never be defeated in life's battles. He has something within him that can never be quenched, which will lead him from victory to victory along life's journey.

Becoming A Better Friend

"Friendship is a single soul dwelling in two bodies."

-Aristotle

"All men," said Socrates, *"have their different objects of ambition - horses, dogs, money, honor, as the case may be; but for my own part I would rather have a good friend than all these put together."*

Indeed, that was an accurate statement. For without friends, the world would be a wilderness and every man would be a beast. An element of love suffused the entire human family. How many we see in the street, or sit with in church, who, though silently, we warmly rejoice to be amid their company. The sweet indulgence with our fellow humans is always a pleasant excitement, like a shower of sunlight in the dark. Everyone, I believe, passes his life in search of friendship. Every breathing man requires some politeness, some friendliness, some kindness, some respect, some acknowledgement, and some appreciation - requires an attentive ear, a caring hand, a friendly eye, and a loving heart. This is natural, for no one is an island, and no human being can claim total independence in the full sense of the word.

It is equally true as well that every breathing man carries around with him some fame, some talent, and some whim of philosophy in his head that he is dying to share. No matter a person's financial status, educational status, or religious status, he more often than not has some fame or talent or ideology that we can learn from, or that we will find interesting.

It is safe to assert then, that based on the requirements of every man, he will surely need a friend. For politeness, friendliness, kindness, respect, acknowledgement, appreciation, and a loving heart are the fundamental components of a true friendship. True friends indeed are the beautiful gifts from God, who daily shows Himself in such images to us. Personally, I embrace solitude, and yet I am grateful to appreciate my lovely noble-minded friends, with whom I exchange joys and happiness measureless to man. Every one of my friends represents a world in me, a world not born until they arrived. They are my asylum and my shelter-house, and I feel privileged to be in relationships with others who are aiming for a better tomorrow, embarking on a meaningful life, and who are keeping my life purposeful and interesting. I am honored to be amongst others who are always seeking a way to lift their community and their country to brighter days.

I TAKE PRIDE IN MY FRIENDS' ACCOMPLISHMENTS AS IF THEY ARE MINE. I feel as warmly when they are praised as when I am praised. I carry a deep admiration for all of them. In fact, I have a deep admiration for all thriving friendships, because a genuine friend is rare and almost impossible to find. Diamonds and gold, I believe, are easier to find than a warm and loving friend with whom we may be sincere without being ridiculed or scorned, with whom we may think aloud without being afraid or ashamed. We all need someone who can improve our happiness and abate our loneliness, one who can be silent with us in a moment of despair, and cry with us in an hour of grief and mourning, one who can introduce warmth in the midst of a storm.

CERTAINLY, A TRUE FRIEND IS FAITHFUL, LIKE THE HAND THAT LIFTS THE GLOBE. Willing to be there until all the world has ceased to roll, in good times and bad, a true friend is the source of hope beyond the gloomy skies. A true friend is kind, compassionate, and warmer than a smile. A true friend is patient. We have arrived, at last, in the presence of someone so real and understanding that we may drop even those undermost garments of dissimulation.

However, the higher the style we demand of friendship, of course the less easy it is to establish with flesh and blood. Honestly, every single human walks alone in this world. Friends, such as we desire, are dreams and fables. It, like the immortality of the soul, is too divine. Still, we go on with a sublime hope that cheers the faithful heart, that elsewhere, outside of ourselves, souls are now acting, enduring and daring, who can love us for who we are, and who we can love for who they are as well. How can these souls be entwined into something heavenly? How can these souls find each other like some biological insemination and metamorphose into something bigger than themselves? How can we discover a genuine kind-hearted friend?

Well, to discover a genuine friend, we have to first be the friend we wish to have. Ewe wisdom says, *"Your goodness is not for yourself only, it is for others."* The only reward of virtue is virtue. The only way to have a friend is to be one. Therefore, let us treat our friends as we would have them treat us. Let us be willing to require of ourselves the same as that we require of others. It is unreasonable to seek a friendship that we are unable to give ourselves. Neither should we expect any personality traits from our friend that we ourselves are not willing to display. The fair course is to first be accommodating ourselves, and then to look out for another of like character. Men who are united by affection learn, firstly, to take delight in fair and even-handed conduct, to bear each other's burdens, never to ask each other for anything inconsistent with integrity, and to not only serve and love, but also to respect each other.

There are people who give the palm to riches, but it gives life a completely new meaning having repose, which we always find in the mutual goodwill of a friend. What can be more delightful than to have someone to whom we can say everything with the same absolute confidence as to ourselves? Even riches are robbed of half their value if we have no one to share them with. Ambition embraces fame, riches embrace pleasure, power embraces reputation, health embraces wellness, but friendship embraces innumerable advantages.

A GOOD FRIENDSHIP GIVES US BRIGHT HOPES FOR THE FUTURE AND EASES WEAKNESS AND DESPAIR. In the face of a true friend, we see as it were, a second self. So that where our friends are, we are; if our friends are happy, we are happy as well. This unearthly bond of which we desire, if it ought to last, MUST spring from a natural impulse. It should be birthed from an inclination of the soul combined with a certain instinctive feeling of love and kindness. Friendship should not spring from a wish for help or from a deliberate calculation of the material advantage it is likely to confer. It should emerge from the indication of good values and high moral standards, to which souls of like characters are naturally attracted. When that is the case, the solidification of alliance is almost instantaneous.

If, somehow, we decide to go the material route, we must be sure to prepare ourselves for a sad disappointment. What can be more irrational than to take delight in many objects incapable of response, such as clothes, cars, jewelry and money, and yet to take little or none in a sentient being endowed with affection, which has the ability of loving us back? Nothing is more delightful than the return of affection, and the mutual interchange of kindness.

We are inclined to think that friends, at times, ought to be in need of something. What scope would our affections have if our friends never need our service or charity? On what ground would we truly display our worth as a friend? How else would we be able to show how much we care? However, it is not friendship that should follow material advantage, but material advantage that should follow friendship.

TRUE FRIENDSHIP, I REPEAT, IS RARE; OF COURSE, ALL EXCELLENT THINGS ARE RARE. Nothing in the world is so hard to find as a thing entirely perfect. However, most of us consider something to be of value only if we can make a profit from it. We choose our friends as a stockbroker chooses his stocks, caring most for those by whom we hope to make the most profit. We fail to learn from our own feelings the nature and the strength of friendship. All of us love ourselves, not for any reward, which such love may bring, but because we are dear to ourselves independently of anything else.

What rational man would choose a life of the greatest wealth and abundance on the condition of neither loving nor being beloved by any creature? That is the sort of life tyrants endure. They, of course, can count on no fidelity, no affection, and no security for the goodwill of anyone. Sometimes the poorest of friends, when they become wealthy, undergo a complete change of friends. They banish their old friends and hurriedly gather new ones. Can anything be more ridiculous than those who have all the opportunities which prosperity, wealth, and great means can donate, securing all that money can buy but not securing friends, who are the most valuable and beautiful treasure of life? Even if those possessions, which are the gifts of fortune, do prove permanent, life, without the consolations and companionship of genuine friends, can never be anything but joyless.

    A friendship derived out of materialism simply will not last. For instance, a man of wealth who has a poor friend. Look how imbalanced the union is. Perhaps, the man of wealth does not even know where his poor friend lives. The friendship, most of the time, revolves around the ideas and activities of the friend of wealth. Such friendship is nothing but a mutual convenience. When our confidence in ourselves is the greatest, when we are so fortified by virtue and comfort as to want nothing and to feel absolutely self-dependent, it is then that we are most conspicuous for seeking out and maintaining friendships. I know this might be discouraging for many readers, for most friendships nowadays are built on expediency. Most of us these days purposely go out seeking friends who can do things for us. We can hardly find people nowadays who are willing to be friends with someone where there seem to be no material benefits. Friendship should not be built on such shallowness. It should spring from similarities in good values and by admiring someone for the person they are, the same virtue that we recognize in ourselves. Even though many great material advantages may follow, they should not be the source from which the friendship is formed. Friendship is not a way of extorting gratitude; do not regard an act of kindness as an investment. Friendship follows a natural inclination to liberality, so we look on it as worth trying for, not because we are attracted to it by the expectation of ulterior gain, but in the conviction that what it has to give us is from first to last included in the feeling itself.

    TO BE A TRUE FRIEND WE SHOULD NOT REFER ANYTHING TO SELF-INTEREST. We should not join the union to see what we can get, without ever thinking of what we can give. We should seek comfort in the friendship by being more inclined to do a good service than to ask a return. Its origin from a natural impulse rather than from a sense of need will be at once more dignified and more in accordance with reality. If it were true that material advantages cemented friendship, it would be equally true that if the resource runs out, the friendship would swiftly dissolve. Therefore, anyone who enters a friendship for self is fated to be terribly disappointed.

NOTHING DESTROYS A FRIENDSHIP QUICKER THAN SELF-INTEREST. That is the reason it is important for me to expound repeatedly on the basis by which a friendship should be formed. If the union did not spring from a natural impulse, it will not last. It should emerge from an inclination of the soul combined with a certain natural feeling of affection and kindheartedness, not from seeking material assistance. So much for the origin of friendship; perhaps some readers would not care to hear any more.

Now that we have secured our friends, not for material advantage, but for likeness in virtue and character, there are traits we need to exorcise to have a lasting bond. One of the most difficult things in the world is for a friendship to remain unimpaired to the end of life. There seem to be more things that disrupt the flow of a great friendship than things that bind it closer together. So many things might intervene: conflicting interests, differences of opinion, natural envy, and frequent changes in character. Indeed, it seems that it takes more than wisdom and virtue to maintain a friendship. I read somewhere that an ancient philosopher said it takes pure good luck. With these premises, then, let us first lay down the most important characteristics of a friendship.

MUTUAL RESPECT: This should be the first rule of friendship. Consequently, the easiest and quickest way to earn respect is to be respectful. The basic principle we owe to each other is that of respect. We do not have to know or love someone to respect them. Every encounter with our fellow humans should be with a level of respect. Respect should be an attitude, not a thing given to a person after they have proven themselves.

There is a varied level of importance placed on respect. Some people, like me, depend only on freely giving respect to gain it. I believe that it should be reciprocal regardless of status. It is not for us to go out of our way to impress a friend. Others respect others because they are seeking some sort of benefit from the gesture. True respect is independent of possession or social status. Genuine respect, as I established before, is an attitude. It supersedes ideology. It is not only about what we admire in ourselves that is worthy of our respect. Certainly, respect is selfless. For example, not everyone sees beauty through the same glasses. If we go out disrespecting our friends because of a quality that we may not necessarily find in ourselves, we will not be able to keep them. When we respect our friends, we listen to them. We listen to their ideas and opinions. We listen to their cares and concerns. We listen to their successes and failures. We listen to their joys and their sorrows. We listen to the good and the bad. Remember that I also mentioned earlier that I take pride in my friends' accomplishments as if they are mine, and triumph in their virtues. I feel as warmly when they are praised as when I am praised. That is respect for a friend's accomplishment.

If we want our bond to last, we have to maintain mutual respect for each other. On the contrary, we should not enslave ourselves by the desire for the respect and admiration of our friends. This may force us to act contrary to our most profound principle.

UNDERSTANDING: A true friend should be full of simplicity, social disposition, and a sympathetic nature. In all of these attributes, we will find that understanding is one of the biggest elements in a lasting friendship. Wholesome understanding, indeed, is one of the fundamental characteristics of a lasting alliance. It helps us to appreciate rightly the point of view of our friends. It helps us to see things from their point of view, to understand their situation that we can have a thorough appreciation of their rationale. This we can never do if we are immersed in the fog, either of their personal selfishness, or our own. By understanding our friends, we can appreciate our differences.

If a friend is in the depths of despair because she cannot afford a dress she so desires, it does not help her by telling her the truth about her character, and lecturing her upon her vanity in wasting grief upon such a trifle, when there are so many serious troubles in the world to bicker over. From her point of view, the fact that she cannot get that dress is a travesty. You should not let such a petty trifle offend you. Instead, you should keep quiet and let her see that you understand her disappointment, while at the same time holding your own standard. She will be led much more easily and more truly to see for herself the smallness of her attitude.

Understanding a friend at times is like understanding a child. We give loving sympathy to a child who cries when he breaks his toy, although we know there is nothing real to grieve about. The object is, perhaps, some cheap Chinese-made plastic of no real value. However, to the child, it means more than that. It is something that comforts him. It is something to grieve about, something very real; but we can only sympathize helpfully with his point of view by keeping ourselves clearly in the light of our own more mature point of view. An unpleasant misunderstanding arises because of a state of mind; it is not because of a person. Therefore, we can stop a misunderstanding if one of us maintains a quiet mind. How do we maintain a quiet mind? We maintain a quiet mind by positively refusing to resent or to resist whatever our friend says or does. Our friend may be remarkably irritating in what he thinks or does; there may not only be no justice in it, but in our view, no sense at all. Still, that gives us no right to resent him. He has exactly the same individual right to be completely wrong that we have to be completely right. In all fairness to justice, and the friendship, we cannot deny him that right. If we try to deprive him of his freedom to think as he pleases by our resistance to his opinion, it is not the misunderstanding that is making the trouble; it is our resistance to it. Suppose, on the other hand, our friend considers our opinion wrong and is resisting it even more than we are resisting his. That again is no business of ours. We have no right to interfere with his or any other man's resistance to an opinion.

I know two people, apparently very true friends, who had a dispute. Each one went separately to a third friend, in great unhappiness, with the whole story. The third person listened carefully, and in his answer, which was given very thoughtfully, he spoke hardly one word of the other, but referred each man to himself and his own mistakes. Fortunately, he was listened to with trustful attention and intelligent agreement. Each friend came to see clearly and acknowledge his own mistakes, and the result was that the friendship was not patched up to go on with further and similar interruptions, but weeds were removed which were obstructing its growth, and these friends have grown in mutual wholesome sympathy to each other and to those about them. Each had grasped the principle taught to him by the loving, intelligent friend to whom they had each deferred. You see, what I am trying to make clear is that peace between two friends does not depend primarily upon both parties; it depends really at first upon only one. The peace grows and may be sooner established if each one of the friends works alone and with equal interest on refusing to nurse resentment or resistance, and so he will be able to give attention with a clear mind to the attitude of the other. That, of course, is ideal in the clearing up of misunderstandings and putting "friendly" quarrels out of the question.

We do not have any right to depend in the very least on the attitude of our friend to bring peace. Of course, if our friend does his work while we are doing ours, so much the better. But if he is delaying or refusing to do his work entirely, while it makes ours all the more difficult, we can, in as far as we are personally concerned, welcome the difficulty. For the greater the difficulty, the stronger and the more positive must be our refusal to resent or resist, and that very effort will result in establishing more firmly within us peaceful intelligence and affection, which is needed to bring our friend to his senses.

The mind of a friend who has been blind to his faults begins to be clarified much sooner if his friend acknowledges openly, and without excuse, his own fault. To begin with, the other man does not want to be outdone in apparent honesty, and that often leads to a genuine honesty on his part, which enables him to see himself as he is in more than one detail, and to meet his friend in compromise.

TOLERANCE is another trait of a lasting friendship. It is living with the things or persons we do not necessarily agree with but cannot change because it is not our duty to change them. We should be willing to accept him for who he is. We should not expect him to be always the best of himself. We should not be surprised at his various forms of selfishness. This will enable us to keep persistently near his best qualities, while enduring his defects. It is a happy fact that getting free from resentment, our friend has the effect of keeping us close to that which is best in him. For instance, we have some friends who are very negative and doubtful. They do not understand that great minds are not without a touch of insanity. They have some things about them that are very discouraging and pessimistic. They often make a laughingstock of our brightest idea, often on the sole basis that it is new and uncommon. This temper of mind, contrary to friendship, too often chokes us with despair to seek the alliance of strangers. Yet, we can only be despairing because of our intolerance to their ignorance. For seriously, as much as we would want the support of the ones closest to us, every new idea, especially the one that ushers in a brighter dawn, is always shunned on the sole basis that it is new. Due to their stubborn hold on tradition, old ideas and conventionalities have never hesitated to make use of the foulest and cruellest means to stay the arrival of the new, unconventional ones. Needless to say, we retrace our steps into the distant past to understand the enormity of resistance, difficulties and hardships placed in the path of every progressive idea. If we understand such an equation tolerably, then we would not take any offense to their "Doubting Thomas" persona. We would be guilty of a grave transgression if we deserted them on the basis that they did not like our view or idea. Friends can co-exist and still maintain independence in their thoughts and ideas. Surely, they have the right to find fault with our idea. Friends have the right to find fault with their friends. Plutarch said, *"I don't need a friend who changes when I change and who nods when I nod; my shadow does that much better."* I would advise you to quickly get rid of friends who approve of all you do. In all times, the honesty of a true friend should always be respected; but certainly, we are under no obligation to comply to the contrary. All we can do is avoid lending too readily an ear to their conflicting opinions.

    LOYALTY ranks among the several qualifications of a good friend as the most imperative. No one appreciates a fair-weather character. Some of us are like shadows; we are only seen when the sun is shining. But when the rain is falling, we disappear quicker than a teardrop in the summer sun. How often we are disappointed by the one we cherish and regard the most, on discovering that he cherishes and regards us the least.

LOYALTY IS FAITHFULNESS AND DEVOTION; allegiance to a person to whom one is bound by a personal virtue. First Samuel 18:1 gives us a perfect example of two people bound together by a personal goodness. The verse reads, *"Now it came about... that the soul of Jonathan was knitted to the soul of David."* Indeed, that is how loyalty brings friends together in such a way so that, in a sense, two become one. Unwavering loyalty in a friendship is of the utmost importance. Proverbs 27:17 states, *"Iron sharpens iron, so one man sharpens another."* A loyal friendship provides support and strength, especially when needed the most. "One man sharpens another."

I consider there to be many components of loyalty in a friendship. When our friends tell us something personal, they expect us to keep it a secret; keeping such a secret demonstrates loyalty. Helping a friend in need is also another element of loyalty. When we help a friend naturally, without being asked to do so, we have truly established the heights of devotion. There is nothing more sublime than voluntary kindness. It shows that we are paying attention to our friend and what is going on in their life. There should be a rule though; do not consent or ask of our friend that which is not honorable or just. Nature has given us friendship as the handmaid of virtue, not as a partner in guilt. Certainly, a real friend will never force upon his friend the obligation to stand by him in cases where he is terribly wrong and in need of defense. I believe loyalty should be exclusively reserved for only that which is just, fair, righteous and honest, even if it is contrary to race, religion or country. Let this, then, be laid down as the first law of loyalty - that we should ask from friends, and do for friends, only what is honorable. Let the influence of friends who give good advice be paramount and let this influence be used to enforce advice not only in plainspoken terms, but also in practice. One of the most wonderful things in the world is the effect we seem to have on others, when we are simply working in ourselves with no thought whatever of influencing them.

UNSELFISHNESS is putting the general needs or good or interests of our friends first. The poem below is one of my favorite poems on this subject and so I decided to share it with you. Enjoy.

> I live to hold companion
> With all that is pure and true
> I live for the wrong that I can cease
> And the right that I can do
>
> I live to share my brother's grief
> And help him when I can
> Knowing Man does not make the charity;
> The charity makes the man
>
> I live to be that giving hand
> That never cease to give
> To be that shining hope
> When you lost the will to live
>
> I live to shelter the shelterless
> To lead the weak and blind
> I live to lift to a deeper destiny
> The best of humankind
>
> I live to raise that weary heart
> From its pillar of stone
> I live for that great cause
> That is still unknown
>
> I live for the ones I love;
> Even the ones who do not love me
> I live for the Gods of lands and seas
> And the ones above me

-Feial Britton

The poem demonstrates the willingness of the author to be unselfish. There is no suggestion in the poem that he has any expectation of charity from humankind, but in every stanza he conveys to his readers his life's purpose. John F. Kennedy once said, *"Ask not what your country can do for you, but what you can do for your country."* The same rule applies to friendship. In having a friend, the objective is not that our friends are compelled to make us a better person, although that is one of the advantages of having friends. Instead, it is how we can be of service to the ones we have freely chosen as our friends. If we tend to sway toward the benefits of friends, we will probably wake up one morning and find ourselves without one.

Another quality in being a good friend is finding the time and patience to listen to a friend. Some of us require of our friends their undivided attention, whether it is a mere achievement we are chattering about, or whether it is a dire situation. Yet, we never have the time to listen to what they have to say. We are always swift to shut them out as if we are the only relevant one in the relationship, and as if there is nothing to learn from them. There is hardly anyone from whom we may not learn much, if only they will trouble themselves to tell us. And even if they teach us nothing, they may help us by the stimulus of intelligent questions, or the warmth of sympathy.

WE SHOULD NOT BE SELFISH IN A FRIENDSHIP. We should always be prepared to lend a hand to our friends unselfishly. *"The humanity of friendship, comradeship, citizenship and brotherhood,"* said Mother Teresa, *"is as such that if thou wilt give the left hand, then I will give the right. That feeling is the hallmark of humanity in intimate intercourse, and without that feeling every friendship, every band of disciples, every display of togetherness, sooner or later becomes a fraud."* As I have said earlier, we have to be the friend we wish to have. The only reward of virtue is virtue; the only way to have a true friend is to be one. We must treat our friends as we would have them treat us, and require of ourselves the same as we require of others. Hence, let us not be caught up into ourselves and let the relationship be about us. The union is not for us to own. It is equally our friends' as it is ours. Since we do not appreciate a self-centered, self-indulgent, self-interested, self-absorbed friend, sincerely then, we should not be one.

KINDNESS IS ANOTHER TRAIT OF A LASTING FRIENDSHIP. Ever-flowing is a heart that is being fed by human kindness. There is nothing more celestial than that little trait of benevolence. Can another be so blessed, and we so pure, that we can offer him tenderness? When a man becomes dear to me, I have touched the hem of fortune. I find very little written directly to the heart of this matter in books. I have a few lines that I can't help but remember. Emerson said, *"I offer myself faintly and bluntly to those whose I effectually am, and tender myself least to him to whom I am the most devoted."* He further goes on to say, *"I hate the prostitution of the name of friendship to signify modish and worldly alliances."* Indeed, kindness should not be conditional. We should not cease to acknowledge a friend who is in need of our compassion. On the other hand, when we give time or aid to a friend, we should do so out of love, and not for display. When charity is for show and not for service, it pulls down the host. Everyone is more valuable than his splendor of table and draperies. How sick one gets of the false kindness of a so-called friend! "I wish I could help you - do let me do something for you!" is said from a sugar-coating of "kindness" with arrogance and a sense of superiority seething and sizzling underneath. It is surprising the amount of unconscious antagonism one friend can carry against another in the name of charity. Many of us, from vanity, mistreat even our closest friends, when in the presence of witnesses to whom we wish to make our own preponderance clear.

KINDNESS SHOULD BE A PART OF OUR FIBER SO THAT OUR FRIENDS DO NOT AND CANNOT ROUSE HOSTILITY IN US, WHEN IN NEED AND ASKING FOR ASSISTANCE. As friends, our interests are always the same - to see each other prosperous and happy in this world, and be the best living human being that we can possibly be. Therefore, when a friend is in need of aid of any kind, there is an important interest at stake to which we should always be sensitive. Not helping a friend when we can is a huge conflict of interest. We should not break our treaty when our friends need us the most, and forsake them, and shatter fellowship we have sworn to shelter. Neither should kindness come across as a burden to us, whereas, our friend, upon receiving our charity, thinks we are under a weight heavier than that of the Brooklyn Bridge. Some of us, of course, have no naturally kind sentiment within us, and often find every little kind deed burdensome. When we are assisting a friend, we should be very careful not to let the friend feel less of a person because they are seeking our assistance. Some friends because of their arrogance will tell the world that they have done such-and-such for so-and-so, because they want to be seen as the superior friend or they are seeking some kind of fame. Such kindness is not genuine. It is more for self than for the improvement of our situation. An act of condescension is scarcely accepted as brotherly kindness, nor what seems to be done with a great deal of complaining. We should not be dreadfully condescending, that we cannot avoid seizing upon every small opportunity of making our greatness felt.

  I will conclude this topic by saying that friendship is a partnership. One that combines moral rectitude, fame, peace of mind, vanity and serenity; all that men think desirable because with them life is happy, but without them cannot be so. The sanity and prosperity of humans rest dangerously upon friendship. It makes us not a mere beast but a human being. We all need a caring friend. Friendship is a necessary aspect of every human's life, as we are not self-sufficient in and of ourselves. On this basic then, I am obliged to advise you to please choose your friends wisely. As it is important to be of good influence to our friends, we should choose prudently friends who can also have a productive impact on us as well. Friendship is destroyed by associating with the base, with equals equality is gained, and with the distinguished, distinction. If you want to know your worth you should total all of your friends' worth plus yours and divide it by the number of friends. Therefore, if you are the only friend in the bunch that is worth something then indeed you are worth nothing. The greatest leaders are a reflection of the people surrounding them. They did not become so by attracting to themselves people of lower character.

GREAT MINDS ARE LIKE STARS; THE MORE THEY ARE, THE BRIGHTER EACH SHINES. And the brightest star is difficult to see amidst a fleet of shrouding black clouds. Take for example the animal kingdom. It would make for great comedy for a lion and a deer to be friends. Lions are dominant creatures. Their basic role in the jungle is to divide and conquer, to suppress and tyrannize. They are of a fearless character, determined to remain the king of the jungle. A deer on the other hand is the sport of bravery. Their courage is in their feet. They are preys to every cold-blooded creature thereabout. There is absolutely no way a predator and a prey can be friends. Lion in this allegoric expression represents the proactive friend who is a predator to an opportunity to improve his life or the lives of others. He is always swift to conquer and tyrannize his adversities. Whereas the deer, a reactive prey, always grazing and extremely vulnerable to obstacles and obstructions. He always runs away from the least brushing sound he hears, even when it is nothing but the falling "dry limb" of an adversity. What kind of distinction can a deer offer a lion? He has no effect in forming and maturing the lion's character. Can you imagine a lion calling on a deer for hunting ideas and techniques? I am not saying that we should only seek friends who are wealthier than us, more intelligible, or of a firmer moral fortitude. What I am saying is to be careful to choose friends that can help us grow as we also can help them grow. Conflict of morality, goals, aim and objective, education and buoyancy are just a few thorns which will choke the chance for a productive friendship. Just as there is a contagiousness in every example of a honorable conduct as there is an equally contagiousness in every example of a dishonorable one.

THERE ARE MANY VALUABLE THINGS IN LIFE, BUT A TRUE FRIENDSHIP IS PRICELESS. To live life without the experience of friendship is life without living. Human interaction is a necessity to its survival, but a developed friendship is essential to the successful wellbeing of everyone. I do not remember any other saying that has pleased me more than that of a friend being the medicine of life. If, dear friend, we do not demonstrate these traits as a giver of our companionship, we should try our very best to adhere to this awakening. We should always try our best to keep the characteristics of a true friendship unsoiled. We should live to bring out the very best in our friends. Ironically, the task of friendship is not to put greatness into our friends, but to elicit it, for the greatness is there already.

    Ambition embraces fame, riches embrace pleasure, power embraces reputation, and health embraces wellness, but friendship embraces innumerable advantages. Companionship is one of the greatest of all things which we need to distinguish us as a race, for certainly, without friends, we are mere beasts, unloved and lonely. Therefore, friendship, being one of our best and highest aims, MUST spring from a natural impulse. It should emerge from an inclination of the soul combined with a certain instinctive feeling of compassion and charity. It should not spring from a wish for help or from a deliberate calculation of the material advantage it is likely to confer. It should emerge from the indication of good values and high moral standards, to which souls of like characters are naturally attracted. Let us therefore choose our friends based on good values, not for what they have. And if we deserve so great a blessing, then they will always be with us, preserved in absence, and even after death, in the chamber of our memories.

We Are Our Thoughts

"The mind is its own place, and in itself can make a Heaven of Hell, or a Hell of Heaven".

-Milton

This topic may seem, at first glance, to be a bold and almost ill-advised statement, but please allow me some time to prove the reasonability of my audacious wit.

The Bible tells us that as a man thinketh in his heart, so is he. It is safe to say then, that we are our thoughts: we are what we think. It is reasonable to assert that as a man is, so does he think, and, that as he thinks, so do his outer life and circumstances become.

OUR THOUGHTS CAN BE A SPIRITUAL POWER OF TREMENDOUS POTENCY; BY THEM, WE CAN RAISE OURSELVES ABOVE THE OBSTACLES OF LIFE. Yet, they can also be a deadly scourge that sinks us beneath the crushing tread of defeat. This may sound rather metaphysical, but it is really quite simple, and confirmation meets us at every turn. Take a man from the slums and put him in nice surroundings, and note what happens. Very soon he either drifts back to a slum or turns his new house into a slum dwelling. Take a man of a higher standard, and put him in a slum, and soon he will either leave the slum or change his slum dwelling into a more decent habitation.

Therefore, before we can change a person's environment it is necessary to change inwardly the person himself. When a man becomes inwardly changed and filled with new ambitions, principles and hopes, he, in the course of time, rises above his lowly surroundings and attracts to himself an environment that corresponds with his new state of mind.

How many times do we see a mother laboriously tidying her children's room only to have it all in a mess within minutes? She has to first get her children to understand and appreciate the idea of neatness, cleanliness, order and spotlessness, and then they can start to connect their room with their mental ideal or image.

A Khemetic wisdom: *"As you think, so shall you become."* I honestly could not agree more. **A WELL-CELEBRATED THOUGHT HAS THE POWER AND THE ABILITY TO CHANGE OUR BODY, SOUL AND ENVIRONMENT DRAMATICALLY!** A man who stands united with his thought conceives magnificently of himself. The transformation of thought is as such: Thoughts to Words, Words to Action, Action to Character, and Character to Destiny. The mind is extremely intriguing. It is the seat of everything possible. Very often, the failures of our lives, and their disharmonies and poverty, either comparative or real, are outward symbols of our weakness of mentality. We may have ability in plenty, but lack application or steadfastness, and thus we fail in all our undertakings. I assure you that the actual cause of our failure is in our mental character. A poor mental approach can ultimately reduce a king to beggary and impotence and a rich one can raise a beggar to the status of king. Mother Teresa said, *"To keep a lamp burning you have to keep putting oil in it. To want to achieve your goals you must put positive thoughts into them."* If, therefore, our physical poverty, or financial difficulties are owing to the weakness of mentality, which manifests itself in our work and intercourse with others, in the form of inefficiency, poor service and bad judgment, it follows that we, ourselves, should change before our circumstances can be permanently altered for the better. The difficulty in dealing with unsuccessful people is in getting them to realize that they, themselves, are the cause of all their troubles.

Until we realize the root of our downfalls, our case is hopeless, and it is impossible to help ourselves. It is only when we acknowledge that the fault is ours that we can be shown that there is a remedy for our ills and a way out of our difficulties, by means of self-improvement.

Everything comes from within - first within, and then without, this is the law - therefore, the change should always take place within. It is necessary to point out that the cause of all manifestation is the mind. **OUR MIND IS INFINITELY INFINITE.** It is also of a higher order. Just think how one can hold a mental picture in his mind that does not physically exist. He can give that picture color, frame, life, and substance, whatever he wants. Yet, physically, that picture does not exist, and as soon as he stops imagining the picture, it disappears like dreams at the break of dawn.

Think further how this picture, which exists only in his mind, can trick the physical body that a picture does exist. The eyes see the color, the frame and the life as it sees a painting on our bedroom wall. The picture exists in the infinite space in his mind, which he projects outwards and, not knowing any better, his senses think it is real.

I was in New York City recently, watching one of those street artists painting a tree. Being the kind of people-person I am often thought to be, I engaged him in light conversation about his work. The picture was brilliant. It looked almost too real, as if he had plucked it from some nearby forest. It was only surprising because I was in Manhattan, and anyone who has ever been there knows that there is no nearby forest. I asked him how he was able to be so accurate in his depiction of the plant. Of course, he was apt to reply, *"It is easy! I've been doing this all my life!"* I am no expert in guessing ages but I know he was in his late sixties.

"It is easy for you," I responded promptly, almost too forcefully, because his answer did not reveal much.

"I am an artist! A true artist! This is my bread and butter. Drawing and painting has become a part of me."

His reply still did not relay much at all. I stood there for a moment looking at the busy streets. I was thinking maybe I was disturbing the artist and that I should move right along.

Moments before I had fully committed my thought to easing on down the road, the artist paused from his craft, looked me dead in the face as a mother does her child who is found at fault and said, "Painting is a narration of the mind. Nobody can draw a tree without in some sort becoming a tree; or draw a child by merely studying the outlines of his form. By watching for a time his motions and plays, the artist enters into his nature and can then draw him at will in every attitude. That is what I am doing for this tree; entering into the innermost nature of it. If the spirits are identical, so too are the facts. For the spirits are the facts. By paying deeper attention, and not primarily by a painful acquisition of many academic skills, I attain the power of awakening other souls to a given activity."

We can conclude now that every object we see around us is the product of our minds. **IF WE SEE POVERTY AND HOPELESSNESS, IT IS THE OFFSPRING OF OUR IMPOVERISHED MIND.** Those minds that see such a thing will forever be poor. They will go through life closely fettered by limitation. They can never escape from poverty; it traces their footsteps like their shadows. It is a shadow or reflection, in the outer life, of their state of mind and mental attitude.

OUR MIND IS THE MOST ACCURATE OF PROPHETS; IF IT TELLS US THAT WE ARE GOING TO FAIL, MOST DEFINITELY WE WILL FAIL. IF IT TELLS US THAT SUCCESS IS INEVITABLE, THEN SURELY, SUCCESS WILL CERTAINLY ARRIVE.

Our failures are based upon a fundamental error in our mindset. "I did not attend such-and-such a school so I will never be able to make the money I want to make." "My mother did not love me as a child and so I must go through the rest of my life not loving myself." "I am too old to learn a new skill." "She will never go out with someone like me." "I am not good enough because I am overweight." "Only politicians can make a difference in our society." "I do not think that I am a good parent." "I am worthless." "It is what it is and there is nothing I can do about it!" These might sound like some overly exaggerated quotes but I am sure that many readers will wonder how I gained entrance into their minds. Perhaps it may alarm you to wonder what else I might know. On a serious note, **WHEN A MIND IS LIMITED IN QUALITY, THE BODY WILL FOLLOW.** The body will act upon these negative thoughts and cease to act in a way that would elicit success. How do you see the world? If you see it as a trap of ignorance and misery, then so it is. Do you see it as being full of possibility and hope? Then so it is. The world as we see it is a perception of our state of mind. Our inner state has a profound influence on how we perceive the world; the content and the fabric of these thoughts become who we are.

Many of us live this immaculate life of utter dependence upon our mentality that we never become rich, but all our needs are supplied. Something always arrives in time to meet our requirements. Such a life requires a live and active state of mind. Poverty is the product of lack of faith, which is due to lack of outlook. It is the product of fear, ignorance, and weakness of character, all of which originated in our minds, and is the unreality that our weak minds deemed reality. We are all under the spell, more or less, of a grand illusion. Indeed, this illusion is of historic proportion. The evil, disease, sickness, poverty and other scourges that are blighting our human race have no reality, in reality, but have an existence in unreality, for it was not so in the beginning; therefore, it cannot be "real" as we often imply. They are not real in a real sense, yet they are terribly real to our present limited consciousness.

IT IS ALMOST IMPOSSIBLE TO SEPARATE US FROM OUR THOUGHTS. We are, as the title implies, our thoughts. We are the offspring of our minds. We are what we think we are. Take, for instance, a girl who thinks she is not beautiful; who believes and thinks that she is a mere useless material being, then she lives the destructive life of a useless material being, and is never able to rise above it. Take a man who thinks that his work is difficult and that he is not equal to his tasks; he finds that really his tasks are difficult and beyond his powers. Yet on the other hand, if he believes his work is easy or, at any rate, within his powers, he finds that such is the case, and that he can do his work with ease.

Is the glass half-empty or half-full? Those of us who are always thinking negatively, because of the divinity of thoughts, frequently experience the manifestations of those negative thoughts. It is as if they had breathed them into life through the mere repetition of their thoughts. Negative thoughts produce a negative state of action. Allowing the thoughts to dwell upon failures is a sure way to failure. It is far more difficult to change the way we think than to change the things we do. It is imperative to know that if we ought to make the best of our brief existence on earth, we should be conscious. We should become well-established mentally, before our victory can manifest in the outer life. No matter what we are going through - joblessness, moments of despair, sickness or loneliness - our state of mind will help us through it, only if we remain positive.

The entering of this higher consciousness where we know and realize the truth, that all our success, happiness and peace begin mentally, to always beware of this, a constant mental activity and watchfulness is required of us. It necessitates persistence and perseverance in positive thinking. The power within us is infinite! However, we should have the frame of mind to manage that power before our body can reap the fruits of such strength. Like the prodigal son, we should "come to ourselves" and leave the husks and the swine in the far country, returning to our *Father's house,* where there is bread of life enough and to spare.

I once was talking to a friend who kept telling me how bad the current state of the world was. Not only that, he spoke of how bad the economy was and the fact that everything seemed dim and gloomy. I, on the other hand, spoke of the good news I had heard and witnessed lately. I counteracted his stories with achievements, optimisms and the remarkable stories I had read of people who were doing fairly well.

The more he spoke of troubles, the more I spoke of delightful news. He told despondent stories, I told exuberant ones; he spoke of impossibilities, I spoke of possibilities; he spoke of sickness, I spoke of health; he spoke of crimes, and I spoke of law and order. I simply refused to honor his negative outlooks. Sure enough, he accused me of not facing reality. As far as I was concerned, both of our stories represented reality. The issue at hand was which we chose to esteem. The stories he had observed may have had some sort of merit. I would be utterly naïve or ignorant to deny the fact that what he said existed. However, the scenes that I observed were equally as evident as the ones he observed. Why then, should I not lift aloft the positives that I saw? Why should I cripple them with all the negatives that surrounded us? Angel Kyodo Williams said this about thoughts: *"They are the seed of intentions. So they are the original source of every action we perform. Even if an action does not follow the thought right away, the thought will hang around until it can reveal itself in some kind of way. Thoughts find themselves with voice and become speech. In turn, speech eventually gives fuel to action."*

In 1989, Rumeal Robinson, from Michigan, sank two free throws with three seconds remaining in overtime to give the Wolverines an 80-79 victory and the school's first national championship. It was a historical moment of greatness.

It is alleged that after the foul occurred, Seton Hall coach, P.J. Carlesimo, immediately took a timeout. Michigan coach, Steve Fisher, looked at Rumeal Robinson and saw that he was very timid. History was weighing heavily in his hands. He was very sensitive to the frenzied disturbance of the screaming fans. But Steve Fisher was of an impressive personality and extremely calm demeanor. He took advantage of Seton Hall's timeout to tell Rumeal Robinson this and only this: *"I see that you are disturbed by the noise of their fans in the conduct of their affairs; pardon me if I leave with you an infallible recipe for peace in the midst of commotion: Hear only what you will to hear, see only what you will see, and in the end glory will be all yours."* With this brief counsel, the coach quietly bade Robinson adieu in an attempt to prepare for all the interviews that would follow. Twenty seconds later, the game resumed and the seemingly nervous Robinson felt unaccountably calm, and was constrained to meditate upon his coach's advice, and no sooner did he seek to put it into practical use than he learned for the first time that it was his rightful prerogative to use unseen ear protectors and blinders - to hear only what he wanted to hear and see only what he wanted to see. Despite the pestering fans, he nailed the two free throws and secured glory for Michigan and himself. He had successfully practiced the simple though forceful injunction, that he had reached a point in self-control where the Babel of tongues about him no longer reached his consciousness.

Our environment, as far as it affects our judgment and our conduct, is made up not of physical realities, but of mental pictures. Our environment is within us. Let us get this conclusion clearly in our mind. Hold fast to the point of view that the environment that influences our conduct and our life is not a chance massing of outward circumstances, but is the product of our own thoughts.

Think what this means to us. It means that by deliberately selecting for attention only those sense-impressions, those elements of consciousness, that can serve our purpose, we can free ourselves from all distractions and make peaceful progress in the midst of turmoil. Our thoughts are the instrument by which all our work begins. The will-power at the center of our system, which first determines what is to be done, and then sets the hands to work to do it, and in the doing of it the thought and hands become one, so that the hand is none other than the thought working. Thoughts have no limitation; so too is life then without limits to its glorious possibilities.

All human achievement comes about through bodily activity. All bodily activity is caused, controlled and directed by the thought. **THE MIND IS THE INSTRUMENT WE SHOULD EMPLOY FOR THE ACCOMPLISHMENT OF ANY PURPOSE.** Realizing this distinction and applying it to our daily life, we can at once set to work to acquire mental poise and practical self-mastery, the essence of personal competence.

The greater man within us is our perception - our thought - the true human principle in us. We should believe in ourselves wholeheartedly, believe that we have the capacity of achieving whatever it is that we are bent on doing. *"All is opinion,"* said Marcus Aurelius. A single footstep may never advance us on the road of life, but a single thought will. **THE HAPPINESS OF OUR LIFE DEPENDS UPON THE QUALITY OF OUR THOUGHTS: IF WE ENTERTAIN**

NEGATIVE THOUGHTS, THEN OUR LIFE WILL BE NEGATIVE. IF WE ENTERTAIN POSITIVE THOUGHTS, THEN CERTAINLY OUR LIFE WILL BE POSITIVE.

We should believe in ourselves. We should know that we were born equally to our fellowmen; therefore, if they can do it, so can we. We might be going through trying times, and perhaps we feel like giving up, but we owe it to ourselves to try. Do not give up! We should be strong mentally, knowing that we can overcome any circumstance and rise and shine gloriously. However, we should understand that our thoughts have everything to do with our success or failure. A positive thought causes a chain reaction of positive attitude. The more we meditate upon good thoughts, the more we will view the world in a favorable light. **WE ARE MADE OR UNMADE BY OURSELVES.** By the right thought we ascend; by the wrong one we descend. We hold the key to every situation because we are a being of power, intelligence, love, and the lord of our own thoughts. We should always think positively and maintain a positive thought in our undertakings. It can only make whatever we are going through a little better. The winners in life think constantly in terms of I can, I will, and I am. Losers, on the other hand, concentrate their waking thoughts on what they should have or would have done, or what they cannot do. *"Such as are your habitual thoughts, such also will be the character of your mind; for the soul is dyed by the thoughts,"* Marcus Aurelius.

If we are feeling like our life is a constant failure, we are absolutely thinking wrongly. Think of all the good things we have done. Think of all the people we love, or the ones who love us. If we find even one person we love or one person who we know in our heart truly loves us, then our life can never be a failure. Find hope through that person and live for them. We should use this as a ladder to rise above our depression, to rise above our hopelessness, to rise above our losses and longings, to rise above our hurts and sorrows. Yes, indeed, life can be difficult, and sometimes the strongest of us feels the need to cry. There is nothing wrong with that. Cry if you have to! Cry if you want to! Just never give up! Maintain a positive thought. Remember:

THOUGHTS LEAD TO WORDS, WORDS TO ACTION, ACTION TO CHARACTER, CHARACTER TO DESTINY. Our thoughts, then, are the master of our destiny. If we could only carry this thought within us; the thought that all we are sprung from our thought, that our thought is our father as well as our God, surely we would never conceive any negative or conflicting thoughts of ourselves. The body we share with the rest of animals, but the thought is of a higher order.

We all have to deal with each thing according to the view that we form about it. If we hold that we were born to fail, surely failure will come our way. Those who hold that they were born to be of substance, worth and purpose, surely, will apply themselves accordingly. We should not be afraid to talk to ourselves and ask ourselves, "Who am I? Who is this wretched human creature with this miserable flesh? Do I have something better than this worthless flesh? Can I rise and shine and take my place, and display a character that runs deeper than this frail and fading flesh?"

Once the initial difficulties and temptations have been subdued by our frame of mind, it is not difficult to pick the triple-bolted gate of prosperity. And to maintain our stay in the State of Success, we should live a double life: we should live rich in consciousness, but careful and thrifty in actual practice.

In the end, we are our thoughts. It is from thinking about failure and sickness, believing them to be inevitable, that they do come through. **THE WAY OF LIFE IS TO WALK, THINK AND ACT POSITIVELY.** The wrong mentality destroys the will, faith and hope, even our peace and happiness. Thinking thoughts of lust and envy is a fruitful cause of unhappiness and anxiety. The divine forces of our thoughts should be directed into the right channel. If our thoughts are allowed to dwell upon purity, good results will follow. Therefore, they should be controlled and reversed continually. Not repressed, but reversed, be it noted, for there is a tremendous difference between the two. Repression creates tension, but by reversing or transmuting the thoughts, the life becomes transformed, and the bodily deeds greatly improved.

On the other hand, if we indulge in thoughts of hatred, resentment, ill will, fear, worry, care, grief, and anxiety, we will eventually manifest all of those. We therefore see that the state of the mind and the character of the thoughts are important factors that cannot be ignored. It is useless to treat any kind of ill as if it is merely the external effects of hidden causes of the mind. To achieve a cure, we have to get back to the source of the trouble.

Thought-control is a great assistance. Substituting a wrong and negative thought for a right and positive one will, in the course of time, work wonders in our life. We have an illimitable power of extraordinary intelligence in our subconsciousness. This wonderful power either builds up health, harmony, success and beauty in our life and body, or tears us down, according to our thoughts. The power is good, the intelligence is apparently infinite, but it goes wherever our thoughts direct it. By our thinking, therefore, we create or destroy, produce either good or bad. If, consequently, all our thoughts are positive and constructive, it follows that both our body and our life should become built up in harmony and perfection. This can be done if we have the desire, and are willing to discipline ourselves and persevere in the face, often, of seeming failure. We may say, "Yes, I want to control my thoughts, but how can I cease to worry when I have so much to worry about? How can I cease to have negative thoughts when everything that is happening around me is negative?" Well, I would ask you, when can positive thoughts and attitudes be more important than in times of great difficulties? We should be the most positive when all we see around us is dark and gray. That is the time we should demonstrate our mental endurance. Remember (and once again, I am not trying to come across as your favorite pastor), the scripture says, *"As a man thinketh in his heart, so is he."*

I challenge you now. What are you thinking in your heart? What is your thought? Are you thinking that you will never rise about poverty? Are you thinking you will never step up in your job because your boss is biased? Are you thinking that you will fail your finals next week? Are you thinking that this marriage will not work because everyone thinks so? Are you thinking that you are too in need to be charitable? If you answer yes to any one of these questions you should start thinking the reverse. Think positively. Believe in yourself. We are our thoughts! Our thought is the narration of our action. We should know that our powers are not contained between our hat and boots. By losing sight of this truth, we surround ourselves with limitations and see only the inferior part of us. We can be anything we want to be, if only we breathe it into life by our thoughts. I am, I can, and I will, should be our watchwords.

As we go to the gym to get fit and in shape, so too should we exercise control over our thoughts. It is the one and only instrument we have to work with, but it is an instrument which works with the greatest certainty, for limitation if we think limitation, for improvement if we think improvement. Our thought is the magnet that draws to us those conditions that accurately correspond to itself. Thoughts are actions. Again we ask, "How can I think differently from my circumstance?" Certainly, we are not required to say that the circumstance at the present moment is not what it is. To say that, we would be hiding from the truth. Nevertheless, what is wanted is not to think from the standpoint of the circumstance at all, but to think beyond it. We should realize that this is only a circumstance; something that we are bigger than, and will overcome. We should not be afraid to articulate with confidence, "I will not be defeated by this circumstance, and neither am I prepared to be overcome or overpowered by it. I must apply myself and tackle it accordingly." If we think anything contrary, then surely the circumstance will definitely get the best of us and we will fail terribly.

Even at the point when we are barely hanging on by a thread, please, I beg of you, my dear reader, let your thoughts create an advertisement for betterment. It should run thus: *"Think success, for I can be successful; think prosperity, for I have all that it takes to be prosperous."* Let it run repeatedly like our current weight loss commercials often do. This is a perfectly sound statement of the power of thought, although it is only an advertisement; but this will push us to make an advance beyond thinking "success." And before long, we will find ourselves doing the necessary things to procure that "success" we are thinking of. We should think like an Olympian who thinks gold medals and practices for four years religiously. He devotes numerous hours of every day in practice, and devotes himself to a diet that befits his training. He does so continuously, always carrying in his mind the thought of standing on the platform, his hand placed gently to his chest as he recites the national anthem of his nation, listening proudly to the chants and cheers of his fellow supporters. Every time he thinks of such a scene, it pushes him to train more religiously and to diet more sincerely, until at last he realizes that he is indeed at the place where his thoughts were, four years previously.

Surely, he has many obstacles to overcome, but his thoughts will not submit to circumstances. A lion does not submit to a fox. **SUCCESS CONSISTS PRECISELY IN COMBATING THIS DEVASTATING DOCTRINE OF SUBMISSION.** The natural process of growth is not submission. It is not the pouring-out of ourselves in weakness, but the gathering of ourselves together in increasing strength. There should be no weakness in our thoughts, and we should always be watchful against the insidious approaches of the negative that would invert our true position. The negative thought always points to some external source of strength. Its formula is: *I am not, I cannot, it is too difficult.* It always seeks to fix a gulf between our infinite power and us. It would always have us believe that we are inferior, that we are incapable, and that we were born a mere weak and failing creature of flesh and blood.

Let us inscribe "No Surrender" in bold characters upon the banner of our thought, and advance undaunted to claim our rightful heritage of liberty, life and prosperity.

Our Special Calling

"A person often meets his purpose upon meeting himself."
-Marcus Garvey

Man is heir to astonishing and unlimited talents, but until he becomes aware of them and consciously identifies himself with them, they lie dormant and unexpressed. When he becomes awakened to the great truth that he is more than just a physical being, when he learns that the little petty self and restricted personality are not his real self at all, when he realizes that he is blessed with an inner man who is limitless in nature, then the universe will be at his mercy.

EVERY MAN IS A CAUSE, A COUNTRY AND AN AGE. HE CAN LIVE ETERNALLY THROUGH HIS DESIGN. A man called Napoleon is born and decades later millions are sheltering securely under the laws which he imposed; a man called Caesar is born, and for ages after we have a Roman Empire; a man called Christopher is born and today we have "A New World"; a man called Socrates is born, and centuries later nations are guided by his philosophy. Every institution, as Emerson acknowledged, is the lengthened shadow of one man.

There is a popular fable in the Arabian Nights about Hassan. Hassan is a drunkard who was picked up dead drunk in the street, carried to the king's palace, washed and dressed and laid in the king's bed and, on his waking, treated with all flattering ceremony like the king, and assured that he had been insane and he was cured and that he was now existing in his real self. This fable owes its popularity to the fact that it symbolizes so well the state of man, who is in the world a sort of drunkard, but now and then wakes up, exercises his reason, and realizes that he is a true prince.

To give ourselves a reasonable prospect of happiness and completion we should realize our true purpose and then make the most of our opportunities. **LET EVERY MAN THEN KNOW HIS WORTH AND KEEP HIS PURPOSE CLOSE TO HIS HEART. LET HIM NOT PEEP OR STEAL, OR PROWL UP AND DOWN WITH THE AIR OF A BEGGAR OR AN INTRUDER, IN THE WORLD THAT EXISTS FOR HIM.**

There is an ultimate aloneness to human existence. No matter how close we are to someone, it is an illusion to think we truly understand him or her, or that he or she truly understands us. At some level, we may share an experience, but ultimately we are alone in this world. No one can feel another's pain, even when we have been through the same experience. If we are willing to accept this truth, we are willing to figure out our uniqueness as a human being wherein our life's purpose lies.

We are all unique. We are unique in experiences, thoughts and emotions. Discovering our distinctive self puts us in a position to celebrate such uniqueness. It gives us a natural monopoly on something that is truly unique in the world. Most of us, when we discover our uniqueness, are afraid of it, and often hide from it. We engage in everything that is not us, accepting the standards and expectations of others. In our flight from our ultimate aloneness, we end up living under the constraints of the widely divergent social traits of others. In doing so, we are never truly happy no matter how we appear to be. We are fated to follow tradition. We go to school, secure an education, get a job, get married, have a family and work toward retirement, because this is what tradition tells us to do. We do this, then, systematically, without trying to find our unique self.

I hate to discourage any of my readers but the only way to be truly happy, peaceful, free and successful, is to discover that unique person lying unexpressed within us. **MANY OF US DO NOT HAVE**

ANY CONNECTION WITH OUR INNER SELF BECAUSE WE ARE BEING BRED LIKE CATTLE FOR A PARTICULAR MARKET. We have been cultured to behave according to the norms of our society; to walk like it, to talk like it, to dress like it. These concepts exerted a great influence on our morality. This means that what we know of ourselves may just be a result of the cattle-like rearing we have received. It does not represent the real and unique us. These false values are only concepts that we have absorbed from popular society. All this time our true self is unexpressed, lying dormant, since the day that we were born. Taking on the values and standards of others or of tradition can lead to severe unhappiness and wholesale discontent.

Those of us whose thoughts and feelings are not our own live perpetually in disappointments and vain regrets. It is difficult for us to find our true purpose. We are forever looking outside ourselves for the true instruments of our ambition, interest or pleasure. It will be difficult for us to secure any great change in the world around us. Instead of opening our senses, our understanding and our hearts to the resplendent fabric of the universe, we hold a crooked mirror before our face, in which we admire a different person and pretensions. We habitually become a slave to opinion. We are a tool, a part of a machine that never stands still, and is tired and shaky with the ceaseless motion. We have no satisfaction but in the reflection of others. All this time our true soul wrestles with the tiring attempt to emerge from obscurity.

It has become a way of life for us to do things not because we want to do them, but only because it is expected of us to do them. We are in college taking a course that has no interest to us just because our parents want us to pursue such a course. We are engaged in activities at our church, not because we have a passion for them, but because our pastors will be displeased if we do not participate. We dress and speak a certain way because this is how all of our friends are dressing. We are trapped into all of these activities that we enjoy the least, because if we do not participate, our spouse will be disappointed. We have absorbed all these standards and values that are inconsistent with our true nature, and while everyone around us showers us with praise, we are unhappy and all alone. We are living under the dead weight of always having to make "a good impression" that is creating a shameful internal conflict within us. Even when we discover our brightest self within, we still suppress it. We do everything to discourage it. We do not speak properly because our friends will think that we are *"acting like we are brighter than them"*. We do not dress according to our standard because our friends will think that we are *"too old-fashioned"*. We do not strive to be a better person because our neighborhoods do not encourage it; therefore, we will look odd.

WHY SHOULD WE LIVE UNDER THE OBLIGATION OF PLEASING EVERYONE AT OUR OWN EXPENSE? Why are we such a slave to the common fad? Why are we so willing to just "go with the flow", like a straw in a river? The fact that a lot of us are willing to adhere to values and standards that are way beneath us just *to "have a place in society"* always baffles me. Who made these rules anyway, and why am I supposed to live by them?

What is said by one is often heard by all. **THE SUPPOSITION THAT A THING IS KNOWN TO ALL THE WORLD MAKES ALL THE WORLD BELIEVE IT, AND THE HOLLOW REPETITION OF A VAGUE LIE OFTEN DROWNS THE FAINT VOICE OF TRUTH.** We may believe or know that what is said is not true, but we know or fancy that others believe it; therefore, we dare not contradict or are too timid to refute them, and so give up our internal and, as we think, our solitary conviction to a sound without substance, without proof, and often without meaning.

The ear is quicker than the eye and often hears things long before the eye sees them. For instance, a man who is arrested and cast into confinement is often deemed guilty, long before any evidence of his guilt is found. We give him up with bound hands and feet into the power of his accusers. And if he tries to defend himself, it is a high crime, a contempt of court, an extreme piece of impertinence. Or if he proves every charge unfounded, we never think of retracting our error or making amends to him. It would be a compromise of our profoundest dignity; we consider ourselves as the injured party and the unfavorable outcome as a grave miscarriage of justice. We know that certain things are said; by that circumstance alone, we know that they produce a certain effect on the imagination of others, and we conform to their prejudices by mechanical understanding, and for want of sufficient self to differ with them.

I am sometimes accused of being a stiff-necked person and I will not refute the charge. For I do not necessarily stand by an opinion because it is old, neither do I fall in love with every extravagance at first sight because it is new and popular. I conceive that a thing may have been repeated a thousand times without being a bit more sensible than it was the first time. I also conceive that an argument or an observation may be very just, though it may so happen that it was never stated before.

The public is faint-hearted and cowardly, because it is weak. It knows itself to be a great dunce, and that it has no opinions but upon suggestion. Yet it would have us think that its decisions are as wise as they are weighty. It is hasty in taking up trends, and hastier in laying them aside.

To be sure, the public is not ignorant, it is a coward! My dear reader, instead of drawing any offense from these words, pay close attention to them. For if we should ever find our true purpose, we MUST know the truth, regardless of how cold and ruthless it might sound. Do not be swift to shun my thoughts on the sole basis that they are uncommon.

The public is as envious and ungrateful as it is simple-minded. It reads, it admires, it praises, only because it is the fashion, not from any genuine love of the subject or the man. It praises us up or runs us down out of mere notion and lightheartedness. If we have pleased it, it is jealous of its own involuntary acknowledgement of merit, and seizes the first opportunity, the first shabby pretext, to pick a quarrel with us.

In saying all this about the public, I did so with no personal malice or grudge. Instead, I am trying to educate you, if you do not already know, about the profoundest hindrance that impedes us from finding our true self.

Every creature that gapes and wonders, only because others did so, is glad to find us (as he thinks) on a level with himself. And he will do almost any malicious act to prove that an astronaut is not then, after all, a being of another order, neither is an author, a musician or an actor.

I find that most of us, who have this admiration for current fashion, do so by passive force. We do so because we are afraid to be ourselves and go against the grain. Deep inside we are not sincere. That is the reason as soon as another fad comes along we promptly change sides, and the thing we just now admired so greatly is an image of scorn. The greatest number of minds seems utterly incapable of fixing on any conclusion, except from the pressure of custom and authority.

TO FIND OUR TRUE PURPOSE, WE CANNOT LOSE OURSELVES IN THE DAZZLING MAZE OF OUR OWN IGNORANCE. Neither should we be afraid to engage an ambition, whether it has or has not been done by others before us. Strange as it may seem, to learn what an object is, we should look at the object itself, instead of turning to others to know what they think, say, or have heard of it. For want of this the real powers and resources of the mind are lost and dissipated in a conflict of opinions and passions, while truth lies in the middle, and is overlooked by both parties.

To find our true purpose, we should not be willing to conform to any common practice or trend, or to subscribe to any fleeting fad. As a general rule, all those who live by opinions not only starve, they will never find their true identity. Most poets never reach the height of their career until after death. Only then, we erect monuments to their memory and celebrate their works in speeches. While they were alive, however, they went by unnoticed and hungry.

To find our true calling, we should look deep within ourselves with our own buoyancy. We should be able to bear the dead weight of public opinions without surrendering to them. We should carry with us an independent consolation like a man in exile.

If we dig deep within ourselves, we will find the resources that a man may always find within himself, and of which the world cannot deprive us. The providence of God has established an order in the world, that our greatest possessions and most priceless treasures can never be fallen under the will of others. Our deepest self lies out of the reach of human power and can neither be given nor taken away.

One of the problems is, I think, we are afraid to be alone. We are like children who are afraid of the dark. Yet, it is surprising how much closer we get to ourselves when we spend time with ourselves - when we walk with ourselves, when we talk with ourselves, when we spend quality time with ourselves. After all, it is our self, why are we so afraid to be alone with it? Only a coward is afraid of himself and trembles at his own shadow, and even at the very sound of his name. He is so in awe of others' opinions that he never dares to form any of his own, but catches up the first idle rumor. The idea of what the public will think prevents him from ever thinking at all.

I enjoy solitude. It is where I truly hear and speak my natural, unadulterated mind, and out comes my most stupid self as well as my most sublime. It is where I realize who I am and what I am capable of doing or enduring.

If we do not like to be by ourselves, then quite likely we like to be around others. This, by no means is a bad thing. Nothing is wrong with being a social being. We are a part of the human family. Nevertheless, if we cannot spend time with ourselves, we are exposed to being constantly influenced and inhibited by others. At times, we have to be alone. Loneliness is not after all a bad thing. The greatest discoveries were made in loneliness. The greatest books were written in loneliness. Because we are alone we should not be lonely. We simply have to get away from society sometimes to have that intimate experience with ourselves and get to know ourselves better, without that inhibiting influence of others. We can then discover things about ourselves that we might not otherwise have known. When I vacation by myself, I do different things from when I vacation with others. When we are not being influenced by others, we are most certainly being influenced by ourselves. We are more likely to do what our true self really wants to do. Harry Browne said, *"Our life can be an adventure - a continuing stream of new pleasures, excitement, and satisfactions. We can have meaningful, problem-free friendships; we can have love that is intense and exciting without burdens and compromises; we can produce income in ways that are fun; we can have thrilling experiences that don't lead to bad consequences."* How do you suppose we do so? By finding ourselves or by letting everything around us shape us into what they want us to be?

If our names are supposed to ever be dear to history, if we are supposed to ever be happy, if we are supposed to ever be contented, we should discover our true purpose on this earth, in this life. Indeed, every one of us owes it to ourselves to find our true purpose and meaning, independently of our surrounding influences. Those who are in connection with themselves are often great geniuses. They are the ones who draw the admiration of all the world upon them, and stand up as the phenomenon of humankind who, by the mere effort of their natural ability, have produced works that are the delight of their own times and the wonder of posterity. They are like a rich soil in a happy climate that produces a whole wilderness of noble plants rising in a thousand beautiful landscapes.

There is always something noble and divinely extravagant in the natural geniuses that are infinitely more beautiful than the ones who try to master a purpose through artless repetition. The great pity is the fact that the imitators choke their own abilities too much by imitation, and form themselves altogether upon models and repetition, without ever considering their own ability and purpose. They wobble through life taking a kind of color from the natural geniuses and fall unavoidably into impersonation.

MOST OF US LIVE OUR LIVES MECHANICALLY. THE DAILY ROUTINE OF WORK KEEPS US CONSUMED AND WHOLLY AWAY FROM WHAT WE ENJOY IN SERVICE. We do not have much to look forward to. Then one night we are lying on our back staring at the ceiling after another exhausting day of work. We are fatigued, empty, bored, and even somewhat lonely, and the question suddenly hits us: what is my purpose in life?

Living life with an external purpose can be quite agreeable, but this by no means implies that we are living our purpose. One of the key elements to our happiness is how we employ our time in labor and in service. It helps to have a solid foundation in reality, or the truths of life, before we sit down to find our life's purpose.

GENERALLY, OUR TRUE PURPOSE IS THE ONE THAT NATURALLY FINDS US. Some of the time it is our family or friends who call our attention to our true calling. We go on with this natural ability and do not even know until a friend says, "I think that is your true purpose. You are always doing such-and-such. And you do it very well, in fact." The more we hear it, the more we start to believe that it is true. We start to believe for more reasons than one. We, for the first time, start paying closer attention to the advice of many and indeed, it all makes sense, because we do get fulfillment from this natural ability. We realize that we do this service not just for pay, if ever we even get paid, but because it is what makes us feel complete.

In the totality of life, there is no purpose that is too small or too big. Even the services that society may scorn are very important in life. There is no firm that is too small or insignificant to make an impact on our society and move it forward.

Oftentimes, it is our inherent talent that truly defines our purpose in life. It is amazing how many of us go through life with some incredible talent within that we do not discover. I hear these complaints all the time: "I feel lost. It is as if I am not interested in anything right now. I keep asking myself what the purpose of my existence is and there is no meaningful answer coming forth. It is as if I am just living causelessly. I feel lost. I feel empty! I feel purposeless."

The emptiness that we often feel is because we are not connected to our wholeness, to the totality of who we are. **SELF-REALIZATION LEADS TO LIBERTY OF THE SOUL.** When we discover our true nature, every moment of life is seen in true beauty and is found to be fulfilling, no matter what the circumstances are.

If we do not find our self, we cannot find our purpose. My mother told me how much I used to fix things when I was a little boy. She told me that I was always fixing this or that. I never had any passion to be a scholar. In fact, I never enjoy reading. I was not one of those "bookworms" who was always forecast to do well in life. I had a genuine passion for practical applications. When I left Nigeria and was living with my uncle in Yugoslavia, it did not take him long to predict that I would find my life's purpose with my hands. I have a vast admiration for him because he did not discourage me from academics. He helped me mentally fashion my passion for being creative with my hands. He saw how I was always able to perform certain repairs without any formal training. He never hesitated in telling me that, because of my ability to learn quickly from mere observation, I would be a success in whatever I put my mind to and did from my heart. I carry those words with me even until this day.

When I am scouting a property to purchase, I always find myself looking for the most dilapidated buildings and at first glance, I know what I want to do with it. I always find a deep excitement in this ordeal.

A LOT OF US LIVE WITHIN AN IMMENSE ILLUSION: A FALSE SELF. The blur of everyday life has created a world in which most of us have forgotten our unique and sacred existence. It is our true self, once discovered, that enables us to understand more clearly the nature of our world, and our own existence.

It is only when we are aligned with our inner self that we can discover our true purpose. And only our true purpose can lead us to true happiness and peace in this world. *"There are three things extremely hard: steel, a diamond, and to know one's self."* - Benjamin Franklin.

Truly, we take vacations to wonder at the heights of leafy mountains, at the huge gleaming waves of the oceans, at the long courses of the pearly rivers, at the circular motions of the tropical stars, and every day we pass ourselves without ever marveling. All the wonders in us remain undiscovered and unappreciated. "All wonders we seek are within ourselves." It is a deplorable sight to see the lengths a lot of us go through in trying to avoid ourselves, like a politician who dodges a question as if he thought it was his conscience who had asked it. Our dear self is so wearisome to us that we can scarcely be with it for a few minutes.

OUR LIFE'S PURPOSE CAN ALSO BE AN EVOLVING PROCESS; IT MAY NOT NECESSARILY BE ETCHED IN STONE. It can change in accordance with changes and new realizations inside us.

Time gives perfection to the soul and adds fresh luster to her beauty and makes her live in eternal youth.

OUR PURPOSE MAY NOT NECESSARILY BE THE SAME AS WHAT WE DO FOR A LIVING. Therefore, our purpose does not mean that we should prosecute a scheme of personal ambition. Neither should our high standards be lowered by the gravity of our aspiration. We should be very careful not to get the two mixed up. There is a universal greed nowadays for office. This is nothing but an indication of the appetite for distinction that has been diligently fed from childhood. We are very willing to leave lucrative employments, and subject ourselves to mean humiliations, simply to get our names into a newspaper, or our faces onto a television screen, all in an effort to demonstrate social distinction. We seek to be "somebody," mainly for the purpose of becoming "somebody" and not for any objective connected with the good of our society. We all want to "be something," and to "be something", we seek to leave our proper place in the world, and assume a position that we are not naturally fitted for.

OUR PURPOSE IN LIFE DOES NOT ALWAYS REQUIRE BEING IN PUBLIC LIFE. We should not feel as if we are being cheated out of our birthright if we are not in an air conditioned office. We should not be a mental slave to those who wear suits and ties. We are still "somebody" even if we are engaged in an "ordinary" occupation. We should not be disappointed. We should not be envious. We should not feel less of a citizen. Neither should we feel as if fate has been unkind to us.

If we want to discover our true purpose in life, we should not rush into professions for which we have no natural fitness. Yes, we are supposed to "aim high" in life; nothing is wrong with being ambitious. However, we are not supposed to do so indiscriminately.

I maintain that the secret to our success in this world resides in our insight into the knowledge of ourselves. *"To be yourself in a world that is constantly trying to make you something else is the greatest accomplishment,"* said Ralph Waldo Emerson. We all can be the master of our fate, but first we have to be the master of ourselves.

TO FULFILL OUR DESTINY, WE GREATLY NEED AN INCULCATION OF SOBERING VIEWS OF INNER SELF. We have within us a laboratory wherein we can analyze our own purpose. Yet, most of us chase after high places, and nearly all of us fail to get one. We sometimes dress beyond our means, and live beyond our necessities, to keep up a show of being what we are not, and what we were never born to be, as if to refute the dictates of plain reason. The farmer's daughter does not want to become a farmer's wife because a humble purpose is held in contempt; there is no respect for it. It is only the high distinctions that are recognized.

EVERY BREATHING MAN HAS A PURPOSE. The invisible intelligence that flows through the universe in a purposeful fashion is also flowing through us. None of us was born by mistake or mere coincidence. All of us are a blessed gift to this earth. What constitutes our true happiness is devotion to that purpose for which we were born. I know in my heart that we all are good. If only we can channel our purpose in the right way, then beauty will always triumph. Mahatma Gandhi said, *"The main purpose of life is to live rightly, think rightly, and act rightly."* Of course, the purpose for which we were born is to have a purpose, a meaningful purpose. I have this profound conviction that we, with a settled purpose, can accomplish the zenith of such purpose and fulfill the destiny of hope, peace, happiness and prosperity.

NO MAN WAS BORN FOR HIMSELF. INSTEAD, HE WAS SENT AS A GIFT FROM HEAVEN TO BE OF SUBSTANCE TO HIS SOCIETY, THAT THE INTERESTS OF HUMANITY ARE TO BE CONSIDERED EXCLUSIVELY, AND NOT THOSE OF THE INDIVIDUAL. We all should dig deep within ourselves and find our true calling. It is through this medium that we will be able to perfect ourselves, to further perfect our society. The development of usefulness is therefore the object of living, and the attainment of this great end is the significance of our lives.

WE HAVE A DEEPER PURPOSE THAN JUST LOUNGING AROUND IDLY. We have a deeper purpose than just being a consumer of earthly things. We have a deeper purpose than just raising a successful family. We have a deeper purpose than hoarding for ourselves. Our purpose, indeed, is not for self. It is for advancing the welfare of the whole human race. Consequently, we should try our very best to evolve our functions as a citizen of this world. We should try to evolve chiefly in value, purpose and will. By developing our values, we gain respect, by developing our purpose, we strengthen our will, and by developing our will, we expand our hope. The development of these elements is merely a material development. It is an indispensable moral development. It is impossible for us either to think too much, or to do too much in pursuit of these developments. Our life is to be passed in a moral and material development until we have perfected our purpose. This is the destiny of humankind. We should have a heightened consciousness of our purpose so that we can properly facilitate these forms of development. We should not be artificial in our purpose. Instead, we should be natural. We all have a role to play in the esteem of the human constitution and should be prepared to sacrifice everything we own rather than fail in our purpose. The Apostle Paul, inspired by purpose and faith, declared himself as not only *"ready to be bound, but to die at Jerusalem."*

We should not be a mere grumbler of the injustice and inequality of this world, who complains about everything that is wrong, yet will do nothing to set matters right. A sense of purpose will prompt us to make a change in whatever situation displeases us in this world, instead of only bickering about it.

PURPOSEFULNESS GIVES COLOR TO OUR CHARACTER. This abiding ideal of duty seems to be the governing principle of Martin Luther King's character. It was always uppermost in his mind and directed all the public actions of his life. Nor did it fail to communicate itself to those to whom he spoke, who looked to him for justice, peace and civil direction.

Simple honesty of purpose carries us all the way through our lives, once founded on a just estimate of ourselves and a steady obedience to the fire we feel within our soul. A sense of purpose and duty holds us straight, gives us strength and sustenance and forms a mainspring of vigorous action.

Our time is limited on earth. Therefore, we should not waste it living someone else's life. We should not be trapped by a code of beliefs which is living with the results of other people's thinking. We should not let the noise of others' opinions drown out our own inner voice and most importantly, we should always have the courage to follow our own heart and intuition.

Across the disk of existence, each decade, there glide millions of souls that disappear forever in the dim and dusk of the eternity that lies behind. Out of the bare handful that is remembered, we cherish only the memories of those who stood alone and expressed their honest, innermost thoughts and these thoughts are, always and forever, the thoughts of liberty. Exile, banishment and death may have been their fate, but on the smoke of martyr-fires, their souls mounted to immortality.

LIFE IS A BATTLE TO BE FOUGHT VALIANTLY. A great character stands by its opinions and convictions, and dies there, if need be. Its determination should be to dare nobly, to will strongly and never to falter in the face of adversity and opposition. The power of will, which God has given us, is a Divine gift and we should never let it perish for want of use. The ones who really succeed are those who live purposefully.

I herein beg of you in the mild tone of gentle humility, with which a slave addresses his master, to please search your soul and find your purpose. That purpose cannot be discovered by anyone other than ourselves. The elements of human development should be a growing confluence in our minds. **LET OUR PURPOSE BE THE FLOWERING OF OUR SOULS THAT SHEDS A GRACE BEYOND THE LURE OF LUXURY.** It should show the true colors and characters of our innermost morals. Let our purpose be not just a balm for ourselves but for all humanity. Let it be one of the pillars on which we can all safely climb the slippery steps of human fate.

The Importance Of Faith

"Faith consists in believing, when it is beyond the power of reason to believe."

-Voltaire

Faith is the very sum and substance of life. It is an armor that screens off the gulf of uncertainty that surrounds us. It is the instrument of deliverance from hopelessness and doubts. Faith is the owner of our destiny, and bigger still, it is the lungs of every life. If it has fled, like a dog who cannot reach his assailant and quarrels with the stones that are thrown at him instead, nothing is possible. **HAVING FAITH IS THE HIGHEST BRANCH OF PRUDENCE.** For to believe in things not yet verified is very essential to maximize our right thinking and also our right attitude.

Faith gives us the attitude of tenacity that pushes us to keep our eye on our destination rather than on the hardships along the road. Faith gives us the attitude of buoyancy to carry on, with the expectation that our efforts will bear fruit. Faith gives us the attitude of hope that shines when all around us seems dark and full of sorrow.

If ever we are to rise above the dead weight of failure, faith will have to play an indispensable role. One who is properly attuned becomes, through his faith, a recipient of strength that is above human, and endurance that is unearthly. The power of faith is so strong that there are cases where it creates its own proof.

Faith carries a great psychological advantage. I once read a fable about a miser who had been led by the association of ideas to prefer his gold to all the goods he might buy therewith. This psychology bore easy on him and he lived all his life with two bare legs and a griping stomach, without finding any difficulty in keeping his gold, which indeed had no value unless he exchanged it for some material property. Faith works the same way. If we have this superior reaction to obstacles, we can apply the right approach and gain all that comes of right action, while our less gifted neighbor, paralyzed by his pessimism and waiting for more evidence, which he dares not anticipate, much as he longs to, what law can forbid us to reap the advantages of our superior native sensitivity?

The course of nature is not uniform; neither is it straight. We cannot always mark the day by the morning. We cannot always mark the man by the boy. The same law nature follows today is not necessarily the one she will follow tomorrow. With this proven philosophy in mind, we should not be swift to assert that things will be worse because they are bad, or that things will not get better because there is no help in sight.

If we have faith that stimulates our determination, diligence that keeps us on course and courage to fuel our will, we can, no doubt, achieve anything we set our minds out to accomplish. Faith is the essence of things hoped for. It is a persistent embrace of our highest aspirations and yearnings, a humble trust that can become reality.

FAITH IS NOT ONLY LICIT AND RELEVANT, BUT ALSO ESSENTIAL AND INDISPENSABLE. The truths cannot become true until our faith has made them so. Faith is an assurance within the soul, outside the reach of proof. Voltaire declared, *"Faith consists in believing when it is beyond the power of reason to believe. Consequently, faith always outstrips scientific evidence"*. Tell me, how else one will be a genius, unless he can reach more truth with the same scientific evidence than his counterparts? We see this individual initiative exemplified on a small scale all about us every day, and on a large scale in the case of the leaders of history.

Faith and the midnight oil have produced motor cars, great fleets, the printing press, the incandescent lamp and the many other great inventions of civilization. Without a doubt, the monumental inventions we esteem so highly - railroads, steamships, power plants, telephones, airplanes, etc., are but the relics of faith. These things are only indications of circumstances, mere measurements that register the faith of Man.

We are told that with sufficient faith we can move mountains. Have mountains ever been removed or tunneled without faith? The mile-long ships, the building of satellites, the launching of space shuttles, and the creation of all industries are dependent on the faith of somebody. Too much credit is given to both capital and labor in the current discussions of today. The real credit for most of the things that we have is due to some human soul that supplied the faith that is the mainspring of every enterprise.

The road to success lies along the old highway of steadfast well-doing, and those who are the most faithful and work in the truest spirit will usually be the most successful. Those who look into practical life will find that success is usually on the side of persistency and faith. The winds and waves are on the side of the best navigators. In the pursuit of even the highest branches of human ambition, faith is often found to be one of the most useful instruments in such pursuit.

MANY OF US FAIL AT OUR ENDEAVOR NOT BECAUSE WE DO NOT HAVE THE TALENT TO ACCOMPLISH THE TASK, BUT RATHER WE DO NOT HAVE THE PATIENCE AND THE FAITH TO SEE IT THROUGH TO THE END. The writer of the Book of Proverbs says, *"Where there is no vision, the people perish."* Do you suppose that vision can survive without faith? Statistics teaches that where there is no faith, nothing gets started! Faith not only ignites our best efforts, it keeps them aflame.

We have, indeed, but to glance at the biographies of great men to find that the most distinguished inventors, artists, thinkers and workers of all kinds owe their success, in great measure, to their untiring faith.

It is owing to faith that President Obama maintained hope that he could be the first African-American president. It is owing to the faith of George Washington and his freedom fighters that, during the American Revolution, they fought so courageously and freed America from the fangs of the British Empire. Faith prompted the great Alexander to march along with his troops to conquer the whole world. Such was his spirit that he never lost faith in his abilities and lived the life of a great warrior until his last breath. It was faith that motivated Edison to keep trying for many times before he discovered the electric light bulb, without which, further inventions and discoveries in Science seemed impossible.

TO BE SUBLIME, TO BE EXTRAORDINARY, TO BE ONE OF DESTINY, TO BE ONE OF THE LEADERS OF HUMAN FATE, WE SHOULD HAVE, BY NATURE, UNYIELDING FAITH. All leaders of humankind, leaders of human thoughts and ideas - great legislators, great philosophers, great poets, great artists, great scientists and great musicians - possess this indispensable quality. Men of great faith stamp their minds upon generations - as Luther did upon modern Germany, Knox did upon Scotland, Napoleon did upon France, Washington did upon America and Dante did upon Italy. Their faiths now beacon every generation that follows. Even today, Washington is one of the greatest treasures of America. He is an example of a stainless life, of a great, honest, pure, and noble character - a model for us to form ourselves by in all time to come. In the case of Washington, as in so many other great leaders of men, his greatness did not so much consist in his intellect, his skill, or his genius, but in his rare unmatched faith. Men such as these are the true lifeblood of the country to which they belong. They elevate and uphold it, fortify and ennoble it, and shed a glory over it by the example of life and character that they have left.

If we observe the reasons behind the failure of any person, we find that one of the main factors responsible for the failure is the absence of faith. Truly, lack of faith is one of the main reasons why so many of us do not improve ourselves. We do not have the will and the drive that will lead us to a better way. We are easily weakened and discouraged. This deficiency prevents us from making the long-term sacrifices necessary to alleviate many immediate difficulties. But if we lose faith during the period of struggle and suffering, we give up hope for any success and succumb to the unfavorable situations. There is just no getting around it; we must have faith if we are to get beyond self-estimation.

A few years back, I was reconstructing a property in the Washington D.C. area when a Hispanic man, who was seeking employment, approached me. He was an older man, late forties or early fifties, dressed casually in some inexpensive third-world garb, standing at about five feet five inches. He had a skinny frame out of which two slender arms and legs protruded like the legs of a spider. At first sight, he did not impress me much - I thought nothing special about him - just another immigrant looking to earn a quick buck. In fact, I was somewhat tired and told him to come back and see me some other time. I did so with the intention of discouraging the intruder, so that he would leave and seek assistance elsewhere.

Surprisingly, the man showed up bright and early the following morning. I had no choice but to accommodate him, even for a moment. Therefore, with the help of a Hispanic employee, I conducted an informal interview and learned that the laborer was born and raised in the grime of El Salvador, where he had worked all his life as an on-and-off day laborer. He had managed to save enough money to pay for his trip from El Salvador to Guatemala, where he spent months waiting for the go-ahead to enter Mexico, where once again he spent several more months waiting to enter the United States when the opportunity presented itself. His entire trip from El Salvador to America took thirteen months and some days. He had no relatives in America. To put this into context, in a country of over three hundred and fifteen million people, he was a complete stranger. He told me that he had never seen his father a day in his life and his mother was in El Salvador old and sickly. He assured me that he came to America with the hope of working and saving enough money to build her a nice home in the country and to supply her with the medications she needed to counteract her diabetes. The more I interviewed him, the more I was impressed with his remarkable will and faith. As he spoke, his eyes grew crimson as the all-surveying sun with hope. His soul seemed to be a wandering wind, and he was searching for salvation to void the grief that he was in. Though he had searched for work for months without much luck, his faith still hung sublime, like the moon on a stormy night. Despite the fact that he was without a formal education, crippled in consequence of having to live off two fast-food burgers a day, he had a careless faith that things would eventually get better and he would find employment.

We stood there beneath the cold glare of the Washington sky and acquainted ourselves. I was pushed to give him a break. Two lines of a verse I once read swiftly came back to me:

> With Christian faith and virtues, we shall find
> None ignoring the great needs of humankind

He may have entered America illegally, which was a political crime, but opportunity is the strongest of all temptations, and it would have been a moral crime not to help a brother in need.

He worked for me gracefully, gratefully and faithfully for as long as the project lasted and after its completion, I employed him thereafter for about two years. I paid him well and treated him humanely. He was diligent, never missing an opportunity to stay late or come in early.

After the real estate market took a downturn, I was forced to let him go. I did not think much of our relationship after his dismissal until four years later when we ran into each other at a grocery store. He told me that he was getting ready to return to El Salvador. He had secured enough money to build his mother the house he had in mind. He told me that ever since our last encounter he had done various kinds of employment, cutting lawns, painting houses, cleaning roofs, walking billboards, dishwashing, even brick laying. He told me that he never took a holiday, a day off, or vacation, and neither did he miss an opportunity to do overtime. He looked delighted and exuberant. I asked him out of deep curiosity how much money he was able to save and he proudly told me it was over thirty thousand dollars. I was terribly astonished.

A man, who is barely able to speak English, comes into a foreign country and against all odds is able to save over thirty thousand dollars in five years. He has no formal education. He has no special talent or skill, but through untiring faith that fuels his will, he was able to achieve his goal not just by working tirelessly, but also by denying himself of all the luxuries this great nation has to distract him - by working overtime and living purely off necessity. This man should be a professor in self-discipline.

We may set goals for ourselves only if we have the faith that ultimately we will achieve these goals. Thus, **FAITH FORMS THE FOUNDATION OF EVERY NEW PROGRESS.** Progress, however, of the best kind, is comparatively slow. Great results cannot be achieved at once and we should be satisfied to advance in life as we walk, step by step. To be patient is the great secret of success. We should sow before we can reap, and often we have to wait long, content meanwhile, to look patiently forward in faith. The fruit best worth waiting for often ripens the slowest; this at times can be discouraging. Yet, we should never give up. Instead, we should continue to walk with faith. This blind faith can only come from deep within us. There is no leader of knowledge that can teach it. The greatest professors in all the great universities of the world cannot teach it. All the desks, ledgers and professors of Harvard cannot do so either. Neither can it be imposed upon anyone. It comes from deep within our souls. The quantity of faith possessed by us depends upon how positive our approach toward life is. All the motivators, all the psychologists, all the inspirational writers cannot put into a man the vision and the will to do things that are gained by an untiring faith. Most of us today are frantically turning to everyone and everything outside ourselves to solve our problems, when all the while we have the machine within us, if we will only set it going. That machine is the human soul, from which all our characters spring.

I know it is very difficult for some of us to have faith these days. Faith, to many, seems almost a vain hope or a wishful superstition. How can we be faithful when life has always been an uphill climb? How can we be faithful when life has always been a steep challenge with perpetual struggles? **A LOT OF US WOBBLE THROUGH LIFE WITH VERY LITTLE HOPE TO CHEER US, WITH FEW**

FRIENDS TO ENCOURAGE US, WITH NO FAMILY THAT HONESTLY BELIEVES IN US. Perhaps we have wasted a few great opportunities. I guess it helps to know that nothing great has ever been achieved upon first trying. If we have faith in ourselves, we will be naturally armed with a great force of character, indomitable courage, much worldly shrewdness and far-reaching vision. We are only defeated when we give up on ourselves. I strongly assure you that it is only by having a tireless faith that we will be able to brave the trials and tribulations in our lives successfully. Difficulties are common in everyone's life, but a person having faith knows deep inside his heart that the period of struggle will become a pastime if he faces all the miseries with a brave heart. Tolstoy has correctly said that faith is the force of life. Only faith can help surmount the most disheartening difficulties. With enough faith, anyone can breathe any ambition into life. The most ordinary occasions will furnish us with opportunities or suggestions for improvement, if only we have the faith and vision to see past the moment. With faith, vision and perseverance, the very miscellaneous items of time may be worked up into results of the greatest value.

WHERE THERE IS A WILL, THERE IS A WAY. CAN THERE BE A WILL WITHOUT FAITH? This is highly doubtful. To become an able man in any profession, three things are necessary: character, study and practice; but above all is the practice of faith. A strong conviction in what we wish can dissipate any obstacle that hinders it.

In light of the great gloom that is currently veiling earth's darkening dome, our wheels of faith should never cease to turn. We should press on with faith and hope. There is always something worth striving for. For many, happiness seems to be impossible and to be hoped for only in a future life. Nevertheless, our faith must reach beyond the horizon of our present limitations and difficulties. The man of faith is the author of greatness, for faith is the chain that links us to success. It is also the ladder on which we must climb out of depression, helplessness and monotony. Without faith, we are exposed to the influences of hopelessness and are left defenseless.

Above all of which we speak, what is faith if it is not to believe in ourselves, our own thoughts, and our private heart? What is having faith if it is not learning to detect and watch that gleam of light that flashes across our mind from within? Indeed, faith teaches us to abide by our spontaneous impression with steadfast inflexibility even when everyone else thinks that we are absurd. With faith, we will not be ashamed of that divine idea which lingers within. For success will not have his work made manifest by cowards.

HAVING FAITH MEANS HAVING SELF-TRUST. It is to keep our heads above our shoulders, lay aside the corpse of our insecurities and walk upright in confidence. The faith a man has in himself is the chief element in his success. Where unthinking gazers observe nothing, men of intelligent vision penetrate into the very fiber of the phenomena presented to them, attentively noting differences, making comparisons and recognizing their underlying idea. Many before Galileo had seen a suspended weight swing before their eyes with a measured beat; but he was the first to detect the value of the fact. Men of higher order whose eyes are in their heads. It is the faithful eye of the careful observer that gives these apparently trivial phenomena their value. So trifling a matter as the sight of seaweed floating past his ship enabled Columbus to quell the rebellion that arose amongst his sailors at not discovering land, and to assure them that the eagerly sought New World was not far off. There is nothing so small that it should remain forgotten, and no fact, however trivial, may not prove useful in some way or other if carefully interpreted. When we look with faith, even the darkest of nights seems sunny.

MANY WORK TIRELESSLY WITHOUT A TRACE OF APPRECIATION. Our employer takes our best efforts for granted. But as a rule, the longer our worth is likely to last, the later it will be in coming; for all excellence, as it requires time for its development, so too it requires time for its realization. We should never forget that most people are more likely to appreciate the man who serves the circumstances of his own brief hour. Consequently, we should not lose faith in ourselves. We should continue to push on faithfully. The general history of art and literature shows that the highest achievements of the human mind are, as a rule, not favorably received at first, but remain in obscurity until they win notice from intelligence of a high order, by whose influence they are brought into a position that they then maintain forever.

MANY ARE LADEN WITH NEGATIVE COMMENTS WHEN WE MENTION DOING SOMETHING THAT IS UNCOMMON TO OUR PEERS' ABILITY. We are swiftly discouraged. We are told to be more realistic, called a dreamer. I remember when I mentioned to some of my friends that I was planning to write this book. I faced a great deal of ridicule. I was frequently told to stick to real estate. But I did not take any of those comments personally. Because I know, as history has often shown, a man can really understand and appreciate only those things which are of like nature with himself. The dull person will like what is dull, and the common person what is common. Hence, have faith in yourself and continue the fight. We should not lose faith in ourselves when no one else sees our worth or talent. It is so with great and noble thoughts, with the very masterpieces of genius, when there are only little, weak, and perverse minds to appreciate them. A dull ear mocks at the wisest word.

SOMETIMES WE GET DISAPPOINTED EASILY AND TRY TO "REINVENT" OURSELVES TO SUIT OTHERS. We find ourselves doing things that our morals do not approve of. I urge you not to sell your uniqueness. We should be appreciated for who we truly are. We should maintain faith in our character, faith in our personality and in our purpose. When a head and a book come into collision, and one sounds hollow, is it always the book? The best gifts of all find the fewest admirers, and many mistake the bad for the good; a daily evil that nothing can prevent. The average person has no critical power of his own, and is incapable of appreciating the difficulty of a great effort. People are always swayed by authority, and where fame is widespread, it means that ninety-nine out of a hundred take it on faith alone. Many will pass through this life not knowing the true value of it. For we only see with the outer eye but never with the mind, and praise the trivial because the good is strange to us.

WE SHOULD HAVE FAITH IN OURSELVES, DESPITE THE RESOUNDING ECHO OF EMPTY HEADS, AND STRIVE TO BE

SUCCESSFUL IN OUR PURSUIT. Everyone lives and exists on his own account; therefore, if we do not have much faith in our worth, we cannot be worth much. The idea which other people form of our existence is something secondary, derivative, and in the end affecting us but very indirectly. Besides, other people's opinions are a wretched place to be the home of our true value.

Our greatest pleasure consists in being appreciated, but those who appreciate us, even if they have every reason to do so, are slow to express their sentiments. Hence, he is the happiest man who, no matter how, manages sincerely to appreciate himself. There can be no doubt that appreciation is something secondary in its character, a mere echo or reflection, as it were, a shadow or symptom of merit - and, in any case, what excites appreciation should be of more value than the appreciation itself.

FAITH IN OURSELVES LEADS TO ALL SORTS OF POSITIVE OUTCOMES. It protects our profoundest hope and shelters us in times of despair. Without it we are a mere cynic; with it, we are led to a truer and kindlier view of the nature of ourselves. It will help to tackle the unavoidable adversities that are fated to confront us. When we believe in ourselves we will face setbacks, certainly, but we will not be overrun or defeated. Instead, we will maintain the right approach and weather through until we are beyond the mist and back to brighter days.

We should not forget the latent power within ourselves upon which all prosperity ultimately depends. I cannot perhaps emphasize this any more strongly than by saying that the foundation of progress depends almost exclusively on faith. Only faith can help us surmount the most disheartening difficulties. With enough faith, anyone can breathe any ambition into life.

The necessity of hard work and faith may, indeed, be regarded as the main root and spring of all that we call progress in individuals and nations. It is doubtful whether any heavier curse could be imposed on man than the complete gratification of all his wishes without effort on his part, leaving nothing for his hopes, desires or struggles. The feeling that life is dry of any motive or necessity for action should be of all others the most distressing and insupportable to a rational being.

A lot of us who fail in life are very apt to assume a tone of injured innocence and conclude too hastily that everybody except ourselves has had a hand in our personal misfortunes. We are even swift to consider ourselves born to ill luck, and make up our minds that the world invariably goes against us for some unapparent reason, when it is lack of faith, drive and will that inspire the failure. We cannot lay our faith at the door of our family, friends or the government. We have to carry it deep within our souls wherever we go and nurse it so that it can provide the will we need to go on in times of great difficulties.

In closing, human character is molded by a thousand subtle influences - example and precept, by life and literature, by friends and neighbors, by the world we live in, as well as by the spirits of our ancestors, whose legacy of good words and deeds we inherit. However great, unquestionably, these influences are acknowledged to be, it is nevertheless equally clear that we should necessarily be the active agents of our own wellbeing and well-doing. However much the wise and the good may owe to others, they themselves must in the very nature of things be their own best helpers. If we do not have faith in ourselves, we are doomed to failure and misfortunes. Faith makes us active, earnest, full of promptness and stirring. It makes us bold and unbending. The array of great names, cited within this book, of men springing from the ranks of the lowly classes, who have achieved distinction in various walks of life, shows that at all events the difficulties interposed by poverty and labor are not insurmountable if we believe in ourselves and toil on with faith that yields to no adversity.

HISTORY CONFIRMS THAT IT IS NOT THE MAN OF THE GREATEST WEALTH AND RESOURCES WHO ACHIEVES THE HIGHEST RESULTS, BUT HE WHO EMPLOYS HIS VISION AND FAITH WITH THE GREATEST CONFIDENCE AND THE MOST CAREFULLY DISCIPLINED SKILL. My dear reader, I urge you to believe in yourself and have faith in your abilities. Please do not be deterred by obstacles and naysayers. Press onward toward your goals and ambitions with faith, knowing that nothing sublime happens overnight, knowing that all world-renowned excellence faces ridicules and adversities, but in the end, victory is yours - only if you believe.

Unbending Hope

"If you lose hope, somehow you lose the vitality that keeps life moving, you lose that courage to be, that quality that helps you go on in spite of it all. And so today I still have a dream."

-*Martin Luther King Jr.*

The history of civilization has always been the history of dark struggles amidst economic absurdities. Billions acknowledge that society is terribly arranged. Countless are living in black despair, unutterable grief and shameless injustice. Our days are blemished with an overhanging darkness and our nights are filled with oppressive loneliness and tyrannizing coldness. We are exhausted with a quenchless dejection. To many, life is simply not worth living; not worth fighting to keep; not worth the irrevocable sorrows, piercing joblessness, brutal homelessness, crippling sickness, biting loneliness, lamentable helplessness, deep-seated depression, and the pressing weight of hopelessness.

We desperately search for work and cannot find any. Our bills are insurmountable. This has brought our domestic life to an immeasurable scorn, which further led our social life to an insufferably gloom. Now we are a stranger to peace and happiness. We have done all we can and simply do not know what else to do. Even our prayers are so long that they outrun discretion.

Well, I am here to tell you, no! Do not lose hope. These are the times when hope is most needed. It will not only get us through our popular day-to-day obstacles, but also shape our thoughts, uplift our attitude, inspire our vigor and nourish our wills. *"Hopelessness is an immense conspiracy against victory,"* remarked George Washington. **WHEN WE HAVE LOST HOPE, WE HAVE LOST EVERYTHING.** When we have no hope, we have nothing. When we think all is lost, when all is terrible and bleak, there is always a way out. We owe a binding obligation to ourselves to fight on even in the midst of the storm and overcome our insatiable desolation, blistering loneliness and crushing longing. I ask of you desperately, please, hold on to life with a boyish appreciation. All our sorrows, all our pains, all our fears, all our emptiness, should be bravely vanquished! *"Only in the darkness can you see the stars,"* said Martin Luther King, Jr. Let us stand against our adversities with an ardent protest and a disapproving sharpness.

If we meet our obstacles faithlessly and without hope, they will break us. If, however, we meet them bravely and hopefully, we become stronger through experience, thus becoming better fitted to bear life's responsibilities and to overcome its difficulties and circumstances. One who meets the setbacks, grief and disasters of life in the right attitude, becomes a strong and rich character.

WHEN THINGS ARE GOING SMOOTHLY AND LIFE IS FREEWHEELING, NO CHARACTER SEEMS NECESSARY, AND AS FOR AN INWARD STRENGTH, WHAT OF IT? WE CAN DO VERY WELL WITHOUT IT. But there comes a time in every life when a power and will, of which the limited self knows nothing, is needed to raise the soul out of the dust and ashes of its despair. It is one thing to try to meet troubles and adversities in the right spirit and quite another thing to have the strength, hope and will to do so. One who thinks that he has no power within him, but that all the power is in circumstances, can never rise victorious over his troubles and become a conqueror over life's difficulties. But one who realizes that he possesses a wonderful power that can raise him up, no matter how crushed he may be, can never be a failure in life no matter what may happen to him. He will rise from the ruins of his life and build it anew in greater beauty and splendor.

Our political and social problems are destroying many a dream, many a cherished hope, and many a prospective opportunity, ruthlessly causing endless despair and suffering. Nothing has ever occurred to change the monotonous order of our existence, for no event affected us except the discouraging heaviness of our daily life. Subsequently, there is a constant source of bitterness that hopelessly vanquished our peace, and we now stand indifferent to all happiness. Nonetheless, we should prove ourselves a firm contender on the battlefields of life. We should stand up and fight with a dashing gallantry, with a dauntless courage, and in the end, we will secure a dazzling triumph.

LET US RELINQUISH ALL OF OUR DEBASING TENDENCIES. Let us not be easily discouraged. Though life is steep, we must welcome the climb. We should not be caught in the blinding mist of faithlessness. Let us have the killer instinct often seen in a beast of prey. Hope should be deeply seated within us with a desperate defiance and a frightening boldness, as we hold on with an absolute and eternal courage.

No matter how unkind fate may be, it is possible for us to make our lives a beautiful thing. At different times in our lives we meet with influences that are sometimes adverse. These influences are, however, only influences after all, and one who will stand firm during periods of adversity and refuse to give in should spark the great power of hope to carry him through when he is weak and struggling against the storm.

We cannot prevent obstacles no matter how hard we try. Our best efforts can merely reduce them. But we can all rise superior to any challenges. We will meet with failures and setbacks, but we will make of these stepping-stones to greatness. We will experience sadness and desolation, but we will dig within ourselves, find that store of hope, and use it to strengthen our will to fight on and rise to higher things. If we lose hope, however, we lose the will and condemn ourselves to further suffering, thus making an utter shipwreck of our lives.

We have within us the strength to lift ourselves above average excellence and rid ourselves of life's accumulated burden. As a result, we should never lose faith in ourselves; neither should we lose hope. Even when the world does its worst and then turns its back, there is still always a way out of our struggle. There is always a way that leads us back to happiness. It is often in the darkest skies that we see the brightest stars. Be optimistic and fight on with a brazen determination and a defiant will to overcome.

HOPE IS FIGHTING WITHOUT A THREAD OF DOCUMENTARY EVIDENCE THAT WE WILL WIN. To hope is to know that we will win, we will overcome, we will triumph, and we will get beyond the stumbling-block that we have tripped over. This should be the dominating influence that we live and die by. It is what we need to light our dormant abilities. We should not live in the echoing sadness of hopelessness. To find hope is to find grace, is to find salvation, is to find redemption, is to find a way where there seems to be none. Having hope is having faith, strength, will, endurance and patience. It is to know unquestionably that we can get past our current situation only if we stay the course and press on. Hope is not to be faint and fragile. Neither should it be weak and fearful.

I know at times we find our backs against the rope. All our friends and families have turned their backs on us. Even the mere acquaintances who are hanging around do not understand fully what we are going through. We close our eyes and realize that we are a stranger among even the ones with whom we are most intimate. Nevertheless, we should stand firm and strike back at adversity with an unshrinking determination. We should shun despair with an eloquent refutation and an enduring courage.

These are the moments when we should look with eyes that pierce through obstructions. Greatness often emerges out of these moments. More often than not, those who history best remembers were faced with numerous obstacles that forced them to dig deep within, with an untiring will, and take their rightful place in human destiny.

Throughout all time, from the dawn of history, men have being nibbling off hope. Primitive men set out to distant lands in search of new homes and possibilities. They found commonwealths, empires, constitutions, religions, commerce, and innumerable welfares of our race. Surely, it was hope that pioneered their progress. Even in those moments when the night gathered round them darker than before, they pressed on. At last, glory be to God in the highest! - they saw the overflowing light of victory!

Every factory that hums with marvelous machinery, every railway that spans our nation, every fleet that sails upon the ocean, every airplane that decks the velvet sky, every breath-taking invention - all are, in their largest part, the expression of unbending hope.

MOST, IF NOT ALL, THE GREATEST MINDS ARE THE SURVIVORS OF RUTHLESS OBSTRUCTIONS: Albert Einstein, the name that is synonymous with genius, did not speak until he was four, and did not read until he was seven, causing his teachers and parents to think he was mentally handicapped, slow and anti-social. Eventually, the genius was expelled from school. These are just the mildest of obstacles he overcame to win the Nobel Prize and change the face of modern physics.

Isaac Newton is undoubtedly a genius when it comes to math, but he had many failings early on. He was considered a dull boy at school and was discharged to his family farm. He failed miserably at that too. So poorly, in fact, that an uncle took charge and sent him off to Cambridge where he finally blossomed into the scholar we know today.

Socrates is regarded as one of the greatest philosophers of the Classical era. This prestige was not easily attained. He was called an immoral corrupter of youth because of his new ideas and was forced to write and teach in exile. Eventually he was sentenced to death. However, he did not let these adversities stop him and kept right on teaching up until he was forced to poison himself.

Winston Churchill, the Nobel Prize winner and twice-elected Prime Minster of the United Kingdom, was not always as well regarded as he is today. He struggled in school and failed the sixth grade. After school, he faced many years of political failures, as he was defeated in every election for public office until he finally became the Prime Minister at the ripe old age of sixty-two.

Stephen King, one of the biggest selling authors of all time, had his share of misfortunes and disappointments. The first book by this author, the iconic thriller *Carrie,* received 30 rejections before it was finally published and etched his name on the wall of history.

Jack London, another one of our well-known American authors, was not always such a success. His first story received six hundred rejection slips before finally being accepted.

At times we all feel exactly what Napoleon felt when he was exiled to Elba - lonely, friendless, despondent, abashed and ashamed. But do you think if he was not hopeful he could have escaped from the barren island and reclaimed his glory? It was hope that led him through. He never lost faith in himself. He never stopped believing. He had an unyielding disposition driven by a youthful exuberance and zealous devotion. For a little under ten months, he mused helplessly on the events of French life with great interest, haunted by his very hope, never losing focus or sight of his ambition, until he schemed his way to mainland France and reclaimed the throne as Emperor of France. That is the way it is with greatness.

Life is a wonderful adventure and we all have a great opportunity to make the best of this exploration. Our current situation may not be affably accommodating, to hope may be much harder than to despair. All that lingers may be barren opportunities and base intrigues. Nevertheless, we should never cease to look at life with a complimentary glance, with hope and with possibilities. Let us see beyond the storm, see the cloud beyond the silver lining.

HOPE ITSELF IS LIKE A STAR, NOT TO BE SEEN IN THE SUNSHINE OF PROSPERITY, BUT IN THE BLINDING DARKNESS OF HARD TIMES. During the Civil War, Robert Lee declared that: *"There is nothing more desperate, more horrible, more incredible, more intolerable, shining over our destiny like a winter rain, than hopelessness."*

I know some of us might be thinking that our lives are irreparable. We might be going through the lowest time of our lives. We might be buried in debt. Possibly, we have just lost our job and are struggling resolutely to keep our home. Perhaps we have just concluded a bitter divorce and are alone in a cold and lonely room, afraid and undistracted, having nothing else to do but to take up this book and scan through the pages. Well, whatever the situation might be, it is never too late. If you are reading this, you are alive. Therefore, not all is lost. While there is life, there is hope. You have to be strong, patient, faithful and most of all hopeful. Hope is the only element that separates men from beasts. Hope gives life a purpose and a meaning. Think positively and optimistically. *"Everything that is done in this world is done by hope."* -Martin Luther. You can get through your adversity if you just think positively and optimistically.

HAVING HOPE COMFORTS US IN THE HEIGHT OF ADVERSITY AND SOLACES US IN SOLITARINESS, EASES US OF AFFLICTION AND RIDS US OF DEPRESSING THOUGHTS. In fact, adversity is an opportunity to get intimate with our hope. When I am troubled and burdened, it is my hope - that soothing balm - to which I turn. It stills my natural inclination of despair, sorrow and the habit to be angry and regretful.

We should learn to take control of our soul. No doubt, every day a new problem is sprouted. When one is solved, another swiftly takes its place. Our sorrows keep on growing, ever rising. Our present circumstance only sets the tone for a long course of future suffering. But Emily Dickinson said, *"Hope is the thing with feathers that perches in the soul and sings the tune without the words and never stops at all."*

EVEN THOUGH OUR LIVES MAY BE FULL OF WITHERING SCORN, THERE IS STILL A LOT OF BEAUTY LEFT IN THIS WORLD, AND A LOT OF KINDNESS AS WELL. We should reach out and touch that hope found in the birds with broken wings, touch that hope often found in a dying dog in a ditch, fighting courageously for survival with an augmented force. If we lose hope, we lose everything.

Let us think deeply of the things that mean the most. Aren't they worth fighting for? Whatever our environment, whatever our ambition, we need to believe in ourselves, we need to be patient, we need to be enduring, we need to be hopeful to do the things we want to do, and become the person we want to be.

LET US SET SHORT-TERM GOALS AND TRY OUR VERY BEST TO UPHOLD THEM. Find the discipline within ourselves to stay focused. The fundamental secret of success is the mastery of one's soul, the mastery of all the powers we have within us. The way that works for me is to create a society in my head. This society is independent of the one around me. Indeed, every man is a society. He must be, if he is to find his true self, independent in thoughts, independent in imagination and independent in concepts, if he should be successful.

When we set our own importance in our head, when we set our own moral rules and regulations, we operate more effectively, more freely and more logically, because we are under no obligation but our own and we are not pressured to go out of our way to keep up with the common fad. We are not pressured into getting that brand name dress because it is what the celebrities are wearing. Rather, we think logically and know that it is very much irrelevant and a conflict of interest to what we are trying to achieve. We then start to see that it is okay if we wear the same clothes over and over as long as they are clean, seeing how much money we have saved toward the things that are important in our life. Always remember that a follower has no influence!

So too should we think when we are going through trying times and needing to overcome our obstacles. It is within our reach to achieve our aim, just as long as the aim is not influenced by anyone other than our own soul. To give up is to sting ourselves, scorpion-like, with the virus of failure. Our days might be monotonous and colorless, but we should stand firm with a matchless will, finding peace in the comforting reassurance of hope. Some of the finest qualities of human nature are intimately related to the infinite use of hope.

In the darkest dawn, armed with a burning hope, we should await the sunny day. Our approach, though, should be first to confront our adversity, laying siege to it, depriving it of oxygen, and then to insult it, ravish it, abuse it, and defeat it, as if it is a callous and conscienceless beast.

LET THE LIGHT OF HOPE GUIDE OUR STEPS THROUGH THE EVER-DARKENING CHAMBERS OF DESPAIR, AS WE WALK

WITH A FIRMNESS OF CONVICTION THAT KNOWS NO WAVERING. Let this light shelter us through the raining darkness of despondency and rock us gently upon the wings of faith. Of course, this may not be easy. *"Being full of hope and optimism is a quality rarely acquired from inheritance, if ever at all,"* said Mark Twain. Hope, the blossom of all success, may be found in the heart of him even lowest in the social scale, provided that he has faith in himself and believes strongly that he has what it takes to accomplish his purpose. It is not an affair of genetics. It has no pedigree of birth, chivalry or heredity. In this sense the true dealer in hope does not have to be concerned with the genteel code of social background, but by his own code of character.

    We do not work and strive for ourselves alone, but for the benefit of those who are dependent upon us. It may be our parents, our children, or even complete strangers. If we choose to give up now, we will let down the ones who rely upon us, but even worse, we will let down ourselves. We own this battle. We owe it to ourselves to work diligently to elevate our social state, and to secure our peace and happiness.

    To accomplish anything great, or anything at all, we must be swollen with hope and face our struggles with an admiring confidence, knowing full well that we will break free of our imprisoning limitations and secure victory. We should cease our sadness. *"There is neither happiness nor misery in the world; there is only the comparison of one state with another, nothing more. He who has felt the deepest grief is best able to experience supreme happiness. We must have felt what it is to die, that we may appreciate the enjoyments of life,"* - the encouraging words of Alexandre Dumas.

NEITHER LIFE NOR PRAYER IS UNDER ANY OBLIGATION TO GIVE US WHAT WE WANT SIMPLY BECAUSE WE ASK FOR IT. This is not an excuse to dislike it. Life is always there to live. We should learn to love it, or at least endure it. To love it even when we are at our lowest point and our days are the darkest and our nights are the coldest. We should learn to love life even when we have just about lost all our faith, even when our strength is gone and our heart is worn. We should appreciate life even when nothing is going our way and adversity has us trapped and there seems to be no open door; when loneliness has got us chained and we do not have a place to run. Even when we stand in the cold, torn and broken without a home. Indeed, we should learn to love life, to appreciate it, and to endure it, even when our biggest dreams are going up in smoke and our souls are filled with the ashes of it. We should never give up or lose hope, even when the untamed emptiness of grief sits with us, thick and heavy as water more fitting for gills than lungs. We should keep on fighting, even when our soul longs to feel a caring hand; when our heart longs to feel an unconditional love; when our spirit feels like a rose in a desert. Mountains may be steep, rivers may be deep, no doubt, but there is a way, and we must find it. There is always a way, and with hope, faith, will and perseverance, we can find it, if we just fight on.

This is a brilliant poem called Ode to Hope. I fell in love with it the very moment I read it. I hope you will find inspiration from this masterpiece, as I did.

> You are an ever-blooming flower
> Here with me through Life's lowest hour
> Time slowly treads on, and at her footprint
> You keep me superior to her troubling hint:
> That gone are the friends that I have known
> And my soul must now beat against Grief's hard stone
> I have lost everything; my whole life is gone
> Oops! You are still here that our fates might be one
> Faithful, enduring and devoted; rocking me slow
> Like a ghost that refuses to leave its naked bones below
> I rest my whole being upon your shoulder
> For you keep me warm as life grows colder
> Inseparable twin, you are a giver of life -a life giver
> Weathering me through Time's dark-flowing river
> My strength, my will, my faith, all turned to clay
> For grief is dark as that gloom that strangles the day
> I am lost in obscurity; in the hush of time
> Shamed – humbled - in a meditation sublime

> Gazing at forgotten moments - forgotten days
> Muttering like a mournful river over stony ways
> Glory is far-flung, away from sadness and me
> Yet you are here dependably to stay eternally

-Feial Britton

Indeed, hope is the giver of life. It gives life to the farmer who struggles to get his produce in the store, to the student who is failing in her studies, to the single mother who is struggling from hand-to-mouth, to the homeless and desperate orphan sleeping in the cold, to that father searching desperately for employment. It gives life to the lonely widow without a neighbor, to that talented young prospect trapped in the slum, to that dying patient on that hospital bed who has no cure for her disease, to the innocent prisoner locked away in a dungeon for all eternity, to the author who struggles to get his work to the masses, to the performer who struggles to capture the watchful eyes, to the scientist who struggles to vindicate his discovery. It gives life to that martyr suffering painfully for his beliefs. Hope is life itself. It is the lungs of every breathing creature. It is the lifeblood of every blood-using mortal. A man without hope is like a body without a soul or a tree without a root.

WE SHOULD NOT DESPAIR BECAUSE WE ARE GOING THROUGH A TOUGH TIME; BUT SMILE TO KNOW THAT IT WILL SOON BE OVER. Handling life at its lowest fortifies us to appreciate it at its highest. *"In three words I can sum up everything I've learned about life,"* said Robert Frost, *"it goes on." "Finish every day and be done with it. You have done what you could. Some blunders and absurdities, no doubt crept in. Forget them as soon as you can, tomorrow is a new day; begin it well and serenely, with too high a spirit to be cumbered with your old nonsense. This new day is too dear, with its hopes and invitations, to waste a moment on the yesterdays,"* advised Emerson. It is so true; every day is the first day of the rest of our lives. This means everything is possible again. Every day is a new beginning that brings a fresh withering of possibilities and leaves the troubles of yesterday behind.

THE STORMS OF LIFE ARE THE SAME AS THOSE OF THE OCEANS. The harder they rage, the quicker they die in their very own self-kindled flames. There is a line in Shakespeare's play *Hamlet* that says, "The world is "a goodly prison;" in which there are many confines, wards, and dungeons..." Nevertheless, my dear friend, I am here to tell you that our lives do not have to be one of them. Oscar Wilde, another great writer, said, *"To live is the rarest thing in the world. Most people exist, that is all."* We can all do better than that. We can all reach our desired destiny.

In life we have never really failed, we just found another way that was not the right one to achieve our aim. However, when we discover another closed door we should not despair. We should not lose hope. We should not be discouraged. For every minute we are angry, upset, sad, depressed, disappointed, lonely and bored, we lose sixty seconds of precious irretrievable moments of happiness and exuberance.

We are all special. There is always more to us than what meets the eye. We are beautiful, beyond the mere definition of mortal measure. We may not have monuments dedicated to us to preserve our names, but as long as we try our best with all our hearts and souls to be the best human we can be, this should be enough.

Now think carefully of what you hope for. Are you willing to live within those hopes? Are you willing to marry those hopes for richer or for poorer, for better or for worse? We can rise above any obstacle. This depends, however, on the essence of our soul.

Sometimes we falter through the muddy halls of adversity that wind through darkness to victory. Sometimes we altogether fall with our weight of cares. But as we stumble and fall and grope, we should never cease to trust the larger hope. For life is the greatest of all gifts. We may rise from the mud to a free nation and have that same nation betray us. We may fall from the throne of wealth to beggary, and back to wealth again. We may recover from a devastating relationship to live happily ever after in immortal love. But the greatest gift of all, which is the gift of life, is only given once. However, if we live it right, if we live it honestly, if we live it to the fullest of our potentials, if we make the best of every opportunity, as well as making the best of every struggle, if we learn to accept the things we cannot change, and change the things we cannot accept, then surely, once will be enough.

Forgiveness

"To err is human; to forgive, divine."
-Alexander Pope

The understanding and the breaking down of this subject has greatly eluded me. I have gone from draft to draft, doing my very best writing on this matter, to find that each of my drafts was far different from its ancestors. In all of my notes, I have truly come to realize that I am not an expert on this subject. I have advised you on how to find the greater happiness and peace within. I have advised you on how to find your purpose and how to entertain positive thoughts, but how can I advise you on forgiving someone who has done you grievous wrong? This is challenging. It is perhaps not so hard to forgive a single great injury, but certainly, it is very demanding to forgive the incessant provocations of daily life. How can I advise you on letting go of the terrible tragedy your neighbor has inflicted upon you and ask you to *"Love them as you love yourself?"* Is all this humanly possible? I would like to think that all of my essays are practical, and I would love to keep them this way. But would I be asking far too much if I ask my readers to FORGIVE an "unforgivable" offense? Forgiveness is the topic of discussion. This is a very sensitive theme. Most people who have been wronged only have one thing in mind, and that is revenge. After all, that is the shallowness of mortal justice. In fact, human justice implies that the punishment should always outshine the crime. It is one thing to ask someone to forgive a mere transgression that does not really leave a dent in one's character, but it is a whole different thing to ask someone to forgive when their whole life has been torn apart by an intentional rumor, act or instigation. Can we be kind, tenderhearted and forgiving to a brutal and reckless transgressor, as Ephesians 4:32 recommends? One of the most difficult things to do is to forgive, especially when the transgressor is someone close to us. Sometimes the extent to which our character has been breached makes it seemingly impossible to forgive. Consequently, forgiveness, I believe, is the greatest exercise of mortal virtue.

IT IS THE GREATEST SHOW OF CHARACTER. To be sure, it is the finest sense of justice that the human mind can frame. To demonstrate forgiveness is to show how to truly enforce any law. The famous saying goes: *"To err is human, to forgive is divine"*. To forgive someone, to have mercy upon someone, to excuse their faults when we have the ultimate power of condemning or prosecuting them, is godly at the very least. When someone offends us they give us an opportunity to display the greatness of our character, and we should always try our very best to make use of the occasion.

Peace is possible only after forgiveness has cleared the way which resentment, ignorance and tyranny have encumbered. Forgiveness is the attribute of the strong and merciful. To be found in a position to forgive is unearthly, but we should not abuse such opportunity. Instead, we should have humanity enough to believe in our offender's capacity to be transformed by our pardon. There is a quote that says, *"Forgiveness is the economy of the heart; it saves the expense of anger, the cost of hatred, the waste of spirits."*

WITHOUT FORGIVENESS, LIFE IS GOVERNED BY AN ENDLESS CYCLE OF HATRED AND RETALIATION. For as I mentioned before, when we feel violated the first thing that often comes to our mind is revenge, which is a kind of irrational justice that often puts peace out of work. Surely, in taking revenge, we have brought our moral and integrity to that of our offender; but when we forgive them, we display uprightness, for it is godlike to have mercy and forgiveness on those who have done us wrong. *"It is the glory of a man to pass by an offense,"* said King Solomon. That which is past is gone and irrevocable, and we have enough to do with things present and to come. As a result, we should not walk around with resentment over past matters. We should understand that if we nurse revenge we keep our own wounds open and infected, which otherwise would have healed if we found it in our heart to forgive. Revenge belongs to those who love to destroy; forgiveness belongs to those who love to build. Everyone who enjoys thinks that the principal thing to the tree is the fruit, but in fact the principal thing to it is the seed; herein lies the difference between those who create and those who enjoy.

WE SHOULD ALL HAVE AN UNWAVERING ADHERENCE AND DEVOTION TO THE SACRED HUMANITY OF FORGIVENESS. The practice of forgiveness is our most important contribution to the healing of the world. The very nature of humans is to get angry and feel resentful toward those who have hurt us or did some harm to us in any way. This emotion is almost impossible to quell without some kind of favorable resolution. We should all seek to extinguish such emotion utterly from our heart. This kind of emotion is like an enormous sledgehammer; it breaks whatever it falls upon. Anger is the staircase to disaster. It is certainly a kind of baseness as it appears well in the weakness of those subjects in whom it reigns. Forgiveness is there as the remedy to lift us above our anger rather than sink us below it. Marcus Aurelius said, *"Remember, on every occasion which leads thee to vexation, to apply this principle: not that this is a misfortune, but that to bear it nobly is good fortune."*

WE ALL CARRY TWO BAGS OF FAULTS AROUND WITH US; ONE IN FRONT OF US AND ONE BEHIND. It just so happens that the one in front contains the faults of our fellowmen and the one behind contains ours. Consequently, we always see the faults of our fellowmen but not our own. When we forgive others for their imperfections, we are also admitting that we too are imperfect and have flaws as well.

Forgiveness helps us feel light and helps us to get rid of bitter feelings that occupy our hearts and eat away our peace of mind. Without forgiving our offender, we can have no peace because we will never cease to foster aggrieved feelings by having been badly or unfairly treated.

FORGIVENESS IS A WAY TO SELF-FULFILLMENT. It is true that the more easily we forgive our offender, the less likely we will suffocate ourselves and keep bad intentions out of our heart. The ability to forgive gives us a sense of freedom and makes us suffer less and feel less misery and pain. People who can readily forgive others are much more responsible and satisfied inside than those who keep grudges against others and develop feelings of hostility. The feeling of anguish only results in arguments, fights, mistreatment and conflicts. Those who forgive help create positive energy on this planet. Martin Luther King, Jr. believed that *"Darkness cannot drive out darkness; only light can do so. Hate cannot drive out hate; only love can do so."* Consequently, he led a life of perpetual forgiveness that is worthy of praise and admiration.

When we praise any moral excellence we should regard only the motives that produced them and consider the actions as signs or indications of certain principles in the character. The external performance should get the least merit. We should look within to find the moral quality. This is why forgiveness is one of the brightest qualities of human virtue, because it is the ability to understand our fellow human who has erred. It has no external interest. There is nothing material to gain from forgiving. To be sure, it is solely to give; to give tolerance, compassion, understanding and mercy where it seems most undeserving. It is the sense of morality or duty that produces the act of forgiveness and not any other motive.

However displeasing other people may be, however unfair they may be, however true it may be that the wrong is all on their side, whatever we may suffer at their hands, we can only resolve this when we are entirely free from resentment and bitterness. If we are unwilling to rid ourselves of anger and hatred, this unresolved feeling can leave us with a long train of grief, terror, indignation and other negative emotions. The demonstration of mercy is man's highest ideal. Without the will to forgive, man is a busy, hateful creature, no better than a wild beast.

There is a tale of a Lion, a Beagle and a Wolf who were on a hunting mission to secure an Ox for a meal, when the Lion accidentally fell into a ditch. Immediately, the Beagle and Wolf began rejoicing, laughing and mocking the Lion. They accused him of always taking the best parts of the catch, leaving the worse parts for them. Although the Lion begged for mercy and forgiveness along with a promise to change his ways, his friends did not yield and continued the mission, leaving him to his fate.

Upon reaching the scene of the action, they saw a herd of Oxen all ready to engage them in a battle. The trembling hunters turned around fearfully and would have fled had not a sea of Zebras barred their way, equally eager to employ the pair in a fierce conflict. There was nothing left to do but surrender themselves to a dreadful fate.

The Oxen and the Zebras began closing in on the intruders, vexed as a volcanic stream. The Lion, who had managed to free himself from the ditch, watched through the thickets with a childish grin. However, as soon as his friends were about to be severely harmed, he charged their attackers, who were very familiar with the ferociousness of his fangs.

The herd of Oxen and Zebras fled the scene, but the Lion maintained chase until he had secured one of the Oxen.

He dragged the catch to the Beagle and the Wolf and gave it to them, went to the shade and watched them eat as if they were on the verge of starving. And after their bellies were full, they invited the Lion to join the feast.

Upon the Lion's arrival at the feast, he was surprised to discover that they had saved the best part of the Ox for him. He smiled and shook his head and they all laughed contagiously.

Had the Lion promoted resentment for his friends, the outcome would have been much different. Instead, he had the courage to overlook their misdeed. Clearly, **FORGIVENESS ALWAYS WINS AN EASY VICTORY OVER RESENTMENT.** When we are walking around with bitterness and anger, there is a great big beam in our eye, which we cannot see through, or under, or over, but, as we gain our freedom from these terrible emotions, the beam is removed, and we are permitted to see things with a truer sense of proportion.

I know there are offenses that seem too grave to be overlooked or merely ignored. There are deliberate transgressions that seem impossible to forgive. Others who have faced the same form of violation have swiftly taken vengeful action. However, that does not say we too should do the same. Encouraging resentment, or carrying out revenge, has no positive outcome, and there is nothing to gain from it. It is difficult to resent another after a violation without an underlying notion of punishment and revenge. Nevertheless, we should know that revenge is truly a weakness that only produces a series of new cruelties and anger, and hatred often goes beyond the duty of justice. We are not supposed to make others' standards our own, unless, of course, they are higher than ours. We can never excuse ourselves for feelings of resentment or revenge simply because other people foster resentment or revenge. We should never pin our morals against the morals of others. If we want to do right and the other man wants us to do wrong, we should pass by his moral; step over it like a trap, but never on any account yield to it.

It is difficult to have any form of resolution when we are apt to be unforgiving. We should always remember that it is not the repression or disguise of bitterness, or the forbearing to express them that can free us from bondage to the ones who have done us harm, it is overcoming any trace of antipathy within our own hearts and minds. If the hatred is in us, we are just as much in bondage as if we expressed it in our words and actions. If it is in us at all, it will eventually express itself in one way or another. To rid our hearts of hatred and dislike, we should look firstly to ourselves, instead of looking to the offender for an apology. Surely, one would make the damage easier to bear, but how many times does our offender apologize and we are still left with resentment? Some of us, even after a sincere apology, still go on to plot and execute revenge. Clearly, we have a role to play in repairing our peace. In fact, our transgressor may never apologize. He or she may think their action is justifiable, or they may not see any wrongdoing in it at all. What are we supposed to do? Rage an eternal war? Absolutely not! This can only lead to further anger and hurt, even if we have won the contest. The proper way to resolve the matter is first to become conscious of our own resentment and anger, and then we should acknowledge them heartily and fully, and then go to work firmly and steadily on dismissing them completely from our heart. We should never cease until we banish them completely from our heart, not just stopping at merely accommodating a futile show of exterior modesty. This, however, takes a lot of strength of will. For we all have pride and egos that at times are swift to generate obstinacy which weakens our character. At times, our egos tend to lean more toward hatefulness.

FORGIVING EVEN OUR GREATEST ENEMY IS PRACTICAL. Indeed, we have suffered great injury by some malicious words or deed. Yet, if we refuse to let go and move on, the resentment and resistance will only cause us to suffer more. We can only heal ourselves of the hurt by shunning the anger and hatred within.

Unless we live a life of seclusion, there will always be acquaintances with whom we are brought into constant or occasional contact, and by whom we are made to suffer; not to mention the frequent irritations that may come from people we see only once in our lives. Imagine the joy of being free from all this irritability and oppression; imagine the peace that would accompany the readiness to forgive those who have offended us instead of avenging them.

The fable is told of a farmer who was greatly annoyed by a fox, which came prowling about his yard at night, carrying off his chickens into the darkness. He set a trap for the predator and caught him, and decided to have his revenge on the beast. Therefore, he tied a bunch of dry hay to the tail of the fox and set it on fire, then cut the scourge loose.

As ill luck would have it, the fox headed straight for the fields where the farmer's corn was standing ripe and ready for harvesting. It quickly caught fire and was all burned up, and the farmer lost all his harvest. This tale is worth much. The moral of it is: Revenge is a two-edged sword.

Throughout the whole sweep of human history, we see the effect of rising up against crimes by hating and avenging the criminals. It simply does not get us very far. By forgiving our offender, we are helping them to overcome their mistakes or blunders. Without compassion and forgiveness, human peace is insupportable. We should have some regard for any comprehensive purpose of good for the race of man. In doing so, we should be prepared to dismiss all insults and injuries from our memory and forgive our fellow erring brother. That is the true essence of a faithful and noble character. When we display mercy, understanding, tolerance and forgiveness to those who have done us wrong, in spite of the injury, it is the deepest degree in perfection and self-accomplishment. These traits are the highest branch of moral prudence. The ability to cast hurts, malice and injustice behind is rare and heavenly.

This world is our heritage - we all have so much vivacity at our disposal - so much opportunity - so many wonders - so much beauty - so much to live. The pillars of our social structure rest upon the fundamental fact that everyone sincerely considers all that he is. And whoever wishes to add a stone to our social structure should be implanting in humankind this saintly philosophy of forgiveness, tolerance, compassion, kindness and understanding.

A GREAT SOUL IS NOT ONE THAT IS CAPABLE OF THE HIGHEST FLIGHT, BUT ONE THAT MAKES THE BEST USE OF THE ALTITUDE GIVEN. The difficulty in climbing a mountain is not the height one has to reach; it is the method which one uses. That is so, too, with any obstacle we have to overcome; even the obstacle of learning to forgive.

He alone is happy, and is truly so, who can welcome whatever life brings! There is no one too careful to escape the foul shame that human hearts must feel. We should learn to accept every circumstance and experience of life, and count it all as gain. Life is a precious privilege. He who succeeds in evading unpleasant experiences cheats himself out of so much life. We know ourselves by watching what we do when we are scorned, scoffed, mocked, jeered, contradicted, deprived and ridiculed. If we judge men by what we have done, or by what we are, then we would incontestably be considered the worst creature that ever drew breath. For this reason, I look for what we can be, through forgiveness and repentance. I believe the forgiveness of which I speak is not a thing outside of us, taught by priests, pastors and theologians of the Bible. It is in the heart of man, and its chief quality is compassion, tolerance and understanding.

Forgiveness is the leading resolution that can cease any war or dispute. Therefore, let us free our thoughts from all resentment and retaliation. Let us learn to forgive and lift ourselves from sublime ignorance and show some compassion to our ever-erring neighbors, for we too are ever-erring. Let us emancipate ourselves from the scourging traditions of revenge and hatred, not only by deposing the idea of these evils, but by actually making the conception of uprightness be the starting-point of all our thoughts and actions.

HUMANITY SHOULD NEVER BE BANKRUPTED. WE, AS A RACE, SHOULD DO OUR UTMOST EACH DAY TO GET BEYOND ALL TYRANNY AND MISERIES. We should try our utmost to get beyond our social, political and economic struggles. It is imperative that we get beyond the yawning gulf that lies between our unity and goodwill. Everyone must play their part in advancing the wellbeing of our race, so that our planet may increase in beauty, goodwill and peace. Let us slope our minds from any thought that produces conflicts and sets up antagonism in society. Each one of us is the cornerstone of the moral structure of our community, and is instrumental in the moral elevation of the world. Forgiveness, then, should be our social attitude, and we should never be afraid to demonstrate it with a touching confidence. Mercy is noble, but we abolish such nobility as soon as we stretch out our hand to exercise revenge.

This world is beautiful! How magnificent is Life that breathes over the world, passing whole and wonderful! The mountains and rivers, streams and brooks, sun, moon and stars, wind and rain, have a gleaming theme, on which the heaviest hearts can moralize. Life! Oh, Life! Having the elements of all that divine hands can frame of loveliness and divinity. Without a doubt, it is an amazing gift. The greatest gift of all! It is heavenly. It is a great miracle. It is bigger than any mere changes of empires, wreckages of dynasties, political systems, birth or extinction of religion. Take a look at the universe of stars and planets, of which this inhabited earth is one, and their motions and their destiny. Indeed, life is the great miracle that should be cherished and preserved. Let us make the very best of it and make it our point of duty to ensure that our birth is remembered, however small the measure might be. Let us make sure that we live on, and in doing so we strengthen the pillars of future generations. Let us not spend it being hateful, resentful or intolerant. It is easier to stoop to intolerance than to rise to the summit of forbearance. A true character is never afraid to believe in love, loveliness, togetherness, oneness, mercy and forgiveness. Neither is it afraid to show them.

FORGIVENESS CREATES AN OPENING WHERE THE IMPRISONED SPLENDOR OF OUR ANGER AND REVULSION CAN ESCAPE. To rinse the world of hatred, discrimination, segregation, bigotry and intolerance should be the never-ending passion of every soul. Forgiveness teaches us to turn away from hatred and liberate our hearts from retaliation and vengeance. Getting even after an injury is a mark of the weakest sort of men. The true gallant deed and masterpiece of a great character does not lie in avenging those who have hurt us, but in the far harder task of extending a harmless hand to them in true forgiveness, without bitterness, hatred, anger or resentment. The sword of vengeance is long and broad, but the sword of forgiveness runs out to a needlepoint. Victory will be the reward of the dauntless and the good, who dare to hurl defiance at selfishness and self-indulgence, at injustice and inequality, at supremacy and tyranny, at segregation and racism. And greatest still will be the reward of those who learn to forgive the perpetrators of these indiscretions.

Let us be a living light; a watch-fire that robes the world in a peaceful glow. Let us be the stars that stud heaven's silvery vault; let us learn to have tolerance, learn to live and let live, learn to forget and forgive. Let us love each other with our deepest blood. Let us be all-inspiring; like the morning sun that tickles the silvery sea - like the purpling sunset that tinges the velvet sky - like the tropical wind that dimples the feathery leaves - like the flowery clouds that speckle the sunshiny brow of heaven. This blessed earth can be a reality of Heaven! However, this cannot be so if we are overwhelmed by hatred and anger. This cannot be so if we are carrying a great deal of bitterness for our neighbor.

THE REFUSAL TO FORGIVE AN INJURY WILL ONLY LEAVE BEHIND AN IMPRESSION OF WEAKNESS AND COWARDICE. Resentment exhausts the soul and brings its very dregs to light. We should not allow our hearts to formulate any sort of hatred or revenge; for he who shuns war and strife finds an eternity in one short life. We all are human, born of flesh and blood, frail and vain at best, born to make mistakes. If there is anyone who you are refusing to forgive, get up now! Go and forgive them, so that you can move on with your life. For he who learns to forgive learns to live in the warmth and fullness of the heart, and as it is, in the summer air of the soul.

Banishing Our Fears

"The only thing we have to fear, is fear itself -nameless, unreasoning, unjustified terror, which paralyzes needed efforts to convert retreat into advance."
-Franklin D. Roosevelt

Billions of us are living our lives in a manner which is purposeless, meaningless and reasonless. We seem to have no desire, no motivation, no strength, and no will. We are too beaten down, beaten up, shunned, scorned, mocked, jeered and rebuked. We have a constant feeling of humiliation, betrayal, oppression, victimization; feelings of inferiority, persecution and discrimination. Even when we are amidst our friendliest neighbors we still feel like an anchorite in isolation, or a martyr in exile. We are very fragile, feeling like an open wound that is being constantly irritated by our clothes. We live our lives hiding behind the obscuring mist of fear, afraid to respond to any new prospect or possibility that knocks at our door. We are so enveloped by fearfulness that we have reached the summit of mortal sadness. Love, peace, happiness, compassion and success are only a few words to be lived and realized in some speculative afterlife.

WELL, THE ONLY WAY WE CAN RID OURSELVES OF SUCH LOWLY EXISTENCE IS TO FIRST RID OURSELVES OF FEAR. Fear is the mind killer. Fear is the strength killer. Fear is the will killer and the dream killer. Fear is a disease that eats upon the will and brings total stagnancy to even our profoundest aspirations. *"Fear is the dominion of the human will,"* said John F. Kennedy. *"There is little to* *be achieved for those of us who live in constant fear. The fundamental ambitions of our social and economic wellbeing can only become a reality through the uncompromising zeal, courage and determination of our very own strength of character."*

Indeed, we will not get rid of the influence of failure until we break our mental chains. The greatest obstacle to our progress is the inability to think, judge and act for ourselves because of the authority of fear. It requires more strength to fear, than not to. Fear and doubts equal defeat. All bodily activity is caused, controlled and directed by the mind, and all human achievement comes about through bodily activity. Therefore, if fear penetrates the mind, it will naturally paralyze the body as well.

FEAR DOES VERY LITTLE TOWARD THE PRODUCTION OF ANY GREAT RESULT IN LIFE. Even the task that is achieved by what is called "luck" can only be made by a bold venture. And if these tasks are carefully investigated, it will be found that there has really been very little that was "lucky" about them. For the most part, these so-called "slips of fate" have only been opportunities, carefully improved by persons of bravery. This art of seizing opportunities and turning even "accidents" to account, bending them to some purpose, is a great secret of success.

Fearfulness characterizes the lowest order of humankind. This pitiful exhibition of weakness is certainly of the lowest rank in a character. A great deal of the unhappiness, stagnancy and much of the indiscriminate vice of the world is owing to the absence of courage. Persons who are resolved to find a way for themselves will always find the opportunities to do so and if the prospect does not lie readily near their hands, they will create it. On the other hand, the passive endurance of a timid coward is always found ready to bend and surrender, to conform and to yield, without so much as an attempt to make a difference.

THE BASIC COURAGE WE CAN HAVE IS THAT OF BEING OURSELVES. Every man should be himself! We should have the crucial bravery of being ourselves and not the shadow or the echo of others. If we are afraid of our neighbors' opinions of us, we cannot exercise our own powers, think our own thoughts, or speak our own sentiments. We would be too much of a coward to elaborate our own opinions and form our own convictions. *It has been said that he who does not have an opinion must be a coward, he who will not, must be a coward, he who cannot, must be a dunce.*

Popularity these days seems to be easily attained by flattering people with lies, by writing and speaking to their lowest tastes. If we are weak and blind, hungry and shelter-less, desperate, uneducated, unhealthy, and cowardly, then surely, we will be easily flattered. We will be easily led to throw off the glimmering robe of our brightest colors and wear those of "the public". In fact, fear is the convicted murderer of individual freedom. It is the virus that is known to decay individuality. In truth, one of the true functions of fear is to aid the decline and insecurity of personality.

A FEARFUL MAN CANNOT EXPRESS HIMSELF HONESTLY. If he is upright, he can easily fall victim to fraud. If he is truthful, he can easily become a liar. If he is an advocate for justice, fear can turn him into a tyrant. A coward may know what is right and yet fail to exercise the gallantry to do it. He may understand the duty he has to perform, but will not summon the requisite resolution to execute it. Fearfulness will deny him the power of standing firmly, when to yield, however slightly, might be only the first step in a downhill course to ruin. Those of us who possess this vice have no security for the preservation of ourselves or others.

There is scarcely a great truth that never had to fight its way to public recognition in the face of detraction, ridicule and persecution. Every progress we have ever made in science and art that has made us better acquainted with the universe, with the earth, and with ourselves, has been established by the energy, the devotion, the self-sacrifice, and the courage of the great spirits of past times. These supreme characters, however much they have been opposed or reviled by their contemporaries, now rank amongst those whom the enlightened of the human race most delight to honor. Even today, these supreme characters continue to present to us some of the noblest spectacles to be seen in history. For men of sterling character have the courage to speak the truth, to hold to their ideas and to be true to self, even when it is unpopular. They will set their feet to a good action, though the entire world dislikes it. They always look on things as they are, not through the dim spectacles of vulgar estimation. That is the only way to represent the moral force of the world. That is the only way to implement any form of positive change in ourselves or in society.

MANY WORLD-CHANGING IDEAS DIED AN UNTIMELY DEATH BECAUSE OF FEAR. As we all know, every great idea sounds absurd when it is first revealed, wholly because it is the victim of newness. Moreover, it suffers great damage from its author, if he is not well-known and much talked about. The entire world is accustomed to mark the author by his fame. Whatever depth, originality, and brilliance the idea contains will suffer as time goes by, under the blinding ignorance of traditional admiration. Perhaps many years will pass and many a spider will have to weave its web about the idea before it is finally renowned. Therefore, if we are a coward, we will lack the impudence needed to reveal the discovery. If, somehow, we gather the boldness to do so, we will lack the courage necessary to maintain the idea, after it has been widely shunned. John Adams, another one of our great presidents, once stated, *"He who has not realized that every great man must not only be encouraged but also, for the sake of the common welfare, opposed, is certainly still a great child."*

INDECISIVENESS IS ANOTHER ADVERSE OUTCOME OF FEAR. Many of us, because of fear, call upon others for help in forming an important decision. This, though at times is the right thing to do, can also be the wrong thing, and when it is, we suffer severely from our cowardice. Therefore, we should train our habits to rely upon our own powers and depend upon our own courage in moments of making a life-changing decision. The will, which is the central force of character, should be trained in the habits of decision, otherwise it will neither be able to resist evil nor to follow good.

In 1995 I was determined to purchase my own house. I was propelled into making this decision due to some issues I was having at the condominium that I had rented. I remember telling some of my friends at the time of my intention. Most, if not all of them, told me to reconsider. All sorts of negative questions attacked me like a score of piercing arrows. It was very difficult to withstand the potency of their negative tongues. But of course, none of us had our own house at the time. We were all paying rent. Therefore, it was easy to see where they were coming from. They never thought that I would be able to maintain the obligations of owning a house, because they themselves could not manage such obligations. This experience is no isolated case; whenever someone cannot do a thing or cannot perceive a thing being done, they will always be the first to tell us that we cannot do it. If we let fear and negative opinions take control of our lives, we will not be able to accomplish much. Sometimes we have to make that great step against the odds. We cannot be fearful and indecisive. The purchasing of this first house of which I speak led me to my real purpose in life as a realtor and a real estate investor. I never looked back since; neither do I harbor any kind of regrets.

It is precisely because of fear that so many of us fall short and disappoint the expectations of our biggest fans. We march up to the scene of action, but at every step our courage oozes out. We lack the requisite decision and audacity. We calculate the risks and not the reward until the opportunity has passed.

Many theories formed end merely in words because of fearfulness. *"Fear represents the stronghold of man's enslavement and all the horrors it entails,"* Napoleon once stated. There are many designs projected that are never begun, all because of fear. For in life and in business, action is better than words; and the shortest answer of all is, DOING. Nothing demonstrates a weak mind more accurately than irresolution - to be undetermined when the case is so plain and the necessity so urgent to make a move. To be always intending to live a new life, but never to find time to set about it. This does to our soul what putting off eating, drinking and sleeping from one day to another does to the body.

INACTIVENESS IS NOT A SAFEGUARD AGAINST FAILURE; NEITHER IS IT A SAFE ZONE. The only way to attack the problems of our lives and render a swift solution is by demonstrating unflinching fearlessness. This life is all we have. It is not a test run or a mere experiment to see if we would really like it here on earth. When this brief life is over, we will not have another, at least not on this planet. Consequently, we should be careful not to leak it away being indecisive. I would rather fail than be afraid to fail. Fear, to me, is holding a sharp two-edged weapon against my neck. Fear makes a mere molehill into a mountain. Ultimately, a victory lingers on the other side of every fear; we gain this victory by each experience in which we prepare ourselves by saying, "I am not afraid! I will not fear. I will face this challenge. I will not permit it to seize control of me and break me." Thomas Jefferson said, *"When the people fear the government, there is tyranny. When the government fears the people, there is liberty."* It is so, too, when we have a fear of failure - when we have a fear of failure, there is failure. When failure seems nothing to us, there is victory.

We cannot advance in life if we remain dormant when it is so clear that it is imperative that we make an immediate move. Indecisiveness leads to stagnation. I know many talented people who procrastinated indefinitely, eroding their confidence, and before they know it, there is nothing their fragile will is willing to try. The fear of failure is perhaps one of the most customary and hardest fears which does not warrant the fear we have of it. When such fear is oppressing a man, telling him that the big move he is about to make will turn to dust, it is difficult to get him to act.

MEN OF COURAGE LEAD HUMAN DESTINY, WHILE THE WEAK AND TIMID LEAVE NO TRACE BEHIND. We can all agree that the world owes nothing to the cowards and everything to the courageous. Every step of progress in the history of our race has been made in the face of opposition and difficulty, and has been achieved and secured not by cowards, but by men of intrepidity and valor.

Fearlessness creates confidence in us. Knowledge is power; this is true, but truer in a much higher sense is that fearlessness is power. Mind without heart is no mind at all, and true graciousness is exempt from fear. Consequently, the first duty of man is to surmount fear. He should get rid of it, for he will be forever stagnant until then. This is because our fears are generally heavier than the danger that is at hand and tends to keep us inactive or overactive, which at such a time often carries an adverse effect.

There is never any real reason for fear because, as we all know, anxiety never helps us to gain, and often is the cause of us not reaching the things that we so much desire. *"I love the man who can smile in trouble, who can gather strength from distress, and grow brave by reflection. It is the business of little minds to shrink, but he whose heart is firm, and whose conscience approves his conduct, will pursue his principles unto death."* -Thomas Paine. I hold the same belief. Fear only stifles our thinking and ability to act.

Marcus Garvey attributed his success as a public man not to his talents or his powers of speaking, for these were but moderate, but to his known store of bravery. *"Hence it was,"* he said, *"that I had so much weight with my audiences. I was but a bad speaker, never eloquent, subject to much hesitation in my choice of words, hardly correct in language, and yet I generally carried my point."*

Much of the fear that exists is the offspring of imagination, which creates the images of failures which MAY happen, but perhaps rarely do; and thus, many people who are capable of summoning up courage to grapple with and overcome real obstacles are paralyzed or thrown into dismay by those obstacles which are imaginary.

There is indeed nothing attractive in timidity, nothing loveable in fear. All weakness, whether of mind or body, is a deformity that can create an adverse effect on the body as inconvenient as a disease.

THERE ARE VERY FEW THINGS THAT WARRANT THE FEAR WE HAVE OF THEM. The fear of failure, the fear of loneliness, the fear of disease, the fear of sickness, and the fear of death -all these fears do not warrant the fear we invest in them. To succumb or be intimidated by any one of these fears is just not helpful or healthy. *"All government in essence,"* said Emerson, *"is tyranny. It matters not whether it is government by divine right or majority rule. In every instance its aim is the absolute subordination of the individual."* The same goes for fear as well. Any kind of fear is tyranny; its aim is the absolute subordination of the mind. Indeed, fear is a ruthless tyrant. Edgar Wallace said, *"Fear is a tyrant and a despot, more terrible than* *the rack, more potent than the snake."* To yield to nervous excitement of any kind is like rubbing a sore. It only irritates it and makes matters worse - or makes matters that were not even bad in the first place become so. This is nothing but instinctive faithlessness. We simply do not have enough faith in ourselves.

> "What are fears but voices airy?
> Whispering harm where harm is not
> And deluding the unwary
> Till the fatal bolt is shot!"
>
> -Wordsworth

THE QUICKEST WAY FOR US TO RID OURSELVES OF FEAR IS BY POSSESSING THE WILLINGNESS TO FAIL. This might seem like a monstrous mockery. Of course, it seems like a presumptuous way of combating fear. But yes, indeed, the way to rid ourselves of fear is by possessing the willingness to fail. For instance, when we attempt a task and fail, we suddenly exclaim, "It's alright!" So soon we discover the good use in it being "alright!" And how soon we settle into the sense of it being "alright!" A circumstance that has seemed to us all wrong at first, suddenly, through our quiet way of non-resistance to it, appears to be alright.

A strong sense of something is being "alright" means a strong sense of willingness to admit that it is okay as it is; it is alright to fail, or to be disappointed. With that clear willingness in our hearts in general, we can adjust ourselves to anything in particular - even to very sudden and unexpected changes. It is carrying along with us a background of powerful non-resistance that we can bring to the front and use actively at a moment's notice.

OFTEN, THE FEAR OF NOT ACCOMPLISHING WHAT IS BEFORE US IS THE ONLY THING THAT STANDS IN OUR WAY OF ACCOMPLISHING IT. If we put all anxiety - whether it may be an immediate anxiety of missing the train, or the anxiety of not meeting the objectives of our lives - if we put it all under the clear light of this truth, it will eventually relieve us of a burden which is robbing our energy.

If one holds failure to be "alright!" after failure, why then can't he, before the failure, be perfectly willing to fail? All this requires is one's utmost power of concentration to enable one to yield truly, and to be fully willing to submit to whatever the law of our being may require.

If a man is wholesomely willing to fail, should such an affliction overtake him, he has dropped all opposition to the idea of failure, and thus also to all the mental and physical contractions that would foster it. He has dropped a strain that was draining his brain of its proper strength, and the result is new vigor to mind and body.

To drop an inherited stress of fear produces a great and astonishing change, and all we need to bring it about is to thoroughly understand how possible and how advantageous it is. If we once realize the benefit of dropping the strain, our will is there to accomplish the rest.

THE FEAR OF FAILURE KEEPS ONE IN A CONSTANT STATE OF UNNECESSARY ANXIETY. The willingness to fail does not make failure more likely to happen, but it prevents our wasting energy by resistance and keeps us quiet and free, so that if an obstacle of any kind arises, we are prepared to act promptly and calmly for the best.

If the amount of energy one wasted in the strain of fear could be measured in pounds of pressure, the figures would be alarming. Whether it might be the fear of our children catching a disease, fear of the dentist, fear of being unattractive, fear of our children not being successful, fear of losing our job after the upcoming job-cut and all the above fears that I cited - whatever the fear might be, fear is slavery - a self-appointed prison. **TO LIVE IN FEAR IS WORSE THAN TO LIVE IN SLAVERY.** It is a terrible thing to live in fear. I tell you, there is no prison as steel-bound as fear. Fear can deny us of the simplest effort.

We are encouraged to view fear as an object, an obstacle we must tackle and bring down at all cost, for the failure to do so is a guarantee of not accomplishing the very thing we fear. Nelson Mandela said, *"I felt fear myself more times than I can remember, but I hid it behind a mask of boldness. The brave man is not he who does not feel afraid, but he who conquers it."*

To conquer this emotion, we should be willing to fail in whatever we fear. The true helpfulness from surrendering to the idea of failure does not come from neglecting to take proper precautions against it, but from yielding with complete readiness to the essential facts of life, and a rational confidence that, whatever comes, we will be provided with the means of meeting it. This confidence is, in itself, one of the greatest sources of mental endurance.

What is your fear? Losing your job? Losing your marriage? Failure? The past? The present? The future? The inevitable unknown? Are you afraid of venturing into a new, mysterious and untested territory? Is that the reason you have been stuck for the past few years without any real progress in your life? Is that the reason you are at home, lonely, depressed and afraid? Is that the reason you are holding onto ancient, comforting (but illusionary) beliefs? The only certain moment is NOW! Get up, stand up and LIVE! How many of us have turned our backs on this mortal life, the only life which is certain, however brief, to seek a future one, which is speculative at best? There is no man with living breath that does not have a purpose, or that cannot be appointed one. It is my thought that we all have some level of immortality that can be achieved by living a compassionate and loving life, contributing to a better, more peaceful world, during our life, thus leaving tender memories and positive lessons behind for those yet living. *"There is nothing to fear but fear itself."* Be undaunted! Do not be afraid or deterred by the prospect of defeat, loss or failure. Do not forfeit this life. There is a lot of magnificence left in it, a lot of humanity, a lot of meaning, and a lot of duties to be performed.

Life is for living in the fullest, helping to make the world a better place for those we share it with, and for those to follow. This world and all its uncertainty is to be embraced and cherished, not feared. Would it not be far wiser for us to have faith in and love for ourselves, and have faith in humanity, followed by faith that we are on a course of betterment, day by day, only through the positive aspirations of individuals, followed by positive actions? We should all move onward in the hope of a brighter, better world. If we sit back in fear, there will never be any progress. Obstacles exist, no doubt, but we should face them courageously. This and only this can shape our character and our destiny.

I URGE YOU TO COME OUT FROM UNDERNEATH THE DEADWEIGHT OF FEAR. This kind of emotion is destructive and nonproductive. A close examination will show that it is nothing but a tyrannical instrument of torture, perhaps even worse than an iron maiden. It keeps the slaves loyal to their masters, the citizens loyal to their tyrants, the weak loyal to their oppressors, and ultimately, the poor loyal to their beggary.

Life may give us stone when we ask for bread, but this is no excuse for hunger. The manner of living is to try to bear with every circumstance, to overcome every adversity, bridging each with courage and defiance. My greatest longing is for us to be able to see with the eyes of history that for victory to be possible, fear has to be, by nature, nonexistent. All the obstacles and adversities of our lives are intimate. The thing is, we all have to bravely confront these burdens that seem to hold us in the net of hopelessness and poverty of will. How else will we be able to defeat the grisly terrors of our age?

THE HORRORS WE FACE ARE MONUMENTAL. NEVERTHELESS, WE SHOULD FIND A WAY TO PREVAIL. WE MUST BE VICTORIOUS. We can only secure a favorable result by being brave, resilient, faithful, hopeful and self-sacrificing, not by being fearful. Fear suppresses our inner voice, subdues our spirit, and chains our body to stagnancy, causing our life to be dull, gray and monotonous. It is the annihilator of individuality, of free inventiveness and originality.

As I said, the quickest way for us to rid ourselves of fear is by possessing the readiness to fail. Yes, let us combat our fears by being willing to fail in our endeavor; by being perfectly willing to fail. With that clear strong-headedness in our hearts we can adjust ourselves to any challenges - even to very sudden and unexpected ones. If we are wholesomely willing to face our adversities and challenge them, regardless of the outcome, it will be easy for us to drop all resistance to the idea of failure. In doing so, we drop both mental and physical contractions that fear would foster, and drop the strain that is known to drain our bodies of its proper strength, and we would be left with vigor to attack the task defiantly.

I repeat, in an effort to make this perfectly clear, the idea of being wholeheartedly and absolutely willing to fail does not make failure more likely to happen, neither does it guarantee that failure will happen, but it prevents our wasting energy by resistance, and keeps us quiet and free, so that whatever difficulty comes our way, we are prepared to act promptly and calmly for the best. It is simple as this: you have to possess the willingness to lose, in order to win. Indeed, to truly conquer this emotion, we should be willing to fail to be successful. The true support from yielding to the concept of failure does not come from neglecting to take proper precautions against it, but from yielding with complete readiness to the essential facts of life, and a rational confidence that, whatever comes, we will be provided with the means of meeting it. This confidence is in itself, as I said earlier, one of the greatest sources of mental brilliance.

Overcoming Adversities

Glory inherited, I feel, is the worst pity
For success is of little account without adversity

-Feial Britton

The rewards and punishments of the economic world are severely unequal. One man earns as much in a week or even in a day as another does in a year, or perhaps his entire life. This man by hard, manual labor makes only enough to pay for humble shelter and plain food. This other, by what seems a pleasant leisure pursuit, fascinating as watching a flock of passing birds, acquires uncounted millions and never has to work because he was born into an easy and sheltered affluence. A third stands hopelessly in the unemployment line asking in vain for work. A fourth lives off his mother, dozing in his lazy-chair, and neither toils nor turns, unless, of course, it is to watch Jerry Springer. A fifth by the sheer risk of a lucky deal acquires a fortune. A sixth, who has no education, scorns work, earns nothing and is an ignorant beggar who cannot sign his name, sleeps all his life without taking his shoes off, and wanders through society like an underground mouse, scrounging his food wherever he can, sunning his tattered rags when it is warm and freezing whenever it is cold. He plays his part, however, as a dependent of the government, eventually slipping through the meshes of civilization. This is the harsh reality of our economic society. An even harsher reality is that of adverse fate, which begins, for many, from the very cradle. Others are the children of inhumane and indiscriminate want. For some, life is but a foolish leisure pursuit with mock activities and avocations to mask its uselessness. For others, the long struggle of life begins in the very bloom of childhood and ends only when the broken and exhausted body sinks into senility.

ADVERSITY, I FIND, IS THE INEVITABLE LOT OF HUMANKIND. It is the mother of success. Every glory has its origin in it. It should be the greatest inspiration for one burning with indignation at some obstacle or abuse, to know profoundly well that the paradoxical circumstance is a divine ladder furnished to mount him to the zenith of his ambition. It is observed that adversity has the effect of eliciting ability, which in thriving situations would have lain latent. All men should acknowledge that this can be for nothing else but a beam of divinity that stirs a mortal body and lifts it to a deeper destiny. Some are born in poverty but rise to embarrassing wealth owing to that inborn energy and capacity that maintain defiance to the ill will of fate. All about us is the moving and shifting spectacle of adversities and glories, side-by-side, inextricable. If success is there, so too is adversity and vice versa. They are symmetrical, inevitable and perpetual. Very few can attain success without being profoundly impressed by the terrible impartialities of adversity. To achieve the simplest necessaries and comforts of life, almost everyone must scale the monumental peaks of adversity. The truest winning often comes first through the halls of adversity. It then is necessary to develop a person and a character. In a time of hardship, people need to find a strength that is beyond their mortal capacity to overcome the situation. Through this divine resilience, the true colors of a person are shown; how enduring they are, how inventive they are, and how faithful they are. More character is shown during difficult times than prosperous ones.

ADVERSITY IS A MEANS TO A HIGHER END THAT ULTIMATELY BRINGS TRUE SUCCESS. IF WE CHOOSE, IT CAN ALWAYS BE USED AS A MEANS TO AN END RATHER THAN AS A RESULT IN ITSELF.

How often do we hear the complaint, "I could do so well if it were not for my circumstances"? How many people are held down for a lifetime by the habitual belief in circumstances as limitations, and by ignoring the opportunities that they afford? "So long as I have Mr. So-and-so as my teacher, I will never graduate." If this complaint could be changed to the resolve: "I will accept Mr. So-and-so until I have so adjusted myself to him as to be contented." A source of weakness would be changed into a source of strength. The quiet activity of the mind required to adjust ourselves to difficult surroundings gives a zest and interest to life that we can find in no other way, and adds certain strength to the character that cannot be found elsewhere.

If we are alive to our own true zeal for success, we should have an active interest in the necessary warfare of life. For life is a warfare-not of persons but of strength and will. Every man who loves victory loves to be in the midst of the battle. How else will he be able to secure that victory other than by fighting?

IT IS NOT THE ADVERSITIES OF LIFE THAT TROUBLE OR WEIGH UPON US; IT IS THE WAY WE TAKE THEM. Wrestling with the hardships of life itself is just as necessary, not only that we may meet the particular problem of the moment truly, but that we may gain all the experience that may be helpful in meeting other difficult circumstances as they present themselves. Practical wisdom is only to be learned in the school of experience. Precepts and instructions are useful as far as they go, but, without the discipline of real life, they remain of the nature of theory only. The hard facts of existence have to be faced, to give that touch of truth to character which can never be imparted by reading or tuition, but only by contact with the broad instincts of life. The whole of life may be regarded as a great school of experience, in which we are the pupils. Many of the lessons learned can only be taken on trust. We may not understand them, and may think it hard that we have to learn them, especially where the teachers are trials, sorrows, temptations, and difficulties; and yet we must not only accept their lessons, but recognize them as being divinely appointed.

A broken man, fed up with all his sorrows, gathered them in a barrel and headed thousands of miles out into the Atlantic. He was bent on drowning them once and for all.

At last he reached his selected ground and tossed the barrel of sorrows into the depths of the sweltering ocean. He stood for a while watching the container descending beneath the monstrosity of the current, and after it was completely submerged, he breathed a sigh of relief and veered to shore.

Upon his return to the coast, the barrel with all its contents was slapped to shore by the angry waves and was comfortably waiting for him. He was utterly astonished. He rushed up to the container to confirm his suspicion.

"How did you reach back to shore?" he questioned his sorrows desperately. "I put you in a barrel, sealed it, and tossed you miles and miles into the hungry ocean!"

His sorrows smiled at him humorously, tapping him on the shoulder teasingly.

"My dear, you have to learn how to get along with us, for indeed, we know how to swim very well.

Of all the sots who try to drown us in a bottle of rum, of all the smokers who try to drown us in a pack of cigarette, of all the gamblers who try to drown us at the casino, tell me, my dear friend, which one has ever been successful?

My friend, think of us as your wife. Your triumph over us is not to avoid us, it is to endure us. And therein lies your hope; that in spirit you might rein over us - your nagging wife."

ADVERSITY IS THAT STRONG WIND THAT TEARS AWAY FROM US ALL BUT THE THINGS THAT CANNOT BE TORN. No matter how bad things seem, we can always make them better…or worse. **WHAT DEFINES A GREAT MAN IS NOT WHAT HE DOES WHEN HE IS ON THE THRONE OF GLORY; IT IS WHAT HE DOES WHEN HE FALLS FROM IT TO RISE BACK TO THAT THRONE.** We should first convince ourselves thoroughly of the truth that obstacles are rarely without opportunities. They are not by any means opportunities for taking us in the direction that our own obstinacy would have us go; they are opportunities that are meant to guide us in the direction we most need to follow - in the ways that will lead us to the greatest strength in the end.

We should know, without a doubt, that there is a destiny that shapes our end and it is in the silly resistance to having our ends shaped for us that we stop and groan. Moreover, much of what we call evil is good in disguise, and we should not quarrel rashly with adversities not yet understood, nor overlook the victories often bound up in them. Pleasure and pain are, as Plutarch said, the nails that fasten body and soul together.

Oftentimes, events that look like misfortune, if boldly faced, turn out to be good. If approached with the right mentality, calamity turns to our advantage, and great ruins make way for greater glories.

There is a power lying deep in all of us, by the use of which we can rise to higher and better things. There is a greater self within us that can raise us above the infinite armies of adversities and lift us sublimely like the mountains towering over the plains. We possess, did we but know it, an infinite power. This power is of the spirit; therefore, it is unconquerable. It is not the power of the mortal life, or finite will, or human mind. It transcends these, because, being spiritual, it is of a higher order than either physical or even mental planes. This power lies dormant, and is hidden within us until we are sufficiently evolved and unfolded to be entrusted with its use.

THE TRUE OBJECT OF LIFE IS THAT WE MAY ATTAIN TRIUMPH THROUGH CIRCUMSTANCES. This cannot be accomplished by giving in to difficulties, but only by overcoming them and taking with us the experience we have learned, so that the next obstacle we face finds us better able to deal with it spiritually, physically and intellectually. The promises of glory are not made to those who fail in life's battle, but to those who overcome. Neither are there any promises that we will have an easy time and be constantly happy.

WE SHOULD NOT MAKE CIRCUMSTANCES A CONVENIENCE TO FAILURE. Failure is inexcusable! We should not bear this unjust thought of drifting through life, learning none of its discipline and then, when in trouble, or things are not to our liking, we give up and blame everything and everyone except our will. I find this idea very prevalent today. We have found a rather terrible way of confiding in prayers and throwing up our hands to our allies beyond the skies to help us, when even the ally himself told us, faith without work is death! To be clear, there is absolutely nothing wrong with prayer and I always take any opportunity to pray. However, I know for sure, indeed, that it takes more than prayers to get me through my trying times. I know that, whatever I am going through, I must be the leader in getting past it.

I CURRY NO FAVOR WITH GOD, AND I DO NOT BELIEVE THAT WE CAN GET WHAT WE WANT FROM THE INVISIBLE BY DEMANDING IT. If we try to look to everyone else rather than ourselves to lift us from adversities, we are merely chasing rainbows. The easy life we seek will constantly elude us, simply because there is no such thing. The only life that is easy is the life of the strong soul who has overcome. To get past our trying times one has to have the wit to see opportunities where there are obstacles and see possibilities where there is hopelessness.

It is a farce to think that our life should be a crystal stream of eternal pleasure, and, if it were possible, then life would not be worth living, for the sole object of life is the building of character and the attainment of knowledge through experience. Our lives then, from time to time, will be plagued with all kinds of difficulties, and it is to help those who, up till now, have found life rather too much for them that this book is being written.

WHAT MOST OF US ARE SEEKING IS AN EASY LIFE, WHICH WE WILL NEVER FIND, AND FOR THEM I HAVE NO MESSAGE. But to those prudent and awakened souls who are seeking truth and honesty, no matter whence it may come, and who desire to overcome the difficulties of life, instead of weakly giving in to them, this book, it is hoped, will bring a message of hope and inspiration.

It is a great deal of mental exercise to most of us to figure out why we are seemingly met with more adversities than others; why others should have, apparently, a smoother life than ours. Honestly, that is not our business. That is the business of fate and destiny. We must therefore be satisfied to know that we have to meet trouble and overcome difficulty, and that it is only by doing so that we can attain wisdom and build up our character. The question, then, is not whether we will meet the trouble and adversity, but rather how we will meet them. Will we be victorious or will we be submerged? Will we overcome our difficulties or will we give in to them?

The majority of us are drifters on the sea of life. We are wafted here and blown there, being carried back and forth by every current. It is only the few who realize that we have the power of the infinite within us, by which we can rise superior to all our difficulties, overcome our own weaknesses, and, through victorious experience, attain success.

At this point, some practical reader may say that attaining success sounds very sweet to the ear, but I am currently drowning; going under rapidly, and in need of practical help. He is perhaps out of work, bills are covering him, he just had his car repossessed, his children are not doing well in school, and to add insult to injury, his wife just filed for divorce. Or, he may be well-to-do, and yet going through a severe depression and crippling loneliness. I would say to any such person that they possess the power by which they can overcome all these difficulties and, through overcoming, attain peace and happiness. Our success depends, more than anything, upon our hope, faith and will - our hope that life has a good purpose, our faith in that good purpose, and our will to believe in ourselves, step up to the task and execute that purpose we deeply believe in. Indeed, all of us have the ability to overcome every obstacle in our path, if we have these three characteristics.

THE EXTENT OF THE POWER THAT WE CAN BRING INTO OUR LIVES IS THE MEASURE OF OUR FAITH IN OUR OWN WILL. If our faith has no confidence in our will, then our lives will be feeble and lacking in achievement. If our faith in our will is enormous, then great will be the power manifesting in our lives. The character our faith displays toward our will can exhaust it or refresh it. Therefore, to get by our moment of difficulty, our will requires of our faith an unquenchable belief and trust. To put it simply, we must believe in our own ability!

There is the same power in the timid and weak as in the brave and strong. The weakness of the former is due to a lack of faith and belief in his will. Dear reader, you should know that will and ability have an immense difference in definition. Ability is the skill to do a particular task; will is the determination to do it. Will, I find, often outshines ability.

Confining myself to the topic at hand, there will be difficulties and troubles in every life, and sometimes disaster and heartbreaks, when the very earth slides from under our feet. Yet, by calling upon the strength within, it is possible to rise from the ruins of cherished hopes stronger and greater than before.

Happiness and true success depend upon how the adversities of life are met. Struggles come to all of us, but if they are met in the right manner even the most tragic moments can be made into stepping-stones to success. Trouble comes to all of us, but, while it makes some of us stronger and better in everyday life, it submerges others so that they never rise again. The trouble is the same; it is how it is met that makes the difference. Those who meet difficulty and adversity in the feeble strength of their finite minds and false personality are speedily overwhelmed and broken by the storms of life. But those who rely upon, and have faith in, the infinite strength within them can never be overwhelmed, neither can they ever be defeated. The inner strength, being infinite, is always sufficient, no matter how great the need may be.

We should realize our own spiritual identity, and know that we can never die, that we can never be defeated, that we can never really fail. We may lose our body through the change that is called death; but we, the true man, can never die! We can never fail either, though we might be knocked down a thousand times, we are never once knocked out, never once defeated. Each adversity is a chance to add another victory to our achievement gallery.

ACHIEVEMENT AND SUCCESS ARE NOT LIMITED; THEY ARE FOR EVERYONE. However, we should have faith in our inner power, in our spiritual power, and all things will become ours. We do not have to be afraid of tomorrow, or have any fear of future happenings, for we should realize that the inner strength within us is infinitely infinite.

Currently, there are many troubles that are upon us. Economic, social, and political unrest spans the planet. Since these troubles are inevitable, and we must face them, let us do so boldly, and we will find that they have no substance or reality, but are mere creations of our own gloomy imagination, and it is as true now as in the time of David that *"Man disquieteth himself in a vain shadow."*

Our will should be strengthened in these troubling times. We should see from the light that shines eternally within. We should endeavor to maintain our will when the burden of adversity casts the heavy and weary weight of obscurity over us.

We should carry a heightened consciousness of the power we have within us and face our adversities with our God in our hearts and our sword in our hand. In the end, we will have no regrets.

MOST OF US ARE SWIFT, IN TIMES OF UNCERTAINTY, TO FEAR THE WORST. While all we should do is arm ourselves for whatever may appear, we have a tendency to fear ghosts more than robbers, not only without reason, but also against it; for even if ghosts existed, how can they hurt us? And in ghost stories, few, even those who say that they have seen a ghost, ever profess or pretend to have felt one. The same goes for difficulties; we know they exist, but who said we have to feel them? Why do we often magnify them, and look at them until they seem greater than they really are?

It would be a great thing if we could be brought to the realization that we cannot overcome our trials by giving up. Perhaps this world is an obstacle course for a greater one. Maybe this is our final destination, who truly knows? Either way, we should not be defeated in this life, the next, or the next after that. There is no glory in defeat, and it is a nobler thing to wear out than to rust. Whatever our circumstance might be, we should get up and try. It is hardly a hyperbole to say that *there is no defeat in trying; trying itself is a success.* The reward of an effort is the effort itself, for nothing is done without effort. If we have done our best in our attempt, we should not torment ourselves about the result.

LIKE A STAR, WITHOUT REST, LET US RISE AND SHINE BRILLIANTLY, EVEN THROUGH THE STORMIEST OF WEATHERS. LET US NOT LIVE WITH A FAINT HEART, BEARING EASILY THE RUINS OF EVERY OBSTACLE THAT WE COME ACROSS. There is hardly a living soul who will not find a number of cases in which circumstances are appearing to be limitations to us, but if we will try with a willing mind to find the gate of opportunity, we will be surprised to learn that it was wide open all the time.

To give ourselves a reasonable prospect of success, we MUST realize, firstly, the importance of what we hope to achieve, and then wade through any circumstances, regardless of the odds, to achieve it. And in the excitement of the struggle, knowing the importance of the victory, we will suffer the least. The deathblow will feel more like raindrops in the sun.

I often observe how a spider is proud when it has caught a fly, an eagle when it has caught a rabbit, a gull when it has caught a fish, and a man when he has achieved a task. See, my dear reader, the joys of glory are not limited to us; they are the pleasure of every living creature.

ADVERSITY IS AN EVER-INCREASING SOURCE OF STRENGTH. IT CAN ONLY BE SURMOUNTED BY ENDURANCE AND DETERMINATION. In the case of difficult circumstances, if we cease to resist, if we accept the facts of life, if we are willing to be disappointed, or to work with people we do not like, we gain a quietness of nerve and a liberty of mind which clears off our surrounding mists, so that our eyes may see and recognize the gate of opportunity. We should not rely on the absence of adversity to flourish, but in the mastery of it.

Glory belongs to the most enduring, for the simple reason that the storms of adversity, like those of the ocean, provoke the ability and stimulate the invention, intelligence, aptitude and courage of the sailor. A little misfortune leads away from glory, but much leads back to it.

I must turn your attention for a moment on this inspiring story. I know it is somewhat long but please bear with me. I am sure you will enjoy it.

Long ago in a land far away lived a king of embarrassing wealth and power. An emperor with extraordinary features and that swaggering air of distinction which marks a high man who is one of the pillars that is lifting his nation upward in the world. There was always something in his appearance remarkably beautiful and engaging. He had a soul that was full of fire and vigor fitted to advance the rich style of his physical beauty. He wore, as a livery, a certain air of self-assurance, blended with cheerfulness that showed he was well aware of his earthly standing.

Yet all of his grand achievements he owed to his trusted subordinate with whom he found great comfort in consulting on matters of importance. This advisor was a man of high class, both intellectually and morally, having that natural magnanimity and generosity of mind which one often marks as characteristic of men of higher order. Indeed, his right hand man was considered a prophet. A god-fearing character who believed wholeheartedly that everything, good or bad, happens for a reason. In fact, his watchword was "God is in control." He repeated the maxim so frequently that even the purest saints would have been irritated by such profound monotony. No matter what happened he would always say "God is in control." "It's okay. God is in control." "Let's not worry. God is in control." Even on the night he was mobbed by a band of vagabonds, and was being beaten to threads, the thieves forcefully rubbing his face against a stonewall, he was still reciting: God is in control. He added considerably to the King's wealth, high morality and spiritual sensibility and advised the monarch with such sharpness and mathematical accuracy that the King placed him in charge of all his great affairs and errands.

One lovely evening they were sitting with chairs closely knitted, discussing some subject with great earnestness. The men chatted with an abundance of zealousness with unmistakable confidence that their new idea would bring immediate success. The King was so full of excitement that he forgot that he was getting a manicure, and lifting his hand in an exalted gesture, the sharpness of the manicurist's instrument cut off one of his fingers. Instantly, the wrinkling face of the hurting man assumed the appearance of deformity and distortion, as he flashed his wrist painfully, his bitter brows drawn into a doleful pucker, as he hobbled about the room, stamping his feet in imitation of a wild horse that is stung by some venomous serpent. It is impossible to conceive of a human creature more wholly dismal and forlorn. The reality of losing a finger, not just any finger, but the one that held the ring that bore the seal, sent the blood backward to his heart and aggravated his despair.

It is insulting to the lowest imagination to mention that the whole palace went into a severe pandemonium and panic. The King's intolerant guards promptly seized the manicurist and began clubbing her mercilessly, doctors and nurses emerged unto the scene, servants rushed to mop the bloody floor. The one person who might have shed some light on the matter was entirely silent, and that was the advisor. He was silent with a measure of ease and calmness settled on his chubby face. Everyone took momentarily glances at him as if to ask him what to do?

Eventually the genius leisurely ambled to the center of the event and in light of the pandemonium stated: "Everyone, let's not worry. God is in control!" At this point, the King had heard the axiom over a million times before, but it was the very first time the saying was a sublime annoyance! Certainly, he wanted none of it! The wounded man stood transfixed, his lips pressed tightly with a whole volcano of bitter feelings burning in his bosom, sending streams of fire through his veins. He breathed short, and his large dark eyes flashed like live coals as he stared his advisor up and down before exploding into a dangerous ebullition and asked that the man be locked up, preferably eternally, in a dark and cold dungeon.

The command smote heavily on the advisor's heart as if someone had struck him a deadly blow. He appeared an entirely altered being from the gallant and cheerful character he always wore. His brows were no longer graceful; instead they assumed a very gloomy arch.

As he moved cautiously along the floor, in the arms of two of the King's watchmen, he paused for a moment at the door and raised *his hands in mute appeal to heaven, then boldly turned to the King, gasped a sigh, assuring the emperor that his reply was not an expression of treason, but, indeed, God is in control. His voice waned into silence thereafter and he wobbled away despondently, pale, shivering, with flaccid features and tottering frame.*

Days turned to weeks and weeks turned to months and the King eventually recovered from the tragedy. Yet, he could not recover from not having such a brilliant advisor. He had become so dependent on his right hand man that he struggled terribly on concluding the simplest of matters. Surely he would have released the man hadn't it not being for his pride. Consequently, he went on lame and insecure.

One day he was forced to journey many miles across town to execute a matter of vast importance, and as the Devil would have designed it, the neighboring province was lurking for an outsider to offer as a sacrifice to their gods.

Upon seeing the stranger, two men emerged from the twilight in hot pursuit, crawled up behind him and quickly knocked him out, dumped his lifeless body in a carriage and sped off into obscurity.

Moments later, he slowly returned to his senses, and saw, as in a dream, a throng of murderers standing over him waving hatchets and spears over his head. They were singing and shouting in some unusual tongue. And it was not before long he realized he was about to be sacrificed. His heart raced to his mouth. He could not resist. He was too fragile to throw a fist in his defense. His head was bleeding and his body was aching unpleasantly.

He closed his eyes hopelessly as if to welcome his inevitable death, and like an echo of some dream, he heard the voice of his advisor saying: Do not worry. God is in control. It will be okay. God is in control.

All at once the frenzy increased dramatically and a man of mammoth built, looking like a priest, parted the throng and strolled up to the body that was wreathed in a white sheet. He ordered two of the murderers to uncover the King and after they did, the man stepped back as though he was struck by a bullet, bowing his head dejectedly. To his disappointment, the King could not be sacrificed. Sacrifice was a hallowed ritual that required the wholeness of the one being scarified. The King however, did not fall under such qualification given the fact that he had previously lost a finger. Even though the den of murders was furious, they had to let the King walk free.

By the time he reached back to his providence the entire city, having heard of his disappearance, was looking for him. When an assembly of loyalists spotted him limping terribly, they rushed over to him and placed the dying man between them. By the exercise of almost superhuman effort, the emperor succeeded in remaining upright. He mustered sufficient energy, the energy of despair, to drag himself to a nearby carriage, too dazed to know what was happening, too weak to care.

He was rushed to his palace. By this time, he was faint and dizzy and could not tell what was going on around him. When an awaiting doctor beheld him in such terrible sight, he hastily had him sped off to the sickroom where immediately a nurse lay him on a bed and put a sponge steeped in vinegar to his nose. After that a team of doctors and nurses worked tirelessly to repair the lifeless monarch.

Hours later, the effect of the treatment brought relief and the King slowly opened his eyes. Now that he had returned to his senses he immediately ordered his watchmen to release his imprisoned advisor.

Minutes later, having heard the fate that befell his king, the advisor appeared unto the scene and stared at the recovering emperor with a profound gesture of graciousness. He hurried over to the King with an expression of thankfulness when the echo of the King's course accented voice stopped him in his tracks.

"Please, please, my honored, obliged me for a moment. I am ashamed to admit how terribly I have wronged you. Needless to say I am very sorry. Please, allow me to make it up to you. Gold, silver, diamonds, money, women, fine wine; anything! Whatever you desire consider it fulfilled. And may you be noble enough to forgive me."

The advisor looked at the King delightfully, filled with untamed admiration. The room was silent as everyone waited patiently for the man to state what he wanted.

"Nothing," replied the man, stepping forward from the multitude. "The gratitude belongs to me. I am lost for words to express my gratefulness to you."

Everyone looked at the man strangely, as if they thought he was locked up for far too long and had gone insane from the ghostly solitude.

"You spared my life. And I will forever be indebted to you!"

"But," protested the King. "I had you locked up for no reason. How horribly you must have suffered sleeping on pillars of stone, eating with the rats and maggots, enduring your own stench. I doomed you to a life of scorn and sorrow and you were guiltless."

"You see, King, we all go through obstacles in life. We often question them. But every event in our lives always leads us to a deeper fate, if we allow them to do so. As we walked through the wilderness of this world, sometimes the burden upon our backs sinks us lower than the grave, but we must define ourselves. We must stand firm and find peace in the midst of the storm."

Everyone stared at the philosophical advisor graciously as if he was some kind of God.

"Yes, I may have suffered greatly sleeping on pillars of stone, eating with the rats and maggots, enduring my own stench. In fact, this is just the beginning of my suffering. But hadn't you not locked me up it would have been me who would have undertook that errand for you. I would have been the one who would have been captured. Certainly, I would have being made a sacrifice for I am not an amputee like you."

Everyone chuckled chorally.

"This is a sublime ironic moment. A case of adversity where we both profited. Now if you don't mind, let the celebration began. Everyone is overly excited for your return."

Just then there was a minor explosion of fireworks and one of the servants buckled to the floor in a panic.

"Do not worry, lady," said the King lightheartedly. "God is in control."

Inspiring isn't it? **WE SHOULD REMIND OURSELVES, IN THE DARKEST MOMENTS, THAT EVERY FAILURE IS ONLY A STEP**

TOWARD SUCCESS, THAT EVERY DIFFICULTY IS ONLY AN EXERCISE FOR THE WILL AND STRENGTH. To live happily, or at least contentedly, we should have the ability to face troubles with bravery, displeasure with optimism, and when the victory eventually appears, face it with modesty.

ADVERSITY IS NOT A BYPASS OF SUCCESS; IT IS PART OF THE ROUTE. Often, we will find a road without misfortune leads to nowhere. It is inevitable to encounter impediments along life's journey. But it is okay to make mistakes. Be grateful for both. Our obstacles and mistakes will be our greatest teachers. And the only way not to make mistakes in this life is to do nothing, which is the greatest mistake of all. Do not be alarmed by challenges. They are a surer thing to enrich one's life than comfort and prosperity.

Our challenges, if we let them, will become our greatest allies. All history bears out that the sublime leaders of human fate have all suffered great challenges. And, more times than not, it is precisely those challenges that lead to victory.

Do not be too quick to deplore your sufferings. In fact, find consolation in them. We should find things that make the situation easier to bear. Enjoy these two epigrams by Britton: The first is called Consolation and the second is called A Lighter Sentence.

"Today I was lagged to fifteen years-
Fifteen years of penal servitude and hard labor
But why you see these joys instead of tears
I no longer have to deal with my nosy neighbor."

"Ten years in a maximum prison!
This will be the hardest time of my life!"
Then he brushed off the teasing irony
Remembering, for ten years he had a wife

It is important that we find consolation to effectively deal with the issue at hand. We should have that inner eye to see hopefulness where there is hopelessness; find joy where there is sorrow; peace where there is tumult. This can easily be achieved by knowing that obstacles are not restricted to us. In 'down' times, we can easily relapse into self-pity, as if the whole world is against us. But be sure, difficulties are universal. They are known to the rich, poor, bound and free. *"If all our adversities were laid in one common heap, whence everyone must take an equal portion, most people would be contented to take their own and leave,"* said Solon.

IN CONSEQUENCE, ADVERSITY HAS ALWAYS RANKED AS ONE OF THE CARDINAL ELEMENTS OF SUCCESS, WHICH EXISTS ONLY TO INDEMNIFY THE WILL. Unlike other species of animal, man is governed by individual desires and collective impulses. He has the privilege of perceiving and designating his own mind to the aspirations that drive him. Tormented by these conflicting feelings, I appealed to reason; and it is reason that, amid so many dogmatic contradictions, forced the thesis upon me; that there is always a favorable undercurrent running beneath the sweltering torrents of adversity, and it is our duty to discover, through endurance, that "favorable" thing and mold it into a shining destiny.

> I love Adversity, not despise it
> For all its overwhelming ways
> For when glory appear, how will I recognize it
> Had it not been for these despairing days?
>
> Brighter Days, I can hear your footsteps
> Running up the stairs of Time
> But it is all decreed -
> Great Men must suffer to be sublime!
>
> -Feial Britton

Regrets

"Make it a rule of life never to regret. Regret is a terrible waste of your soul. For you cannot build on it; it is only good for wallowing in - which is saying it is good for nothing."

-Nelson Mandela

Every day we are forced to make decisions in life. Some of these decisions sometimes lead to disappointments and misfortunes, for we have in life many troubles, and troubles are of many kinds. Yet among the many troubles of life, I do not reckon on the necessity of regret. In all circumstances, we should endeavor to maintain ourselves in that optimistic mood in which the burden of the heavy and the weary weight of our unpredictable world is lightened. Time always seems to pass slowly when we are well employed in grief and remorsefulness, while the moment scurries lightly on the minds of those who accept disappointment as a natural part of life.

It happens, unfortunately sometimes, that we make a wrong decision; we have missed the right road and gone wrong. Can we then retrace our steps? Can we recover what is lost? Surely, this may be done. It is too gloomy a view to affirm that our life is over because of one bad decision. Whenever we think we have made the wrong decision, foresight is very wise, but fore-sorrowing is very useless. We often magnify disappointments by grieving and regretting them. It would be a great thing if we could be brought to realize that we can only add to the sum of our disappointments by regretting them.

DISAPPOINTMENTS COME NOT ONLY FROM MAKING THE WRONG DECISION, BUT ALSO FROM NOT MAKING A DECISION

WHEN IT WAS NECESSARY THAT WE SHOULD MAKE ONE. It can also occur from making a late decision when we should have made one earlier or from making one too early when we should have been patient and waited awhile longer. This goes to show that it is impossible to escape disappointments and mistakes. As long as there is a decision to be made, there is also a chance that disappointment can follow. *There is no armor that can guard against the cruel hands of fate.* Setbacks, mistakes, misfortunes and disappointments are all inevitable certainties. If we could see our future, our lives would be uninteresting. Life, to a certain extent, would be dull and unexciting, without expectancy. Moreover, even sometimes when we see these setbacks coming, there is absolutely nothing we can do about it. We have to just let fate run its course. *"Disappointments are like hurricanes, we can only prepare as best as we can for them, but we do not know exactly how severe their impact will be,"* said Jack London.

Whenever we have made an error, a mistake or blunder, we should not be regretful. *"We all hate to be a failure; yet we cherish regret when we assume that we have made a mistake and honor the very thing we hate. For regretting is the greatest failing. To honor regret is to honor a scourge,"* said Edgar Allen Poe. Indeed, we do honor an enemy when we sit and regret our lives away. When we think we have made an error we should be patient, faithful, hopeful and maintain a heightened effort in trying to lift ourselves above our disappointments and missteps, maintaining at all costs a positive outlook while climbing the misty stairs of redemption. With the right mindset, we will be able to locate that sunny interior within us, divinely furnished with all the implements of mortal endurance and fortitude. However, if we decide to encourage regrets, to cherish failures and to be defeated by disappointments, we will soon be swallowed alive by them.

REGRETS ARE IMMENSELY IMMATERIAL! THEY ARE THE NEEDLESS REHEARSAL OF OUR BLUNDERS. As I said before, setbacks, mistakes, misfortunes and disappointments are all inevitable certainties. Where there are choices, there will always be room for mistakes. Try all we can, the greatest minds cannot be too intelligent, too perfect, or too careful to live above mistakes and errors. However, with the right attitude, right character, right confidence, and right forethought, we might very well look around and discover that our finest days are within reach, by the very same decision we thought was our gravest mistake. All at once, a new light has dawned upon us. What sudden ray pierced the clouds and instantly dissipated not only all the darkness our mistake held us in, but also the pressing weight that disappointment often brings?

Regret is caused by a lack of strength and will, and perhaps by a lack of character. *"All the great captains,"* said Napoleon, *"have performed vast achievements by conforming to the rules of the art — by adjusting efforts to obstacles and disappointments."* In the affairs of life, it is not intellect that tells so much as character - not brains so much as heart - not genius so much as foresight, patience and discipline. The outcome of a situation, in the end, is the outcome of the character that leads it. Disappointments and setbacks are a part of life; regrets are not. The desire to be successful without being burdened with the trouble of acquiring success is one of the biggest signs of a weak and worthless character.

LIFE IS A WINDING JOURNEY THAT OFTEN SLOPES THROUGH DARKNESS BEFORE WE SEE THE LIGHT. This expedition proves a continuous trickery, in great as well as in small things. Life, indeed, is a vast deception! If it makes a promise, it does not keep it. For many of us, life seems to be an eternal hill, full of turmoil and turbulence. We spend all of our time occupied with its wants and cares, exerting all our strength to satisfy its demanding needs without daring to expect anything else in return other than merely the preservation of this tormented individual existence, full of want and misery, toil and hardship, strife and struggle, sorrow and trouble, anguish and fear. Many of us have only heard that life is a glorious inheritance but have no intimate experience of the fact. A good portrait of some of our lives may require an elaborate background, for all we have ever known is sadness, monotony and disappointments. Life, when summed up, has an enormous surplus of disappointments and difficulties. Yes, these elements form the fundamental feature of our existence. Life has been said to be hell *and happy is that man who is able to procure for himself an asbestos overcoat and a fireproof room.* Nevertheless, however disappointing life might be, or become, we all should hold the presupposition that it is to continue, and that it is always worth living. We should learn to treasure every breathing moment of it. For in life, anything can happen anytime! *We can be a peasant today and be crowned tomorrow.* Consequently, we should never cease to try, never cease to put our best foot forward, not just to exist but to live! Once we have the correct view of life, and the correct attitude, we will never take any given moment for granted. We should cherish every moment we have been loaned, for time is hurrying by.

WE SHOULD NOT TAKE FAILURES, DISAPPOINTMENTS, OBSTACLES OR ADVERSITIES PERSONALLY. Certainly, we would like to undo some of the decisions we have made in the past. Perhaps these decisions left our lives very difficult and unbearable. But instead of looking back with regrets, we should look forward with hope and optimism. We should always bear in mind that life owes us nothing, and as I said in another chapter, prayer and fate are under no obligation to give us anything simply because we ask for it. This is seeing life in its true light - in its rational light - in its practical light. Yet all the glories and beauties of the universe are ours if we choose to have them; to the extent to which we can make ourselves what we wish to be; or the power we possess of securing success, of triumphing over disappointments and failures. The ignorance of these marvelous abilities is a serious fault.

Each of us, as we travel the way of life, has the choice, according to our strength, of turning disappointments into satisfaction. The art of doing so, the art of living, is learning to take misfortunes quietly, because we know that very many dreadful things may happen in the course of our life. We should learn to attire ourselves for a world where all is relative and no perfect state exists. We should learn to look misfortunes and disappointments in the face and meet them with courage and calmness, not with regret and self-pity.

REGRET IS CRUEL. IT MAKES US MISERABLE. IT MAKES US ASHAMED. IT IS SYNONYMOUS WITH RESENTMENT, ANGER

AND BITTERNESS. It makes happiness a far-flung illusion. Those who have recognized that regret is immaterial, that it is harmful, that it is nonproductive, will refrain from doing so. Instead, we will find the strength and the will to take the sting out of our disappointment, by getting up and brushing ourselves off. *There is no individual who can do all things equally well. Those who stand out before a groping world as beacon-lights were men of great faults and unequal performances. It is quite needless to add that they did not live on account of their faults, mistakes, disappointments or imperfections, but in spite of them.*

THE JOURNEY OF LIFE SHOULD ALWAYS BE CONTINUED BY PICKING UP THE PIECES AFTER WE FALL AND CONTINUING WITHOUT REGRETS. *We should always try our best. Under any circumstance, let us simply do our best, and we will avoid self-judgment, self-abuse, self-pity and regret.* For success is not always marked by the outcome, but by the effort applied. We should know that there will be disappointments along the rugged highway of life. Nevertheless, every failure, every disappointment, every setback, every misfortune, is an experience we can use to further ourselves in wisdom and good judgment. This experience, however disappointing, gives us an opportunity to revisit adverse decisions we have made in the past and correct them by making better ones in the future. It is something we should learn from instead of languishing over and have our heart wrung by grief and regret.

FOR EVERY ADVERSE DECISION THAT I HAVE MADE, I HAVE NO REGRETS, FOR THEY HAD TO BE SO TO FULFILL A DEEPER PART OF MY DESTINY, AND EVEN IF THEY ARE NOT THE INCEPTION OF A HIGHER FATE, I STILL CHERISH NO REGRETS, FOR THE GREAT CURRENT OF TIME WILL NOT REVERSE THE PAST.

To be sure, regret is not an emotion I am willing to reckon with, for it is not an instructive thing; it teaches us nothing. This world is very beautiful, if we could only enjoy it in peace and without regrets. We should see every mistake not as a mistake but as a lesson learned. Life has many difficulties; we should just take them as they come.

Lucius Annaeus Seneca said, *"It is a rough road that leads to the height of greatness."* In many cases, a lot of these rough roads lead to still rougher roads. Nevertheless, if life is worth anything at all to us, mistakes and disappointments should be nothing at all but motivation. Life, I remind you, is a colossal opportunity that we should always be ready to make the best of at every given moment. We should accept every disappointment with the attitude of a beggar upon receiving bread, instead of being a hostage to them. Furthermore, we should indeed refuse to live a life limited to regrets and misgivings. We should fight on in spite of it all! *Surely, a simple mistake can prove to be an expensive college, but once you stay the semesters and graduate, victory is all yours.*

WE CAN CHOOSE TO REGRET BETTER TIMES, BUT WE SHOULD KNOW THAT WE STILL HAVE THE PRESENT TO FACE. We may wish for a better job, but we should, notwithstanding, accept our current one. We can choose to regret the failure of our marriage or ex-relationship, but we have our current one to focus on. We can spend all our energy regretting a faded opportunity and disregard the present ones that are staring us in the face. We can spend sleepless nights over the fact that our childhood was unnecessarily friendless and ignore the great friends who are always there for us. We may regret the family we were birthed into but what good is regretting when it cannot alter the past? We might languish over the fact that the present status of our life is not terribly exciting, but at least we have life - the greatest gift of all, and with that, everything is possible. Therefore, the least we can do is be thankful and cherish this once-in-a-lifetime gift.

THE PAST IS GONE AND IS IRRETRIEVABLE AND WHATEVER CHOICES WE HAVE MADE ARE IRREVOCABLE. By sitting and regretting, brooding over the past, we merely smash ourselves to pieces. Regretting is equivalent to running our heads against a stone cliff; the harder we charge, the greater the damage to our heads. So too, the longer and more deeply we regret, the longer and harder it will be for us to pick up the pieces, dust ourselves off and continue our life's journey. *"In history, as in human life, regret does* *not bring back a lost opportunity,"* said Abraham Lincoln, *"and a thousand centuries will not recover something lost in a single hour."*

I WILL REMIND YOU ONCE AGAINST THAT A MISTAKE IS NOT A MISTAKE, UNLESS OF COURSE IT HAS BEEN RIDICULOUSLY REPEATED. IT IS A LESSON LEARNED, ALTHOUGH IT MAY ENTAIL SUFFERING AND PAINFUL EXPERIENCES. It is the drawing together of certain corrective experiences, through which the soul could not have learned any other way and thus attain wisdom and better judgment. It is so that if we can learn the errors of the past, and live in such a way as to be careful not to repeat them, we would be on the path of liberation, which is the road all advanced souls have to follow, or rather, have the privilege of following. By following this path, we cease to be bound to the freewheeling wheel of fate. *"It is wiser to look ahead and prepare than to look back and regret."* -Barrack Obama.

Our present life is one of countless experiences, each one of which helps to build up character. Decisions that we have made that affect us adversely should not be counted as mistakes. Thoughts like these are mere limitations of the human mind. In spite of our unfavorable experiences, we must always go on, whether we have the strength to or not.

Every day that we live is an opportunity to improve our present life, as well as to create a better future. Therefore, we should always look with eyes that pierce through obstacles, setbacks and disappointments. *When one door is closed, another is always open, but we often look so long and hard at the closed door that we fail to see the one that has been swung wide open for us.* The way we deal with disappointments either makes or mars, to a very large extent, our human career. Those of us who think that life is unfair, and who regret and complain about a former decision, are simply increasing our own dismays. Until we realize that regret is harmful, we can never do anything to remedy our mistakes, because, obviously, the only thing that is required is for us to alter our outlook: our thoughts and approach toward the adverse experience, to have a favorable transformation.

When this change has been effected, we not only begin to repair our present life, but we create a greater and safer life for the future.

There are those who despair after they have made a mistake, but then there are those who, because of the fear of regret, would rather remain stagnant than make that much-needed move to better themselves. They are afraid to make the move and end up "regretting". When such an emotion is oppressing us, we often remain dormant and our lives become a lake of stagnant water. Theodore Roosevelt said, *"The only man who never makes a mistake is the man who never does anything."*

THE FEAR OF REGRET CAN BE THE GREATEST IMPEDIMENT TO AN OPPORTUNITY. We sit and we ponder, reflecting deeply, reflecting soberly, reflecting thoroughly, and even when all our rational capacities imply that we ought to act upon our intuition, we remain inactive; shackled by the unbreakable iron chain of regret. Days pass us by, which eventually turn into weeks, which leak away into months, and we are still fettered by the fear of regret. We are afraid of making a 'big' mistake. But *"the greatest mistake we can make in this life is remaining inactive when we are prompted to make a move, fearing we will make one."* Inactiveness is not a safeguard against disappointments and mistakes; it is actually quite the contrary. If anything, it is the greatest demonstration of cowardice.

In the end, the ones who know how to shun regret are the leaven that saves the race. But the reader may say, "What am I to do, if I feel regretful? How can I pretend that there is something good to come after such a dreadful mistake? How can I suppress such a doleful feeling after such a great loss - after such a huge disappointment?" or "What if I marry him and end up regretting it? Can I start my own business without regretting it? Should I call her?"

WHEN THE FUMES OF REGRET AND DISAPPOINTMENT FOG OUR BRAINS, THEY CAN WORK NEITHER CLEARLY NOR QUIETLY, AND WHEN THAT IS THE CASE, IT IS IMPOSSIBLE FOR US TO SERVE OURSELVES WITH OUR FULL ABILITY. Everyone has in him certain inherited and personal tendencies which are obstacles to his progress, and his success is limited just as far as he allows those tendencies to control him. If he controls them by external repression, they are then working havoc within him, no matter how thoroughly he may appear to be master of the situation. If he acknowledges his mistaken tendencies fully and willingly and then refuses to act, speak, or think from them, he is taking a straight path toward success and happiness. If we could once be convinced of the very real and wonderful power we have of teaching our own brain, and exacting obedience from it, the resulting ability for use would make our lives far more interesting.

INSTEAD OF WALLOWING IN GRIEF AND REGRETS, WE SHOULD LIFT OURSELVES TO HIGHER AND BETTER THINGS. How can this be done? Firstly by reflection. This is one of the best munitions I have found on this treacherous human journey. However, before we can truly reflect honestly on where we erred, we have to drop our regrets completely. Reflection, when accompanied by regret, however effective it may seem, does not begin to have the power that can come from deliberation, without such emotion. As a result, we should drop the natural habit of regretting entirely.

Now that we are left alone to reflect on our former mistakes, we should do so thoroughly, honestly and soberly. *"When I am troubled and burdened and nothing but despondencies hangs in the gallery of my soul, reflection is the balm I turn to. And sure as the sun rises in the East, I see good of what I first saw bad, and hope and optimism from where I first saw hopelessness and misery,"* - Napoleon the Great.

Reflection stills our natural inclination of despair, sorrow, and the habit to be angry and regretful. It represses even the loneliness that feeds it. When we empty our minds from regrets and reflect severely on our former misjudgment, everything will appear to us in a new light -a deeper meaning, and we will surely give birth to a new soul.

WE SHOULD NOT BE AFRAID TO MEDITATE DEEPLY, THINK SOBERLY, LISTEN WISELY AND FURTHER ON ACT COURAGEOUSLY AND CONFIDENTLY UPON OUR CURRENT

CIRCUMSTANCES. We should always reason with ourselves quietly and earnestly and encourage ourselves repeatedly, gently and without pity, like only a mother can. Great discoveries always derive from the intimacy of reflection. As Napoleon mentioned, *our inner observations often find good of what we first thought was bad and optimism where at first we saw only distrust, doubts and skepticism.*

In times of disappointments, self-pity and regrets can consume us. Reflection helps to comfort us and to advise us to step away from such emotions. For in times of hardship, and in all other times, we should seek to extinguish fear, despair and regrets from our hearts. We should seek to smother our regrets utterly. *"He who learns to escape his disappointments learns the art of glory, for the journey of life is full of many a disappointment and misfortune,"* said Socrates.

Through the balm of reflection, we review our blunder with the confidence that it will not betray us, but rather cleanse and educate us so that in the future we can exercise better judgment. This divine session is not to beat upon ourselves and clobber ourselves with self-abuse and curse-words, but rather puts us in possession of our soul.

Whosoever you may be, clad in the rags of misery, or decked in the thorny fabric of poverty, I restore you to that state of glowing bareness, which neither the haze of disappointment nor the blinding mists of regret can dim. Do not despair. Do not be regretful. What is done cannot be undone. Pick up the pieces, brush yourself off and continue life's journey. It will be difficult and trying, but I am sure, with the right mindset, you will overcome your despondencies.

What is in this world for a man who is born into a world already occupied, his family unable to support him, and society not requiring his existence, when at the great banquet of nature there is no plate laid for him? Why should he not nurse regret? Well, I will tell you why. Regret is a waste of our precious soul. Our soul is far too precious to be choked by the iron girdle of regret and disappointments. Please, my fellow human, do not leak your soul away regretting your circumstance. Fold into yourself and find peace, reach deep within and strum up that courage Jesus demonstrated on his way to his crucifixion. Then go out and fight the great battles of life, and *if you must die, please do so bravely, not like hogs and dogs, chained against the common foes.* Strike back at your unpleasant fate. Do not be afraid of these troubled times. Indeed, there is a lot to be concerned with, but find a way to get beyond the troubled outlook of the present hour. Be optimistic and faithful. Be not regretful or perplexed. For when all is said and done, there is only one way to correct the past, and that is to do better in the present and the future.

OVERCOMING DISAPPOINTMENTS MAY BE SLOW. SADNESS AND ADVERSITY MAY, FOR A TIME, WEAKEN YOU. HOWEVER, WITH PATIENCE AND ENDURANCE, YOU WILL EVENTUALLY INSPIRE THE RESPECT AND COMMAND THE CONFIDENCE WHICH YOU ULTIMATELY DESERVE. Fight on with the attitude of a winner. Do not be afraid to give life your best efforts. And once you stand against the common foes, once you strike back at all your disappointments, mistakes and misfortunes, once you have done all you can to better yourself and mankind, you will have no regrets.

Time Is Immeasurable

"The air we breathe is made of time; therefore, time is the most precious natural resource on earth. The way a man uses it determines his fate".

- George Washington

Time is the most valuable resource known to all creatures. What are friends, family, a beautiful spouse, home or wealth, if we do not have the time to enjoy them? Time is often said to be money, but it is more - it is life. It is a sacred gift that simply cannot be overvalued or over-appreciated. It is not so much the hours that tell, as the way we use them. Therefore, it should be budgeted as mathematically as we budget our medical prescriptions, because every moment we lose is so much character and advantage lost; as, on the other hand, every moment we employ usefully, is so much time wisely laid out at remarkable interest.

Are you in earnest? Seize this very minute
What you can do, or think you can, begin it.

WHEN THE DEVIL THROWS HIS HOOK WITH ITS BAIT TO THE TASTES AND TEMPERAMENTS OF HIS PREY, THE IDLE MAN IS ALWAYS THE EASIEST VICTIM, FOR HE, BEING SO WEALTHY WITH TIME, WILL SWALLOW EVEN A BAITLESS HOOK. Ironically, it is not so much that the Devil tempts an idle man; it is that an idle man, having nothing to do with his abundance of time, will tempt the Devil.

Hours have wings, fly up to the author of time and carry the image of our employment and none of our prayers can entreat one of them to either return or slow its pace. The misspending of every one puts us at a disadvantage as to our purpose in life. As a result, we should be very mindful of how we dismiss our time. We should fill our days with proper habits and not suffer them to fly away emptily, or laden with futile laziness. If we learn to use our days wisely and productively, we can all be inspiring and our departure will leave behind us footprints on the sands of time.

Time is often said to fly and if we do not use it prudently, we waste it. But I beg to differ with such a statement. Time is infinite; we are not. Therefore, we can never waste time; but surely, time can indeed waste us. This brought to my mind an ode I have in my possession written by the poet Feial Britton:

>You are a jealous and savage vulture!
>Torn from some gladiatorial culture
>Devoured races, creeds and nations-
>The very crumb of your regurgitations
>You are ravenous to such a degree
>That you can drink an eternal sea
>Swallow the eight planets one by one
>And make dinner with the high-vaulted sun
>You are always eating and never cloying
>Always consuming, always destroying
>You are a jealous imp, quite extreme in fact
>For you give as though, to quickly taketh back
>Youth, beauty, fortune, science and art
>Are mindful of your malicious dart
>You turn Man into a three-legged thing
>And soar the world with undaunted wing
>I maintain that you are honest and fair;
>The healer of hurts; the balm of black despair

For no matter one's wound or sore
You are an herb that will bring the cure

Britton holds that time is jealous and predatory. Indeed, it is jealous in the sense that it gives us youth, beauty and strength and before we know it, it takes them back: *You are a jealous imp, extremely so in fact - for you give as though to quickly taketh back.* Throughout the ode he paints a depressing picture of time. Yet, the last four lines of the poem are a sublime paradox within which he reveals the brightest personality of the beast: *I maintain that you are honest and fair - The healer of hurts; the balm of black despair - For no matter one's wound or sore - You are an herb that will bring the cure.* This is to say that with time, all misfortunes can become fortunes and all sorrows can become happiness; all injustice can become justice. This, however, can only be so with the right employment of time. Only if we have the proper regard for the value of time can we get the best result from it. A proper consideration of the value of time will always inspire habits of purposefulness. An hour a day withdrawn from frivolous pursuits would, if profitably employed, enable a person of ordinary capacity to go far toward mastering a science, an art or a skill. It would make an ignorant man a well-informed one in less than ten years. Time should not be allowed to pass without yielding fruits, in the form of something learned worthy of being known, some good principle cultivated, or some good habit strengthened. Time is the only little fragment of eternity that belongs to man and, like life, it can never be recalled. In the indulgence of worldly treasure, the frugality of the future may balance the extravagance of the past, but who can borrow hours from the future to compensate for those they have lost today? *Let him who would enjoy a good future waste none of his present.* Benjamin Franklin said, *"Lost time is never found again."*

Consequently, we should budget our time productively. We should try to get the best of every breathing moment that we are alive. There are some hours that are taken from us, some that are stolen from us and some that slip from us. But however we may lose them, we can never get them back. It is bothering, indeed, how much innocent happiness we thoughtlessly throw away. The adversities sent by nature can be avoided or endured, but there is no escape from the ones we bring upon ourselves. It is astonishing that anyone can squander, in absolute idleness, one single moment of that small portion of time that is allotted to us in this world.

Executives are accustomed to quote the saying that *Time is Money,* but it is more; an hour wasted daily on trifles or in indolence would, if devoted to self-improvement, improve the dullest of peasants in a few years, and employed in good works, would make his life fruitful. Fifteen minutes a day devoted to self-improvement will be felt at the end of the year. Thirty minutes a day a few days a week engaged in physical exercise can add years to our life. An economical use of time is the true mode of securing leisure. It enables us to get through business and carry it forward, instead of being driven by it. On the other hand, the miscalculation of time leaves us in perpetual hurry, confusion and difficulties and life becomes a mere shuffle of expedients, usually followed by disaster.

Some do not give any thought to the value of money until they have come to an end of it, and many do the same with their time. The hours are allowed to flow by unemployed, and then, when life is fast waning, they remind themselves of the duty of making a wiser use of it. However, the habit of listlessness and idleness may already have become confirmed, and they are unable to break the bonds with which they have permitted themselves to become bound. Lost wealth may be replaced by hard work, lost knowledge by study, lost health by temperance or medicine, but lost time is gone forever!

TIME, INDEED, IS A SACRED GIFT. IT IS IRREPLACEABLE. AS THE TOPIC IMPLIES, IT IS IMMEASURABLE. TODAY IS THE FIRST DAY OF THE REST OF OUR LIVES. We should know the true value of it, snatch it, seize it, and employ every moment of it meaningfully. Each day brings a new opportunity to enjoy accordingly. Time has an infinite destination ahead; we only have but a few years. As a piece of ground becomes better and more useful by cultivation, so does the mind by good employment of time.

We should all have a deep consideration for the value of time. As the days roll onward, they are irretrievable. Every moment of creation is tied to the wheel of time with a free force that cannot be stopped or adjusted. It is forever fleeting. It is an ever-flowing stream. Determine, then, as Thomas Jefferson puts it, *never to be idle. No person will have occasion to complain of the want of time who never loses any.* Idleness is thought to be killing time but an ancient proverb wisely reminds us that killing time is not a murder; it is a suicide. Time should be treated like gold or diamonds where every ounce of it is put to fruitful use and valued greatly. To squander time is to squander the greatest of human resources. *"The wastefulness of time is the greatest prodigality,"* said Benjamin Franklin. Those who have no regard for time and use it idly generally have no regard for success or prosperity either. We naturally conclude that the person who is careless with time will be careless about life as well, and that he is not one to be trusted with the transaction of matters of even the least importance.

Just think of our advantages here in America! We have access to the whole literature of the world. We may see in our museums the most beautiful productions of former generations and the works of the greatest living artists. We have some of the best entertainers in the world. We have several exciting sporting leagues. We have beautiful beaches, mountains, lakes, rivers, and recreational parks. Most of these gifts are free. And to think, so many of us complain of being dull and bored! We talk of a better life to come as if we have already given up on this one. What? Why should it be so when we have one of the most blessed countries in all the world? I put it to you that it is because we do not know how to employ our time. When we have the natural instinct to enjoy all that this blessed country has to offer we will learn to appreciate life and see that it is beautiful.

MANY OF US HAVE BIG DREAMS AND PLANS TO EXECUTE, YET WE SIT AND DREAM OUR LIVES AWAY WITHOUT EVER TAKING THAT FIRST STEP TOWARD THESE DREAMS. If I should ask you why, all I would get in reply would be stutters, mumblings or some inaudible excuses. All the tools we need are all around us but the "human soul" - the sharpest of all tools - is what we keep locked away like stolen pearls.

I believe in people above everything else. I believe that all of us have the ability to be successful, though success can be difficult. There are no immense differences, at least physically, between a successful person and someone who is a constant failure. The difference is with attitude. We are what we are by virtue of our own attitude - attitude of thoughts and actions, by virtue of what our mind is, what our will is; the resulting combination of both. There are countless cases in which the ones with greater ability or talent fall losers to the ones with less talent and ability, owing to the differences in attitude. Often, a person with no skill or talent knows it and applies the right attitude to combat his deficiencies in the pursuit of his endeavor and a person with tremendous talent and ability knows it as well but he is prepared to just sit idly by, thinking that having great skills and talent is all it takes to get him where he wants to go.

LIFE IS ALL ABOUT MINDSET. LIFE IS ALL ABOUT ATTITUDE. A POSITIVE ATTITUDE OFTEN LEADS TO A POSITIVE OUTCOME. *A single gentle rain makes the grass many shades greener. So too do our prospects brighten on the influx of better thoughts and attitude.* Many men have taken over continents, countries, islands, even the entire world, simply because they know within themselves that they can do it and just get up and do it. They have that mindset that escapes every obstacle that ever tries to contradict their ambition.

The Industrial Revolution taught us that we can build great fleets, airplanes and machines that defy the laws of physics and even mathematics. Modern Science teaches us that we can outdo or oppose nature whenever we want to, if ever we want to.

Tell me, my dear reader, what is humanly impossible? If we have the attitude of success then success indeed is inevitable. Therefore, sitting down and waiting for some heavenly ally to bark at us to make a move is vain hope. We must get up, stand firmly, and take that first great step, as on that day we began walking as a child. Time is of the essence! It is rapidly fleeting! Time wasted can never be regained! Make that move for the better. Execute the strategy you have been toying with for so long. If we continue doing what we always do, we will continue to get the same unfavorable result. Labor, for there is absolutely no substitute for it. Idleness is treasonous - a rejection of prudence, with a conviction that prosperity or happiness can be attained outside of diligence, independent of diligence and in opposition to diligence. Most of us will never wake up one morning and see a clear-cut opportunity awaiting us. We all have to create one; create something out of nothing, for better or for worse - such is life, such is fate, such is destiny! No machine in this world can outdo the human will. It is the human will that makes the machine; the machine cannot make human will.

What is there to contemplate? *Sometimes in life we have to jump off cliffs and build our wings on the way down.* Too much contemplation can be counterproductive. The perfect time is always now! I doubt that anyone has ever missed a bus, a train, a flight, or an opportunity by being too early. However, there are countless cases where many of us have missed all of these by being too late. Time is very jealous! What she gives, she quickly taketh back. She gives us health, strength, youth, beauty, and opportunity, and in the wink of an eye, she dooms us to sickness, infirmity and old age.

THE BRAVE AND ACTIVE CONQUER DIFFICULTIES BY DARING TO ATTEMPT THEM. COWARDS AND IDLERS SHIVER AND SHRINK AT THE SIGHT OF OBSTACLES AND MAKE THE IMPOSSIBILITY THEY FEAR.

"Where there is a will, there is a way," is an old saying that carries the same weight through every generation because of its irrefutable accuracy. He who gets up and approaches a task, by that very bravery, at least secures some favorable result, if not the complete achievement of the task. Often, to try seems to have about it almost a savor of omnipotence. Napoleon said if it were up to him, he would have the word *"impossible"* banished from the dictionary. *"I don't know," "I can't,"* and *"impossible,"* were words that he detested above all others. The greatest character one can have is a resolute determination.

Truly, if we are ever to achieve half the dreams so deeply entrenched in our burning soul, we have to GET UP and throw our whole body, heart and mind behind those dreams and see how obstacles that at first seem insurmountable go up in flames and crumble at the heat of our will and passion.

> Quick favor! I need to get you done
> It is a pressing matter not fitted for anyone
> Quick favor! tailored for an obliging friend
> But I need someone on whom I can depend
> A good friend of mine has ample time to plan
> And another is always a busy man
> The "leisure friend" never has a minute to spare
> He is always busy putting off, until I am buried in despair
> My "busy friend" is crowded with never-ending work
> Forgetting the art of wasting time, he never stops to shirk
> Quick favor! Quick favor! I need you done right away
> And my "busy friend" is working every day
> But he will find a minute that has no other use
> While my "leisure friend" is busy framing an excuse

SUCCESS USUALLY DISPLAYS ITSELF IN PROMPTNESS. This truth is self-evident. It is generally found that the ones who are habitually behind time are as habitually behind success. For it is a rapid decision, and a similar velocity in action, that saves lives or secures glory. Taking instant advantage of an opponent's mistakes is key to success in business or in politics. *"Every moment lost,"* declared the Great Napoleon, *"gives an opportunity for misfortune. I have beaten the Austrians because they do not know the value of time: while they dawdled, I overthrew them."*

It was said by Hulk Hogan himself that he was the first choice to be the spokesman for the grill that George Foreman attached his name to. But because of some delay, the company offered the opportunity to George Foreman and called it the George Foreman Grill.

The household item sold millions. Hogan was left with some unknown canned soup which is yet to sell a thousand items.

In addition to the ordinary working qualities, the businesspersons of the highest class require quick perception and firmness in the execution of their plans. Vision is also very important and though this is partly the gift of nature, it is yet capable of being cultivated and developed by observation and experience. Persons with this quality are quick to see the right mode of action, and if they have decision of purpose, are prompt to carry out their undertakings to a successful degree.

That which improves anyone, that which fortifies anyone, and that which distinguishes anyone - that which spreads their glory, creates their moral influence, and makes them respected and submitted to, bends the hearts of millions, and bows down the pride of their rivals to their knees - the instrument of obedience, the fountain of supremacy, the true gem of human fate, is not a nobility of blood, nor an aristocracy of fashion, nor a generation of wealth; it is a sublime character. That is the true crown and glory of a man. It exercises a greater power than wealth, and secures all the honor without the jealousies of fame. It carries with it an influence that always tells, for it is the result of proven honor, integrity, persistency and bravery - qualities which, perhaps more than any other, capture the general confidence and respect of humankind.

Men of character are the pillar of human existence. The strength, the industry, and the civilization of nations all depend upon individual character and the very continuity of life rests heavily upon it. In the just balance of nature, individuals, nations, and races, will reap just so much as they have sown and nothing more. And as effect finds its cause, so surely does quality of character amongst a people produce its befitting results. One of the greatest displays of character is the way by which one uses his time.

THOUGH A MAN MAY HAVE MODERATELY LITTLE CULTURE, SLENDER ABILITIES, AND NO WEALTH, IF HIS CHARACTER BE OF GENUINE WORTH, HE WILL ALWAYS LEAD AND INFLUENCE. How then can he lead others if he cannot lead himself? If he is afraid to step out and confront his ambitions? If he hides behind the curtain of his own shadow and watches time fleeting by wastefully? The blood of all men flows from equally remote sources. Therefore, anyone can be successful. Anyone can be a great author, a great poet, a great artist, a great doctor, a great teacher, a great philosopher, a great leader, regardless of his pedigree. Hard work is sure to be unavoidable, but no one has any valid reason as to why he cannot move the world forward.

Stand up right now, strike back at adverse fate. Do not bend to man or circumstances. Do not surrender to adversities or disappointments. The time is here and now. What are you waiting for? Boldly step outside your very own self-made boundary and face the world with an unrivaled determination, with an unyielding adamancy. Emerge from the blackness of timidity and face your deepest fears. Whatever your soul desires can be attained. You have to believe in yourself. You have to have faith in your abilities. You have to know that you have the character necessary to lift the flattering flag of prosperity. You have waded through many scenes of sorrows; still, you are still here, ready to show the world what true distinction is. Stand and take that monumental step toward betterment.

HOLD YOUR DESTINY PRISONER IN THE BOSOM OF YOUR SOUL, FIRM AS THE STRING THAT BINDS THE UNIVERSE. An obstacle is an opportunity to display your brilliance. Step from beyond the confines of your deepest fears and walk with confidence. Raise the torch of your courage, and lift higher the status of your defiant reputation. Stand now, shine brilliantly, and fix your name among humankind's brightest stars. Go now and be a character of destiny. The time is now.

Human Compassion

"The Holy Supper is kept indeed
In whatsoever we share with another's need;
Not that which we give, but what we share
For the gift without the giver is bare."

                                                          -Lowell

We are subjected to innumerable pains and sorrows by the very condition of humanity. As if nature had not sown enough sorrows in life, we are continually adding grief to grief and aggravating the common calamity by our cruel neglect of one another. Every man's natural weight of affliction is made still heavier by the abandonment, selfishness, or injustice of his neighbor. At the same time that the storm beats on the whole species, we are still preying on one another with our acts of selfishness.

     I know there are those who will read these words with tears and sorrow. For their existence has been a long struggle with aloneness - indeed, some of our most intimate friends scarcely have any knowledge of our loneliness. Thus, this makes us feel that we are standing quite alone in the midst of the multitude of friends and associates surrounding us.

     The world looks at you with barking eyes. You are a stranger to human kindness. Your life is crowded with great grief and disappointments. You sit in darkness and impotency while life rolls by. You have seen no joy and felt worthless since childhood. You are a heritage of shame and sadness. You wonder why. For deep inside your heart, you know that you are a good person. You have an incorruptible virtue in your heart and honesty in every endeavor. Still, your life and all its earthly expectations are in ruins. And to think that all you are longing for is some human compassion.

I am more and more convinced, as the years pass away, that the best thing this world has for a man is affection - the sympathy and the devotion of true hearts. When a fellow human is overcome by pain and sorrow, it is our responsibility to rescue him from his affliction, for he is one of us. He is a fellow brother of our race, and as we move forward, we do so as a race; as a family; we do so in brotherhood. We should not stand by and watch sorrow destroy him. We should feel his pain with a true sense of kinship.

The new social order rests, unfortunately, on the materialistic basis of life; but while all flesh-wearing persons of a philosophic fabric agree that the main evil today is an economic one, we maintain that the solution of this evil can only be brought about through genuine human compassion. *"The living, vital truth of social and economic wellbeing will become a reality only through the zeal, courage, the non-compromising determination of compassionate minorities, and not through the mass nor government,"* said Ralph Emerson.

Everything I own, material possessions and moral, is allied to human compassion, and is always ready to be disposed of accordingly. This, I believe, should be the general temperament of everyone, rather than hoarding and fleecing society to accommodate our selfish individual interests. A thorough examination of the history of human growth will disclose two elements in bitter conflict with each other; elements that we should admit and understand to bring about any noble change to our social instabilities. These elements are social and individual instincts. The individual and society have waged a relentless and bloody battle against each other for ages, each striving for supremacy, because each is blind to the value and importance of the other. The individual and social instincts - the individual instinct has a very forceful factor for personal ambition, aspiration and self-indulgence. Social instinct has an equally potent factor for mutual helpfulness and social wellbeing.

HUMAN COMPASSION IS AN HONEST TEACHER THAT UNIFIES US ALL REGARDLESS OF COLOR OR CREED. We as common people are the heart and soul of society. We have within our capacity the ability to preserve the essence of social life through compassion and kindness.

Kindness is more agreeable in this world than knowledge, and gives a certain air to the countenance, which is friendlier than beauty. **IT SHOWS VIRTUE IN THE BRIGHTEST LIGHT. IT HEALS THE ACT OF VICE AND SUPPRESSES EVEN THE GRAVEST RUDENESS AND EVIL.**

There is no society or conversation to be kept up in the world without kindness. We should be apt to practice it as a habitualness of our daily life. It is one of the blessings of a happy constitution. We should be passionate about our love for humanity. Benjamin Franklin said, *"When I am employed in serving others, I do not look at myself as conferring favors but paying my debts."* Indeed, we are paying our debts for the priceless gifts that we freely receive every day - the oceans and the rivers, the mountains and valleys, the sun, wind and rain.

IT WAS MOTHER TERESA'S COMPASSION AND KINDNESS FOR HUMANITY AND GOODWILL THAT EMPOWERED HER AND HER INNUMERABLE FOLLOWERS TO SERVE THE ILL, THE POOR AND THE UNDERPRIVILEGED. She left us with an enduring example that will inspire many for ages to come. Philanthropists, such as her, show us that if we would do good to the soul of a starving man, we must first put food into his mouth, and comfortable clothing on his back; this, by way of demonstrating a practical interest in his welfare, and paving our way to his heart by a form of compassion that he can thoroughly appreciate. But there is more in such an act than this;- we change his mood, we change his attitude of despair and discouragement into a mood of cheerfulness and hopefulness, and then we have a soul to deal with that is surrounded by the conditions of improvement.

There is far more to the passage of heaven than going to church, reading a Bible and singing a few choruses, then going on our knees in bitter shame, begging God to forgive us for our sins. There is far more to our faith than that. There is more to be done than waking up religiously every Sunday (or Saturday) and attacking the many miles to church, while passing many in need on the way and never offering them any human kindness or compassion. There is more to heaven than merely trying to save our wretched selves. There is more to worship than attending church. Ministering goes far beyond preaching the gospel or reading the Bible. The true essence of worship is charity, kindness and human compassion toward our fellow humans. Our primary duty as a being on this planet is to encourage each one in his struggle to live up to his own highest idea, not to convert him into who we want him to be, but to help him identify his true soul, and help him to lift it aloft to its highest reach. When we do the least of kindness to our neighbor, we do it unto God as well.

THE NEW TESTAMENT ON THIS MATTER IS, INDEED, WONDERFULLY PERSUASIVE AS OUR SAVIOR TELLS US, IN A MOST EDIFYING MANNER, THAT HE SHALL HEREAFTER REGARD THE CLOTHING OF THE NAKED, THE FEEDING OF THE HUNGRY, AND THE VISITING OF THE IMPRISONED, AS DEEDS DONE TO HIMSELF, AND REWARD THEM ACCORDINGLY. Pursuant to those passages in the Holy Scripture, I truly believe that what we spent we lost; what we possessed is left to others; what we shared remains with us.

Tell me what our creed is for, if it is not to feed the poor? What purpose is our light, if it is not to lead others through darkness? What function is our prosperity, if it is not to make others prosperous? What use is our ear, if it refuses to yield to the piercing call of the suffering? For what other reason were we lent sight, if it is not to lead the blind? Our feet should be but the instruments that direct us to the lame. Human compassion I speak of, my dear citizen - being a parent to the orphans with their charred palms outstretched for alms. Let us take a look around and about our parks and streets and:

See that man who cries for bread

His hands are burnt and his eyes are red
New pains replaced the ones that fled
Laying where crime and disease are spread
The grave would make a softer bed
For the World passes by and turns her head
We can ignore the pains he bled
But not this verse that mourns the dead!

See that man trembling in his lonely dell
Envying his peers who had so long fell
The way he begs with a ghostly spell
No ear should hear, nor tongue should tell
His life is like a death row cell
Yet Government greed and corruption swell
As they stack hell on our current hell
Making wars 'cause they pay so well

-Feial Britton

    Isn't this man of whom the author speaks conceived in a womb and birthed from a woman, the same way we were fashioned? Why, then, should we just pass him by without care or concern? How can our hearts ignore the weeping of an infant whose stomach gripes for the lack of a meal? Human compassion is what I speak of, my friends - the kindness to lend a hand to someone in need, to open our doors to the homeless. We all have the ability to love one another at first sight. *"To treat all men with equal good-humor, and to be kind without distinction of persons, may arise as much from a profound contempt for one's conscience as from an ingrained love of unwavering adherence to humanity. Either one is fine with me,"* said Abraham Lincoln.

    I know that there are multitudes of tenderhearted citizens of abounding benevolence and sensitive conscience who are troubled upon this subject. We have a desire to be charitable, but somehow, we are always suspicious of the beggar. We often think his story is insincere or he is healthy, but just plain lazy. Perhaps we think he is just looking to furnish some narcotic addiction. My thought upon this point is: judge not! The best that we will ever be in this world is to be attained through honest and unconditional compassion for each other. There can be no blunder in kindness. We should not permit the storyteller to prescribe for us, nor should we allow him to make us uncomfortable. Indeed, not all beggars are truthful; not all beggars are liars either. Our reasoning is clear; this man begs for a piece of bread, and I will grant it to him because I refuse to doubt his plea and have him perish from lack of it. Secondly, it is not my duty to disbelieve him or to judge him. My duty is to help him, because I can, and because he says he is in need of it.

HUMAN COMPASSION IS THE APTNESS TO MOVE WITH KINDNESS AND AFFECTION FOR OUR UNFORTUNATE ONES WITHOUT RIDICULE OR SCORN. We should all be sensitive to the influence of hunger. For the greatest virtue of man is kindness and compassion and there will also be unity and peace where this virtue is practiced. How sublime we would become if, whenever one of us is suffering, all of us suffer as well, or become sensitive toward the suffering, like the least hurt to the little finger of the hand that runs through the whole body and vibrates to the soul. For the true community, like an individual, is injured as a whole when any part is affected. This is simply so because no man is a stranger to another. Every one of us is connected by ties of blood, characteristics, and temperaments, connected by common wants and needs, common pleasures and pains.

We cannot get any more out of our neighbors than we put into them. Every man is a social being, and can only attain his highest development in the society that is best suited to him. For as in the vegetable world, the weakest seeds can turn out productive if they fall on the right soil; so, too, can the worst of human characters show tremendous improvement when they fall upon a suitable soil. Generosity, hospitality, charity, liberality - all those qualities that enrich the character, and all those virtues that enlarge it and give it fullness, beauty, and attractiveness - are always wanting among the ones who have nothing.

There are some of us who are often discouraged by the ingratitude we received upon giving our very last. Our biggest sacrifices are sometimes taken for granted. However, we should know that it is not about us or the person we are helping. It is about doing our Godly duty. The purpose of human life is to serve, and to show compassion and the will to help others regardless of the obstacles that discourage us. Kindness is the rent we pay for living. It is the very purpose of life, and not something we do in our spare time. **A DEW OF COMPASSION CAN LIFT AN IMPOVERISHED NATION FROM HOPELESSNESS.** Therefore, there is no need for us to be overly sensitive. Whatever good we do on earth we do not for men, but for God! We do it because doing a good deed is food for our souls. We do it because it is justice and mercy for our disadvantaged citizens and even our erring ones as well. Our general temperament cannot be too mild, moderate, or forgiving. For it is also a part of gentleness to forgive and overlook the faults of others. When we forgive others for their imperfections, we are also admitting that we too are imperfect and have flaws of our own. Subsequently, we should not cease to go on in good spirit and spread kindness and compassion without discrimination.

Those of us with compassion expose the deepest virtue in human nature. If it was up to me, I would propose it as a universal rule, to everyone who is provided with any ability of fortune more than sufficient for the necessaries of life, to lay aside a certain portion for the use of the less fortunate. For with human compassion we can make an end to the terrible struggle for the means of existence - the savage struggle that undermines the finest qualities in man, and ever widens the social abyss.

No government or army is mighty enough to capture the world and turn its wheels of conflict and unrest to eternal peace. Only human compassion and kindness can do so. If we wish to cheer a broken man who is buckled to the earth in bitter grief, we should do so with unconditional love.

Yes, indeed, I say unconditional love - giving and expecting nothing in return. According to Kenotic wisdom, *everything we do is sowing, and all our experiences are harvests.* Once we understand that we are all one on this small planet, kindness and compassion will be natural. Gwendolyn Brooks said, *"We are each other's harvest; we are each other's business; we are each other's magnitude and bond."* This is true in many ways. The maxim runs that if society is ever to become prosperous, it will be so through the prosperity of the lowest individuals whose failing efforts exhaust it. Therefore, when we lift a brother up, we also lift up our society and ourselves as well. What soul is not moved by the act of compassion it bestows on an underprivileged brother?

That is not to say, since we are not doing it as an investment, that we will not reap a reward. *"When you focus on being a blessing, God makes sure that you are always blessed in abundance."* A friend once shared with me her (now) boyfriend's experience with giving back during the Katrina Hurricane disaster in New Orleans. She called her (then) former classmate just to see how he was doing. He was a contractor who had been out of a job for some time and was rather severely depressed. As soon as he got on the phone, he started expressing how he was going through a very trying time. His utility bills were long overdue and his food basket was almost dry. There was a constant flow of sadness in his voice. She said the more she listened, the more the walls of her apartment seemed to be caving in on her, forming only a dull crape-like image where she could no longer be anything but a glowing ember of human flesh. She could feel his pains. She too was out of work and was struggling to make ends meet. She was known to be a comforter, but she admitted that she was lost for words. Nevertheless, she told him to forget about his troubles and use his time and talent to help some of the hurricane victims. His voice brightened at the idea and surely, he obliged it.

Within two months of hard voluntary labor, working for food and sleeping in his pick-up truck, he was offered a multimillion-dollar contract. His life, as well as hers, was never the same since. He was able to pay off all his debts, buy a new house and have money to put away in case another drought occurs. She received everything he did, because they became engaged. Colossians 3:23-25 *"Whatever you do, work at it with all your heart, as working for the Lord, not for men, since you know that you will receive an inheritance from the Lord as a reward. It is the Lord Jesus Christ you are serving."*

Make no mistake about kindness and compassion, they are not restricted to the donation of food, clothes or money. Sometimes that can be the shallowest of compassions. If we adopt this as the principal concept of kindness, all well-to-do persons would be isolated from this virtue. Everyone, whether rich or poor, bound or free, young or old, needs human kindness. Kindness is not limited to material offerings. We can easily show compassion by empowering others with a breath of fresh words. A sentence of kind words can be more effective than a million dollars.

IF A MAN IS MOVED TO DO GOOD, HIS HEART WILL LEAD HIM IN THE RIGHT DIRECTION. An honestly loving heart and an ordinarily clear mind will lead a man where he belongs and teach him what he ought to do. If he has the gift of ministering to the sick, he will do so. If he has the gift of dealing personally with the less fortunate, he will do that. If he has the gift of undivided listening, he will lend an ear to the cry of someone who needs someone to talk to, or a shoulder for someone to lean on. If he is blessed with the tongue of Obama, he will spread words of hope and inspiration to a neighbor who is hopeless. A kind word can change someone's life forever. It can inspire him to put away the liquor glass. It can inspire him to exit the casino. It can lift him from the pothouse. If he has the gift of making money, he will make it and properly apply it to good usage. If he has the gift of volunteerism, he will volunteer his skills where they are most needed in his community - schools, homeless shelters, hospitals, nursing homes, youth clubs etc.

KINDNESS AND COMPASSION ARE IN THE REACH OF EVERYONE. THERE SHOULD BE NO EXCUSE FOR A BREATHING MAN NOT TO BE ABLE TO HELP HIS FELLOW CITIZENS. I do not expect perfection of anyone in this world; neither do I expect impossibilities. However, there are certain duties that we owe to each other, which are very possible to be performed, and which I insist upon.

Every man, high or low, should walk with goodwill and compassion for his fellowmen. We should not ignore it; nor try to shake it off.

We may be at a point in our life where we feel invincible, where we feel like we have arrived and we do not need anyone now. We are doing well and life feels great. Nevertheless, in the midst of our arrogance, we should know that humanity is a very helpless and frail being that is subjected every moment to the greatest calamities and misfortunes. We are overwhelmed with dangers and failures on all sides, and can become unhappy by numberless casualties, which we could not foresee, nor could we have prevented them even if we had foreseen them. For that reason, we should always consider helping a fellow-man when we are on top and riding high. Self-reliance of the best kind does not involve any limitation in the range of human kindness, but the happiness of us all depends in great measure upon our individual completeness of character. Our self-dependence, conjoined with a proper discipline of the heart and conscience, will enable us to be more useful in life by dispensing charity. In all this, we should expect nothing in return other than the delightful feeling we get from seeing a smile on our neighbor's face. We should not feel exhausted from lending a helping hand. To be truly compassionate, we should maintain a loving, honest and brave heart, and a soul that judges for itself. Galatians 6:9 *"Let us not become weary in doing good, for at a proper time, we will reap the harvest if we do not give up. Therefore, as we have opportunity, let us do good to all people…"*

THE LESS FORTUNATE LIVE AMONG US AND EVERY MAN AND WOMAN POSSESSES A MEANS FOR THEIR RELIEF. If we have charity and do not feel that we are the proper person to look after the details of its dispensation, we should put it into the hands of an organization more competent to the business. In the meantime, if a man comes to our door and asks for the supply of his immediate necessities, we should try not to turn him away.

Let me conclude by saying this (I hope I do not sound imposing); all of us must stand with a hereditary devotion and commitment for the betterment of the human race. It is imperative to know that age alone will never perform the promises of youth, and the inadequacies of today will never be supplied by tomorrow just by mere chance.

Only a dramatic compassionate change can cease wars, can advocate for peace, can abolish beggary, can remove the black shadow of selfishness that is blinding the earth. What I am advocating for is a new form of compassion, a deeper form of selflessness. From this day onward, we must have a heightened consciousness of how we treat each other. We must believe in each other. We must stand firm to restore the humanity of our race. We must join hands and hearts together to restore our social fabric. Compassion in its obligation is the will of justice and godliness. Indeed, the souls of our average citizens, who are tied to the tasks of life, burdened by care, oppressed by routine and depressed in many instances by loneliness, need compassion more than counsel, and encouragement and inspiration more than a solemn, professional catechetical probing of their religious state. Compassion is what I speak of, my dear friend; human compassion and kindness.

These are troubled times. Human struggles have reached their highest expression. Many of us are living way beneath the dignity of humanity. This struggle is a mix of many abstract adversities. We live in the midst of a very difficult period of economic depression; exhausted, poverty-stricken and hungry, we work with the industry of a slave and die with the repute of a beggar. Our tear-ravished eyes look over the rim of the human horizon searching for better days like the ghost of our founding fathers. All we see is bleak days under all conceivable circumstances. Vast areas of what was once a fruitfully populated world are overwhelmed in chaos and barrenness. Reaching out to human fate is like a journey we are not meant for. Here rolls over us the eternal sea of human misery. Homelessness, joblessness and depression are deeply entrenched all around us. Most of us citizens have no greater advantage over those of developing nations. However, the majority of these miseries can be vanquished if we all practice human compassion and kindness. Let the spirit of human compassion lift us from our prostrate position, that we can stand erect, with our face toward the light, and see the insatiable, devouring, devastating nature of greed, and strike this poisonous monster dead. The moment that we begin to believe in our lowly class, the moment we regard it as precious and special, we turn over a new leaf in the book of human development, we pass a new milestone on the upward path of progress.

THOSE OF US WHO HAVE GREAT POWER, LET US USE IT TO LIFT UP THE LOWLY CLASS. They are our brothers and sisters, molded with the same flesh and blood, by the same heavenly hands, though they might be of different hue or tongue. Let us use our power not to subdue, to crush, to exploit, to enslave, to outrage, to degrade or to tyrannize, but rather to uplift and inspire. Our country is particularly boastful of great power and her enormous global influence. What is the reward of all her wealth, power and influence, if she cannot extend it beyond her shores? What use is the pride of all her leadership if she cannot send missionaries all over the world to help our poor brothers and sisters who are still living in dirt huts, not by choice but from lack of resources?

REAL WEALTH CONSISTS IN THINGS OF VALUE AND BEAUTY, IN THINGS THAT HELP TO CREATE SURROUNDINGS INSPIRING TO LIVE, WORK AND PLAY IN. But if one is doomed to stand at the corner and beg for a meal, or to dig in a trashcan for food all his life, there can be no talk of wealth or beauty. What he gives to the world is only gray and hideous resentment, reflecting a dull and hideous existence - too weak to live, too afraid to die.

It should be recognized that every man has the right to be clothed and fed. Oscar Wilde defines a perfect personality as *"one who develops under perfect conditions, who is not wounded, maimed, or in danger."* A perfect personality, then, is only possible in a society where an individual has at least the basic human needs satisfied. No society is properly organized until everyone who is born into it has an opportunity in life. Everyone should have an opportunity to be successful. This, as I see it, should be the first and the greatest effort of human compassion.

COMPASSION IS PROPERTY. IT IS THE NOBLEST OF POSSESSIONS. It is an estate in the general goodwill and respect of men and they, who invest in it, though they may not become rich, will find their reward in esteem and reputation fairly and honorably won. It is right that in life, good qualities should tell that kindness, justice and honesty should rank the highest above all other properties. For only by compassion can we grow to our full stature as a race. Only by compassion will we learn to think and move, and give the very best within us. Only by compassion will we realize the true force of the social bonds that knit us together.

We are but infants recently exposed to the world outside the womb. Therefore, we should always put modesty above arrogance, and kindness and compassion above selfishness and hatred. I would freely give my life the day I wake up to see us living in love and peace with one another and avoiding the illusionary telepathic beliefs which foster alienation, hatred and self-destruction. For in the end, my dear reader, regardless of creed, class or color, we are only one blood, one heart, one soul.

> The world is a small one and all who are in it
> As a gesture of the universal principle
> Let us join hands and heart this very minute
> And share a love divinely invincible
>
> Humankind everywhere, both great and small
> By reason of which all effect and cause blend
> Weak and strong, rich and poor, I beg you all
> For love is the ultimate means to the end
>
> Let the heart of humanity speak like crystal springs
> In melody with the infinite righteousness of things
> Please, let us push forward, the world's frontier of love
> And be diviner than those with wings who soar high above.

Defining Success

"I believe that anyone can be successful in life, regardless of natural talent or the environment within which we live. This is not based on measuring success by human competitiveness for wealth, possessions, influence, and fame, but adhering to God's standards of truth, justice, humility, service, compassion, forgiveness and love."

-Jimmy Carter

I often marvel at the many capitalists' books and articles defining "success", or supposedly guiding us to "success". I sincerely and solemnly think they comprise the most inaccurate literature ever known to men. They are further off than the wildest romantic novels and much duller than the dullest religious pamphlets. At least the romantic novels are about romance and the religious articles are about religion, however far-flung the practicality of both might be. But the capitalists' books and lectures on success, I find, are very disturbing.

On every bookstall, in every magazine, we may find literature telling us how to succeed. They are books written to allegedly guide us to success in everything. Ironically, they are written by men who cannot even succeed in writing the very book they set out to write.

As if we are not tired of all these "success guide" materials, we have several television stations with these suit-and-tie people spitting in our ears the mold to success. Their windy speech always hits all around the mark like a drunken carpenter. They say it so forcefully and so profoundly, we would think that they themselves are the inventor of success. They often remind me of a pastor who is so sure of his inauguration into heaven, as if he had copied the keys to the Pearly Gates.

To begin with, of course, success does not have a universal connotation. If we want to be extremely technical, there is no such thing as success, or there is nothing that is not successful, just as it is true that every entrance is an exit and every exit is an entrance. Just as it is true that a glass is as successful at being half-empty as it is successful at being half-full. If we want to look at things from such a perspective, we can say, then: a millionaire is successful in being a millionaire and a horse in being a horse. Any living man has succeeded in living; any dead man has succeeded in dying. However, passing over the bad logic and bad philosophy in the phrase, we may take it, as these writers do, in the ordinary sense of success in obtaining money or worldly gratifications. These writers profess to tell the ordinary man how he may succeed in his trade by terribly misguiding him with the doctrine that suggests that if he is a bus driver, he can be successful as a pilot. If he is a farmer, he can be successful at being a pharmacist. If he is a doctor, he can be successful at being a judge. This is terrible. This is dreadful. This, I will go so far as to say, is very ungodly. This is a definite and capitalist-like proposal, and I really think that the people who buy these books (if any people do buy them) have a moral (if not a legal) right to ask for their money back.

Instead, the doctrine should be: if he is a builder, he can be successful at being a better builder; if he is a stockbroker, he can succeed at being a better stockbroker; if he is a farmer, he can be successful as a better farmer. This is not to say that one is forever buried in their current occupation, or he doesn't have what it takes to rise from being a bus driver to be a pilot if he so desires. To be perfectly clear, our potential is infinite. I will be the first to tell you that we can be successful at whatever we set our minds on achieving. However, success has absolutely nothing to do with occupation or wealth; neither does it have anything to do with status or fame. I think that success is simply to do all that one is able to do to the best of his ability, not necessarily all that one would like to do.

THOUSANDS ARE BEING TAUGHT TODAY TO FORCE THEIR HUMAN WILL UPON FATE FOR THE ACQUISITION OF WEALTH AND POWER. They are taught to wade through blood and swim an ocean of gore to demand "what they want." "How to get what you want" is the slogan of these modern teachers. Not merit, not service, not giving, but demanding, compelling by human will power. This is another evil device that is destroying us, and it is taking many souls down the path of destruction and nothingness.

If, however, our ambition is to serve and to give, instead of to grasp and grab, if, also, we seek success through merit and not through the misuse of our ability, we can go forward and our ability will help us and all those around us as well. When our brightest ability has been aroused, we should cease all our selfish striving. I am not saying, however, that we cannot have a personal motive for success. In fact, everyone should feel free to do so. But we should seek our success through service and through following noble aims; through merit and a fair exchange, instead of trying to wring success from life, no matter who may suffer thereby.

When our brightest ability has been brought into expression, it should only be used in love and virtue, for if it is used otherwise, it will destroy the user.

Yet our modern world is full of books about success and successful people, which literally contain no kind of idea, and scarcely any kind of verbal sense; once a man is wealthy, he is successful. We should shun these kinds of shallowness, for they have no place in our society. It is perfectly obvious that in any decent occupation (such as farming or janitorial employment) there is only one way of succeeding - by doing the best we can in an honest and diligent way.

If we participate in sports, we should do so honestly and not dishonestly like a player who has won by using marked cards or a sportsman who has won by disregarding the rules of the sport. In this case, we should seek a book about how to disregard the rules of the sport to acquire a false success. But we would not want a book about success, we would want one about false success, such as those that we can now find scattered by the hundred about the book-market.

If we desire to be a successful sportsman, we should prepare to bring forth success by observing the rules of the sport. The games are won by winners who play the sport honestly, not by those who "do whatever it takes" to win.

This is an article I read a while back in my college years and I laughed repeatedly over the shallowness of it all. Check it out; you may find inspiration where I found scorn and disgust.

"The name of Vanderbilt is synonymous with wealth gained by modern enterprise. Cornelius, the founder of the family, was the first of the great American magnates of commerce. He started as the son of a poor farmer; he ended as a millionaire twenty times over. He had the moneymaking instinct. He seized his opportunities, the opportunities that were given by the application of the steam engine to ocean traffic, and by the birth of railway locomotion in the wealthy but undeveloped United States of America, and consequently he amassed an immense fortune.
Now it is, of course, obvious that we cannot all follow exactly in the footsteps of this great railway monarch. The precise opportunities that fell to him do not occur to us. Circumstances have changed. But, although this is so, still, in our own sphere and in our own circumstances, we can follow his general methods; we can seize those opportunities that are given to us, and give ourselves a very fair chance of attaining riches."

In such strange utterances, we see quite clearly what is really at the bottom of all these articles and books. It is not mere business, it is not even mere cynicism, it is mysticism; the horrible mysticism of money. The columnist did not really have the remotest notion of how Vanderbilt made his money or of how anybody else is to make theirs. He does, indeed, conclude his remarks by advocating some scheme; but it has nothing in the world to do with Vanderbilt. He merely wished to prostrate himself before the mystery of a millionaire. For when we really worship anything, we love not only its clearness but also its obscurity. We exult in its very invisibility. Thus, for instance, the very pious poet, celebrating his Creator, takes pleasure in saying that God moves in a mysterious way.

Now, I should not think the writer of the paragraph that I have quoted, judging by his extreme shallowness, had ever been successful. Nevertheless, the thing he does worship and wish to be - Vanderbilt - he treats in exactly this mystical manner. He really revels in the fact that his god, Vanderbilt, is keeping a secret from him and it fills his soul with a sort of delight that he is telling the multitude that terrible secret which he himself does not know.

Surely, Mr. Vanderbilt might come across as flawless to the writer, not because he actually is, but rather because of the weakness of the writer's eyes and imagination. No doubt, he is aware of the fictitious character Midas. He probably thinks Midas was a successful figure as well.

Midas was a man who turned everything he laid his hands upon into gold. His life was a progress amidst riches. Out of everything that came in his way, he created the precious metal. The writer will probably write another brilliant piece on the foolish legend.

Indeed, we are always meeting or reading about such persons who turn everything they touch into gold. They are often thrown on our television as if to say: "This is success, anything less is no success at all. Look at his suit, look at his tie. I bet you, you do not have one of these in your closet. I bet you, you do not even have a closet. Look at all the cars he owns. Look at all the houses he owns. Look at his jewelry. You, our underachieving viewers, are not successful. If you were, you would be in his place. He is wealthy! He is wealthy! Why else would he be relevant? For what other reason would he be sitting here in front of me, conducting this interview? His life's pathway leads unerringly upwards. He cannot fail!"

Unfortunately, however, Midas failed continuously and terribly, and so did Mr. Vanderbilt. Their paths did not lead unerringly upward. Midas starved because whenever he touched a burger or a pork sandwich it turned to gold. That was the whole point of the story. The old fables of humankind are, indeed, inconceivably wise, but we should not have them abridged in the interests of Mr. Vanderbilt, Donald

Trump or Bill Gates. We should not have King Midas representing an example of success; he was a failure of an unusually painful kind. He, like most of our prominent and wealthy persons, endeavored to conceal the fact. It was his barber (if I remember rightly) who had to be treated on a confidential footing with regard to this peculiarity, and his barber, instead of behaving like this writer who believes success is only wealth, blackmailed King Midas, went away and whispered this splendid piece of society scandal to the "ordinary" people who enjoyed it enormously.

Michael Jordan said, *"I have missed more than 9,000 shots in my career. I have lost almost 300 games. On 26 occasions I have been entrusted to take the game's winning shot, and I missed. I have failed over and over and over again in my life and that is why I succeed."* Thank you, Michael, for your honesty and accuracy in information. You let it be known that you are just like any one of us. You are not someone that turns everything into gold by your divine touch.

I look reverently at the portrait of Lord Rothschild, Rockefeller, Donald Trump and Bill Gates, not because I think they represent the epitome of success, but because I know that they cannot turn everything they touch to gold; that they are failures in many endeavors as well. But they, in the end, find a way to overcome their weaknesses to achieve their aim and that is enough to attract my admiration.

I know that wealth does not define success. What rational thinker would look at someone who has inherited a fortune and say he is truly successful? What rational human being would look at a man who had doomed a community by flooding it with drugs and guns in exchange for money and tap him on his shoulder and say, "Truly, you are successful. Well done!" Truly, they are successful. That is, if we look at success the way our modern writers and Media define it. Success cannot claim glory if it is independent of virtue. An athlete who has won a medal by taking illegal drugs has won no medal at all and is not successful.

EVERY BREATHING MOMENT THAT I AM AWAKE I SEE SUCCESSFUL PEOPLE. I KNOW THAT THESE "ORDINARY" PEOPLE HAVE CERTAINLY SUCCEEDED IN SOMETHING; THEY

HAVE CERTAINLY OVERCOME SOME STRUGGLE. I know the media will never glorify them because their success is too "ordinary" to be announced or highlighted. I also know that Lord Rothschild, Rockefeller, Donald Trump and Bill Gates are also successful. They are great human beings in the sense that they create markets and help many of us to secure employment so we can have a way of providing for our families. Yet, it always seems to me that there is some small domestic fact that they are hiding, and I have sometimes thought I heard upon the wind the laughter and whisper of the winds.

We as writers and media personnel should not discourage the "ordinary" people who are an everyday example of success. We should not discourage success. We should be practical in our depiction and representation of the art. We should teach people to be successful instead of teaching them to be snobbish. We should not spread a sort of evil poetry of worldliness and greed. What is success without moral truth? In our society, temperance may not help a poor man to attain wealth, but it will help him to respect himself and others and that is success. Honest work may not make him the next Gates, but diligent work may make him a successful worker. Let us all be mindful of the gospel we preach to the new industrious apprentice. Let us not mislead them by not giving them enough credit in their "ordinary" success while on the other hand, lifting aloft the financial tyrants who secured wealth through the vices of monopoly and unfair commerce.

SUCCESS IS THE ACHIEVEMENT OF SOMETHING WORTHWHILE, THAT WILL MAKE THE WORLD BETTER AND RICHER, AND ADD SOMETHING TO THE COMMON GOOD. Our specialty in life may be very humble, but if we overcome our own weaknesses, help others along life's journey and do our daily work to the best of our ability, diligently and honestly, our life cannot be other than successful. If, at the end of our life, we can be thankful for it, realizing that we have made the best possible use of it, we have achieved real success.

Success to the shallow and narrow-minded may mean the accumulation of great wealth and the winning of fame. Yet those who give up their lives to the acquirement of these things are the greatest failures in life. They gain wealth, it is true, but they find that their money can buy only those things that bring no satisfaction: that it cannot purchase for them any of the things that are really worth having. Success of this hollow kind can be won, but at too great a price. It is like a person who has mistakenly dropped a penny in the dark and lights a hundred dollar note to search for it. When he finds it, he jumps around in glory having found the penny at the cost of the hundred dollar note. Jesus Christ once said: *"For what shall it profit man, if he shall gain the whole world and lose his own soul?"*

I truly believe that we should be a striver. We should always try to discover new and better things and try to express ourselves more perfectly. We should not just drift through life, making no effort to rise to better things. We should be forever striving, overcoming, rising and achieving. Failure in life is always due to some kind of weakness in character. It is only strong characters that can resist the buffetings of life and overcome its difficulties. The man who would make his life worthy of respect and who would rise to high achievement and service will be confronted by difficulty at every turn. This is as it should be, for it weeds out the weaklings and unworthy aspirants, and awards the spoils to those who exhibit faith, courage, steadfastness, patience, perseverance, persistence, cheerfulness and strength of character. Success, especially material success, is not, in itself, of much benefit to the one who wins it. It does not satisfy for long, but it is valuable in other ways. For instance, success based on service is a benefit to the community. If it were not for successful people of this type, the ordinary man in the rut would have a bad time.

ONE WHO WOULD BE SUCCESSFUL IN THE BATTLE OF LIFE MUST BE PREPARED TO BE TESTED AND TRIED IN EVERY POSSIBLE WAY. One who survives the adversities along life's journey is built up in character in almost every direction. Even in his success, however, he will be tempted and tried. One who is engaged in the harsh struggle of business, or who takes part in public life, may, if he does not watch himself very carefully, become hard and heartless. Of all failures, this is probably the worst.

Life is a continual battle. To the "ordinary" persons, it is generally a fight with circumstances and the ordinary difficulties of life that are very important to overcome, not hoarding riches. There is no direct formula to success. It is achieved mostly when we fight valiantly to overcome the day-to-day struggles that block our path to peace, happiness, virtue and contentment. There is no one who will be able to have an uneventful walk through life. Every one of us faces challenges and obstacles. Success is overcoming them, day by day, one by one. This is because life is not for mere passing pleasure, but is for the building up of character through experience. Consequently, one who would succeed must be strong, wise, patient and hopeful. Those who aspire to make their lives worthwhile, who desire to serve their fellowmen more perfectly, who want to build up character through experience and overcome all their weaknesses, can already claim success from the very intent of such good values.

When Martin Luther died, he left behind him, as set forth in his will, "no ready money, and no treasure of coin of any description." He was so poor at one point of his life that he was under the necessity of earning his bread by turning, gardening, and clock making. Yet, at the very time when he was thus working with his hands, he was molding the character of his country and he was morally stronger and vastly more honored and followed than all the princes of Germany.

Success should not be about individualism. It should not be a *'look at me, see what I own'* kind of mentality. That is hollow, futile and vain. Even when we are wealthy, we are not successful if we use our wealth for vain and selfish purposes. We should not use our wealth to suppress or tyrannize our fellow citizens, physically, mentally or emotionally. How arrogant is the public display of wealth, with no regard for the struggling masses that are perishing for basic needs? The blatant disrespecting of the "ordinary" people who struggle from hand-to-mouth, living from check to check who, technically, are the real success of the nation. Nay, success could never be that low and shallow.

Simple honesty of purpose in a man goes a long way in life, if founded on a just estimate of himself and a steady obedience to the rule he knows and feels to be right. It holds a man straight, gives him strength and sustenance and forms a mainspring of vigorous action. No man is bound to be rich or great, or to be terribly well-educated, but every man is bound to be honest.

Success does not seek power, demoralizing luxury, pomp, the applause of men, or the glittering things that perish to define it. Instead, it seeks to put service before self and gives instead of hoarding.

EACH LIFE IS SUCCESSFUL AS IT WAS CREATED BY GOD. Each one of us was made precious and unique. To continue the success is to live the life according to the laws of the land and those of the Creator.

Do not imagine, however, that it is the will of God for us to be a failure or lacking in achievement. Far from it, for we have only to contemplate how infinite is the splendor of the universe, to see how the universe is forever wonderful and amazing, and forever achieving. We, too, should succeed, but let our success be not self-centered or shallow. Let our ambition be to better humankind through our talents or our academic skills, and let us work for the benefit of the whole human race, rather than for any purely selfish purpose.

NO ONE CAN HOPE TO HAVE A VERY EASY LIFE AND AT THE SAME TIME A VERY SUCCESSFUL ONE. *"The merit of all things lies in their difficulty."* Yet, nothing is too difficult to a man who has a purpose and the will to achieve it. The more we associate ourselves with the day-to-day success of common life, the easier it becomes to achieve our main goals. The timid, weak and undecided are swept aside by the tide of time. Determination and perseverance can enable us to attain success in any field of life just as long as we maintain the quality of making persistent efforts in spite of constant obstacles.

To be successful is not as difficult as we might think. Most of us who think that success is not reachable are spending too much precious time reading Fortune Five Hundred Magazines. We read of private jets and islands, of millions being spent on this and that. We read of unrealistic extravagant lifestyles and say to ourselves, "I do not have what it takes to achieve that; therefore, I will not be anything in life."

Well, this is breaking news to you. You are already a success! When you did not give up, when you were hunting tirelessly for a job and found one, that is success. When your house was about to be foreclosed and you fought relentlessly to keep it, that is success. When times were low and you were thinking of a divorce and then decided heavily against it, that is success. When your brother was going through a rough time and you stood by him and helped him get through, that is success. Though you are struggling from check to check, you still stay true to sponsoring that stranger in some developing nation - that is a success. When you cut your neighbor's lawn last week, free of cost, that is success. Yesterday evening when you visited your elderly neighbor and made sure she had food, that is success. This morning when you helped the old woman cross the street, that is success.

There is nothing wrong with success of any kind. The problem is when it is ignored or overlooked because of its size. *"The prosperity of a country depends, not on the abundance of its revenues, nor on the strength of its fortifications, nor on the beauty of its public buildings; but it consists in the number of its cultivated citizens, in its men of education, enlightenment, and character; here are to be found its true interest, its chief strength, its real power,"* said Martin Luther. Luther should have also said that it does not depend solely on the elites. All success is important and is needed to move us further as a people. The farmer is no less of an achiever than the doctor; neither is the doctor more so than the scientist. We all have roles to play in this grand play of life. I would like to think that it is to be the best person that we can be through our service to our fellow-man.

It is natural and creditable also for one in poor and unlovely surroundings to have an ambition to raise himself to better circumstances. It is only right that he should desire to make life brighter and better for his family so long as he indulges in his ambition wisely, and seeks success through better service to his comrades. If, however, he does not curb and control his ambition but allows it to "run loosely" he may gain wealth, but at the expense of all real joy in life and, at the last, when it is too late, learn to his sorrow that his life, through too much "success," has been a failure.

Please do not take from this subject at hand that I am reducing or deprecating wealth or wealthy people. There are many wealthy persons who spend their lives in a noble service to our world. There is nothing wrong with wealth. It is the manipulation of it and the way in which it is used that is the issue. The more money we have, the more charity we can bestow upon those who need it most. If it were up to many of us, there would be no ghettos in the world; neither would there be any hunger or poverty. Every man would have at least his basic needs met. Everyone would have a home! Everyone would have a friend. No more lives would be torn apart by poverty.

However, most of us are "ordinary" people. All we know of success is that we should always be progressing, achieving, overcoming and endeavoring to be the best that we can be through the service we display at our job, church and community. We should continue to go forward, continue to achieve, and continue to accomplish things. If we do so, we may find that many things which cost us much effort and hard work are not worth the having, yet all the time we are learning through experience, and are being strengthened and prepared for greater things. Through repeated failure, we arrive finally at true knowledge, wisdom and understanding. We are wise then, and know that if the world is laid at our feet, we can be satisfied with a very moderate material success, and turn our attention and aspirations to higher and better things.

In concluding this chapter, let it be pointed out that success and achievement will not drop ready-made from heaven into our lap. All who succeed are gluttons for work, toiling while others leisure and sleep. Success is not going to come to us unmerited. There is only one way to succeed in the affairs of life, and that is by raising oneself to greater usefulness and service, by doing things better than they have been done before. By bearing greater responsibility, we serve humanity better, and therefore merit success. *"It is more blessed to give than to receive,"* said the Creator, and this is true even in the practical and material affairs of life.

Let us strive to give better and more valuable service; in other words, we should sow before we can reap. Let us strive to grow and expand in every possible way, and as we grow so will our success. Outward success is only a reflection, so to speak, of what we really are, and a result of greater and more valuable service to humanity. It requires great effort and determination to get out of the rut, but so long as our ambition is not ignoble or selfish, we will find within us power sufficient to achieve our innermost dreams.

To achieve success, either in the hustle and bustle of life, or the more difficult path of spiritual progress, demands imagination, vision, courage, faith, determination, persistence, perseverance, hope, cheerfulness and other qualities. These are all to be found within us. All these qualities lie more or less dormant within, and can be called into expression if we believe in ourselves.

Again, we should not seek success as a weapon to dominate others. If success is misused, the results are terrible and disastrous. Therefore, use it only for the achievement of good and noble aims and in service that will enrich the life of our men, adding to the common good. Having arrived at this stage, we should continue to go forward, without holding back; ever onward toward greater achievements and accomplishments. Just as surely as the planets must revolve around the sun and fulfill their destiny, so should we go forward. See to it, then, that our aims and ambitions are based upon righteousness, for upon this does our whole life depend.

Character

"Men of character are the conscience of the society to which they belong."

-Ralph Waldo Emerson

Men of authentic excellence in every rank of life command the impulsive respect of our fellow citizens. It is natural to believe in such men, to have confidence in them, and to imitate and envy them. All that is good in the world is upheld by them, and without their presence the world would not be worth living in.

We can always better understand and appreciate men of real character by their transaction of the seemingly commonplace details of daily duty. They always make every effort to do their duty faithfully, honestly and honorably, and to the very best of their abilities. They always strive to make the best of life regardless of the circumstance, fulfilling the purpose for which they were assigned, and building up in themselves the principles of a manly character. They never cease to aim at reaching the highest standard of character - not to become the richest in means, but in spirit; not the greatest in worldly possession, but in true honor; not the most intellectual, but the most virtuous; not the most powerful and influential, but the most truthful, upright and honest. They put their conscience into their work, into their words and into their every action. *No man is bound to be rich or great or to be well educated; but every man is bound to be honest and forthright.* A man may possess only his diligence and poverty and still stand high in the rank of a true character. There are many persons of whom it may be said that they have no other possession in the world but their character, and yet they stand as firmly upon it as any elected president.

Men of character have a largeness of mind and depth of thought; they are full of selflessness, appreciation of the sublime, modesty and delicacy of manner, with a thoughtful heart that is worth regarding.

Without character, life would be indefinite and purposeless, like a body of stagnant water; instead of a running stream doing useful work and keeping the machinery of a city in motion, it lays dormant and polluted. But when all the elements of character are brought into action by determinate will, there is no reason why we should not be able to reach the summit of greatness.

Human character is molded by a thousand subtle influences; by example and precept, by life and literature, by friends and neighbors, by the world we live in, as well as by the spirits of our ancestors, whose legacy of good words and deeds we inherit. But great, unquestionably, though these influences are acknowledged to be, it is nevertheless equally clear that we must necessarily be the active agents of our own wellbeing and well-doing, and that, however much the wise and the good may owe to others, they themselves must in the very nature of things be their own best helpers.

The best sort of character cannot be formed without effort; there needs to be the exercise of constant self-watchfulness, self-discipline, and self-control. There may be much faltering, stumbling and temporary defeat and many difficulties and temptations to be battled with and overcome. Yet, if the spirit is strong and the heart is upright, everyone can reach their ultimate success. The very effort to advance, to arrive at a higher standard of character than we have reached, is inspiring and invigorating and even though we may fall short of it, we cannot fail to be improved by every honest effort made in an upward direction.

Life will always be, to a large extent, what we make it. Each mind makes its own little world. The cheerful mind makes it pleasant and the discontented mind makes it miserable. Our mind gives to all situations - to all fortunes, high or low - their real characters. If our views of life are elevated, if we regard it as a sphere of useful effort, of high living and high thinking, of working for the good of others as well as our own, it will be joyful, hopeful and blessed. If, on the contrary, we regard it merely as affording opportunities for self-seeking pleasure, it will be full of toil, anxiety and disappointment.

Everyone can be a character of substance in this world, regardless of race, religion, nationality, ancestry or education. We have to first possess the will to be so. We have to believe in ourselves and place some value on our life, knowing full well that we entered this planet with a purpose, and if it is not fulfilled, it will leave this world with a huge void. Emerson said in a short poem:

> There is no great and no small
> To the Soul that maketh all:
> And where it cometh, all things are
> And it cometh everywhere
>
> I am owner of the sphere
> Of the seven stars and the solar year
> Of Caesar's hand and Plato's brain
> Of Lord Christ's heart and Shakespeare's strain

The greatest characters of our country's history - great men of science, literature, art, politics, business and service, apostles of great imaginations and lords of great thoughts - have belonged to no exclusive class nor rank. They have come from all over the country, and perhaps the world. This is certain: however rich a man may be, he cannot pay to have a great character. He cannot pay someone to think for him and to behave in an upright manner. A great character can only be achieved through hard work and discipline. There is no bypassing adversities and difficult toil. Of all the great philosophers, poets, artists, inventors and military generals I have studied in preparation for this book, my intelligence confirms that it is not the man with the greatest natural vigor and capacity who achieves the highest results, but he who employs his powers with the greatest industry and the most diligent disciplined skill - the skill that comes by hard labor, devotion and practice.

THERE IS A POWER LYING DEEP WITHIN US BY WHICH WE CAN RISE TO HIGHER AND BETTER THINGS. There is a greater self within us that can raise us above the infinite armies of adversities and lift us sublimely like the mountains towering over the plains. It is a farce to think that our lives should be a crystal stream of eternal pleasure and, if it were possible, then life would not be worth living, for the sole object of life is the building of character and the attainment of knowledge through experience. *"We seldom break our leg so long as life continues a toilsome upward climb. The danger comes when we begin to take things easily and choose the convenient paths,"* said Nelson Mandela.

A GREAT CHARACTER IS INDEED LIKE A STAR THAT SHINES WITHOUT REST, GLOWING WITH AN ETERNAL RISE, SHINING BRILLIANTLY, EVEN THROUGH THE STORMIEST OF WEATHERS. A great character maintains defiance even when the burden of adversity casts the heavy and weary weight of obscurity upon it. A great character can turn lowness into loftiness, nothing into something, darkness into light, failure into glory, defeat into victory and hopelessness to optimism. It can *see a world in a grain of sand, and heaven in a wild flower, hold infinity in the palm of its hand, and eternity in an hour.* It is incorrigible; if it is thrown out of Heaven, it makes a suitable ideal of Hell. If it is disappointed, it embraces the disappointment with greater ardor than its recently embraced hope.

Adversities will come our way, no doubt, but if we meet them bravely and hopefully, we become stronger through experience, thus becoming better fitted to bear life's responsibilities and to overcome its difficulties and circumstances. One who meets the setbacks, grief and disasters of life in the right attitude becomes a strong and rich character.

The apprenticeship of difficulty is one that the greatest of men have had to serve. It is usually the best stimulus and discipline of character. It often evokes powers of action that, but for it, would have remained dormant. There are natures that blossom and ripen amidst trials, which would only wither and decay in an atmosphere of ease and comfort.

Thus, it is good for men to be roused into action and stiffened into self-reliance by difficulty, rather than to slumber away their lives in useless apathy and indolence. It is the struggle that is the condition of victory. If there were no difficulties, there would be no need of efforts; if there were no temptations, there would be no training in self-control, and but little merit in virtue. If there were no trial and suffering, there would be no education in patience and resignation. Thus, difficulty, adversity and suffering are not all evil, but often the best source of strength, discipline and virtue.

It is not prosperity so much as adversity, not wealth so much as poverty, that stimulates the perseverance of strong and healthy natures, rouses their energy and develops their character. **SUFFERING MAY BE THE APPOINTED MEANS BY WHICH THE HIGHEST NATURE OF MAN IS TO BE DISCIPLINED AND DEVELOPED. HAD IT NOT BEEN FOR ADVERSITY, THE BEST PART OF MANY OF OUR BRIGHTEST NATURE WOULD SLEEP A DEEP SLEEP.**

A great character is always an exceptional thinker and is naturally a leader of human destiny. All leaders of humankind, leaders of human thoughts and ideas - great legislators, great philosophers, great poets, great artists, great scientists and great musicians - possesses this primary quality. Socrates, Lycurgus, Galileo, Einstein, Newton, Bonaparte, Washington, King, Lincoln, Mandela, Obama and every pure and wise man such as they that ever wore flesh are a constant reminder that to be great is to have a great imagination. *"Imagination is more important than knowledge,"* said Albert Einstein, and indeed, he is right. It produced motor cars, great fleets, the printing press, the incandescent lamp and the many other great inventions of civilization. Proverbs says: *"Where there is no vision the people perish."* The monumental inventions we esteem so highly - railroads, steamships, power plants, telephones, airplanes, etc. - are but the relics of imagination. These things are only indications of circumstances, mere measurements that register the vision of great characters.

All great wisdom comes from within us. While books and the written word may be helpful, it is the spirit within the reader that illumines the word, and makes it real and true to the seeker of knowledge.

Imagination is our dictionary; it is our biggest vocabulary. This is the way to learn grammar. Colleges and books only copy the language that our imagination had already made. Imagination, dear reader, is higher than intellect.

There is no leader of knowledge that can teach great imagination. The greatest professors in all the great universities of the world cannot teach it. All the desks, ledgers and professors of Harvard mean nothing without great minds, great freethinkers, great critical thinkers, and great unorthodox imaginations. *"Imagination rules the world,"* said the Great Napoleon. And yes, this is also true. Every invention that makes our lives so much easier is a product of a great imagination.

Intelligence is often mistaken for education. It is information, and what we do with that information depends almost entirely on how we put our imagination to work. The more we put our imagination to work, the greater a problem-solver we become, whether it is by finding ways of saving our hard earn money, solving the simplest of domestic troubles, or inventing new technologies. Mark Twain reckoned that: *"Reality can be beaten with enough imagination."*

The most radical ideas of our day are not apt to be found in our popular newspapers or in queer little religious pamphlets, heretical and propaganda sheets that we occasionally might see. They are hatched in the laboratory of our imagination with a will that runs deeper than pride and stronger than interest.

A GREAT CHARACTER IS NOT AFRAID TO STAND STRONG AND COURAGEOUS EVEN WHEN FACING GREAT ODDS. Nothing that is of real worth can be achieved without guts. We should boldly confront fear, pain, danger, disappointment, uncertainty, adversity and intimidation and make a show of them. It is not eminent talent that is required to ensure success in any pursuit, so much as the will - the character. The determination, the drive and the perseverance define a great character. Men of character find the courage deep within and mold their subsequent destiny. They maintain an unbending individuality so that, by its very force, they exert the most potent influence over the highest barriers that come their way and lift themselves to boundless heights.

A GREAT CHARACTER HAS THE FIRMNESS TO OVERCOME ADVERSITIES. They have little or no regard for it. Indeed, the true object of life is that we may attain triumph through circumstances. These circumstances should be used as a convenience to success. My dear reader, character cannot be developed in ease and quiet. Only through experience of tribulation and sorrowing can the soul be strengthened, ambition stirred, and glory achieved. Indeed, it can only be developed in the storms of life. We will be defeated if we become complacent and nonchalant whenever we face difficult circumstances. *"Weakness of attitude becomes weakness of character,"* said Albert Einstein. "Most people," he said on another occasion, *"think that it is the intellect which makes a great scientist. They are wrong. It is character."* Our character, then, is simply our mental attitude toward a particular circumstance. Some of us do not seem to realize that our outlook on adversity is an affirmation of our character, and indeed our circumstance may not be half as bad as our character perceives it.

A GREAT CHARACTER HAS TO HAVE THE WIT TO SEE OPPORTUNITIES WHERE THERE ARE OBSTACLES AND SEE POSSIBILITIES WHERE THERE IS HOPELESSNESS; IT MUST NEVER BE TO DEPLORE SUFFERING BUT TO PERSEVERE BEYOND IT. *"Unfortunate things do happen; how we respond to them defines our character and the quality of our life. We can choose to sit in perpetual sorrow and regret, immobilized by the gravity of our disappointment, or we can choose to take from the mistake a valuable experience that will be advantageous in the future,"* said George Washington.

A GREAT CHARACTER HAS SELF-TRUST. Therefore, we should lay aside the corpse of our insecurities and walk upright in confidence. The faith we have in ourselves is the chief element in our success. We should have faith in our ability, despite the resounding echo of empty heads, and strive to be successful in our pursuit. Everyone lives and exists on his own account. Therefore, if we do not have much faith in our worth, we cannot be worth much otherwise. The idea which other people form of our existence is something secondary, derivative, and in the end affecting us but very indirectly. Besides, other people's opinions are a wretched place to be the home of our true value.

IT IS A TERRIBLE WEAKNESS OF CHARACTER TO RELY UPON OTHERS TO MAKE THE MUCH-NEEDED CHANGE WE REQUIRE TO MOVE OUR LIFE FORWARD WITHOUT ANY EFFORT ON OUR PART. And even if we are lucky enough to have someone successfully implementing such change for us, we will find that sooner or later we will lose a handle of that torch of success. Napoleon said, *"No mere change of circumstances can repair a weak character, neither can any great test destroy a strong one."* Having faith in ourselves leads to all sorts of positive outcomes. It protects our profoundest hope and shelters us in times of despair. Without it, we are a mere cynic; with it we are led to a truer and kindlier view of the nature of our self. It will help us to tackle the unavoidable adversities that are fated to confront us. When we believe in ourselves we will face setbacks, but we will not be overrun by them or get defeated. Instead, we will maintain the right approach and weather the weather until we are beyond the mist and back to brighter days.

A GREAT CHARACTER IS ALWAYS HOPEFUL. HOPE IS THE GIVER OF LIFE. NOTHING CAN COMPENSATE FOR THE LOSS OF HOPE IN A MAN. It is an excellent wearing quality. It is the bright weather of the heart. It gives harmony of soul and is a perpetual song without words. Hope is the lung of our being - it is what carries men and nations onward. Without it, nothing can be accomplished. All that is great in us comes out when we have hope. Hope is the parent of all effort and endeavor and every gift of noble origin is breathed upon by Hope's perpetual breath. It is the invisible engine that moves the world forward and keeps it in action. Hope is the nurse of duty, the chief mother of all success - the ointment of the soul. It is the great helper of the poor. It is the poor man's daily bread. It is also the sustainer and inspirer of great deeds. It is recorded of Alexander the Great that when he succeeded to the throne of Macedon he gave away amongst his friends the greater part of the estates which his father had left him, and when Perdiccas, one of his right-hand men, asked him what he had reserved for himself, Alexander answered confidently, *"The greatest possession of all - Hope!"*

There come times in every life when a power and will, of which the limited self knows nothing, is needed to raise the soul out of the dust and ashes of its despair. It is one thing to try to meet trouble and adversity in the right spirit and quite another thing to have the strength, hope and will to do so. One who thinks that he has no power within him but that all the power is in circumstances can never rise victorious over his troubles and become a conqueror over life's difficulties. However, one who realizes that he possesses a wonderful power that can raise him up, no matter how crushed he may be, can never be a failure in life no matter what may happen to him. He will rise from the ruins of his life and build it anew in greater beauty and splendor.

There are some characters so divinely constituted that they can find hope in every struggle. There is no calamity so great as to render them hopeless and defeated. They can educe comfort or consolation from any adversity - no sky so black without a silver lining, no tunnel so dark without a ray of light at the end of it. Such a bright character is to be envied.

We cannot be too careful to prevent obstacles, no matter how hard we try. Our best effort can merely reduce them. However, all of us can rise superior above any challenges. We will meet with failures and setbacks but we will make of these stepping-stones to greatness. We will experience sadness and desolation but we will dig within ourselves, find that store of hope, and use it to strengthen our will to fight on and rise to higher things.

Although success is the guerdon for which all men toil, they nevertheless often have to labor on perseveringly, without any glimmer of success in sight. They have to live, meanwhile, upon their hope - sowing their seed in the dark, in the hope that it will yet take root and spring up in achieved result. The best of causes have had to fight their way to triumph through a long succession of failures before the fortress was won. The heroism they have displayed is to be measured not so much by their immediate success, as by the opposition they have encountered, and the hope with which they have maintained the struggle.

HOPE IS THE VERY CROWN OF CHARACTER. WITHOUT IT, THE INDIVIDUAL TOTTERS AND FALLS BEFORE THE FIRST PUFF OF ADVERSITY; WHEREAS, DRIVEN BY IT, THE WEAKEST BECOMES STRONG AND FULL OF COURAGE.

A GREAT CHARACTER MUST HAVE PERSEVERANCE. Perseverance is one of the greatest agents of success and if we but go on zealously, I believe in my conscience that in time we will arrive at a position in our life that we can claim glory. Time and time again, we bear proof of what unbounded perseverance and hard work can accomplish by witnessing men of the humblest ranks in society raise themselves to the highest rank in public estimation by the effect of their own qualities.

> Rich are the diligent, who can command
> Time, nature's stock! and could his hourglass fall,
> Would, as for seed of stars, stoop for the sand,
> And, by incessant labor, gather all.

Anyone - I repeat, anyone! Even those of moderate background - can be successful if we apply ourselves by working diligently with an unimpeachable honesty of purpose and indefatigable perseverance. The power of perseverance is not to be underestimated. With perseverance, we have seen water eroding the biggest reef and sending it buckling to its knees. Marcus Garvey was from a humble background with very little education. Yet, with great perseverance, application, energy and with persistency and practice, he became at length one of the most persuasive and effective of public speakers, extorting the impartial acclamation of even his gravest adversaries. The most distinguished inventors, artists, thinkers, and workers of all kinds owe their success, in a great measure, to their unfaltering perseverance. Without perseverance, such an imperative quality, one can be easily outstripped in the race of life by the diligent and even the dull.

Progress nowadays can be slow - very slow, in fact. Nevertheless, if we apply ourselves patiently and diligently, and hold on with the determination to succeed, as if with a resolute confidence in the result, we will no doubt secure an encouraging outcome.

As I conclude this chapter, as well as this book, I know that I have cited the biography of many great men, and cited all the monumental feats that they have accomplished. The average people may be saying: "I am not necessarily trying to be the next president or the next great inventor. All I am trying to do is get by in my daily struggles and live the best life that I can live." Well, with the application of these fundamental elements, we can surely be the best that we can be. With patience when our life is stagnant and seemingly in reverse, courage amidst trials and difficulties, perseverance when all our strength is gone, faith when our way seems obscure and hope when we are standing against the ropes, there is no star that we cannot reach.

The greatest results in life are usually attained by simple means and the exercise of ordinary qualities. The common life of every day, with its cares, necessities and duties, affords many opportunities for acquiring experience of the best kind, and its most beaten paths offer the true citizen with an abundant scope for effort and room for self-improvement. The most ordinary occasions will furnish us with opportunities or suggestions for improvement, if we are prompt to take advantage of them. The road of human welfare lies along the old highway of unwavering faith, unbending hope, untiring devotion, relentless diligence and inexhaustible patience; and those who are the most unrelenting, and work in the truest spirit, will find success.

It is not chance that helps a man in the world so much as purpose and persistent work. To the feeble, weak-minded, and easily-defeated, the sluggish and the purposeless, the most favorable chance will avail to nothing - it will pass them by, as they see no meaning in it. However, it is astonishing how much can be accomplished if we are prompt to seize and improve the opportunities for action and effort which are constantly presenting themselves.

The extraordinary results effected by dint of sheer diligence and perseverance have led many distinguished men to doubt whether the gift of genius is so exceptional an endowment as it is usually supposed to be. It is only a very slight line of separation that divides the man of genius from the man of ordinary mold. Hence, it happens that the men who have most moved the world have not been so much men of genius, strictly so called, as men of intense mediocre abilities, and untiring perseverance; not so often the gifted, of naturally bright and shining qualities, as those who have applied themselves diligently to their work. Let us all show some character! Let us all prove ourselves contenders on the battlefields of life by tackling every obstacle, every setback, every circumstance, every adversity, with a dashing gallantry and a dauntless courage. Let us not be outrun in the race of life. To achieve anything worth achieving, our character must be capable of standing firmly upon its feet in the world of daily duty, temptation, and trial, and able to bear the wear-and-tear of actual life. Any man can do what any other man has done. However, it is unquestionable that one never overcomes any trials to which he is determined to subject himself.

My faith in the immortality of the soul is firm, but whether we are to live in another world or not, there is no higher intelligence than to live here and now - live our highest and best - cultivate the open mind and the welcoming heart, partaking of all good things in moderation, and disbanding ourselves from all that is unpleasant and unjust.

There is much in life that, while in this state, we can never comprehend. There is, indeed, a great deal of miseries, pains and sorrows in the world today. But, Spirits of Nature, let us lift ourselves above the interminable wilderness of these adversities and glooms. Let us not be weakened and despondent. Let us not be disheartened by all these stirring scenes that are fated to consume all our mortal hope. Though we may not understand it all, though we may not understand the cares and sorrows, helplessness and oppressions, the hunger and beggary, violence and crimes, ignorance and intolerance, though we may not understand why we pray so faithfully and it seems all in vain, though we may not understand why we work so hard with little to show for it, though we may not understand the struggle for financial freedom, the immoral pursuits, the exuberant delight in dishonesty, the high praise of shallowness and vainness, we should press on. There is nothing which the human mind can conceive which it may not execute.

The full meaning of the adversities of life, through which we all have to pass, will give us strength and endurance. Have faith in the completeness of the design, of which our little individual lives form a part, and when we have done our work on earth, like the silkworm that spins its little cocoon and dies, we too depart. But, though our stay in life may be short, it is the appointed sphere in which each has to work out the great aim and end of his being to the best of his power and when that is done, the spirit that is lifted from its earthly lungs will breathe on for ages as if it were a number drawn in the lottery of immortality.

www.ingramcontent.com/pod-product-compliance
Lightning Source LLC
Chambersburg PA
CBHW070736160426
43192CB00009B/1467